Charles L. Chaney

Church Planting at the End of the Twentieth Century

Tyndale House Publishers, Inc. Wheaton, Illinois

Unless otherwise noted, Scripture quotations are from the *New American Standard Bible,* copyright © 1960, 1962, 1963, 1968, 1971, 1972, 1973, 1975, 1977 by The Lockman Foundation. Used by permission. Scripture quotations marked NIV are from the *Holy Bible,* New International Version®, copyright © 1973, 1978, 1984 by International Bible Society. Used by permission of Zondervan Bible Publishers. The *"NIV"* and *"New International Version"* trademarks are registered in the United States Patent and Trademark Office by International Bible Society.

Library of Congress Cataloging-in-Publication Data

Chaney, Charles L., date
  Church planting at the end of the twentieth century / Charles L. Chaney. —Rev. ed.
    p.   cm.
  Includes bibliographical references.
  ISBN 0-8423-1113-0
  1. Church development, New. 2. Church growth. 3. Evangelistic work. I. Title.
BV652.24.C43   1993
254′.1—dc20   92-29524

Printed in the United States of America

99 98 97 96 95 94 93
8   7   6   5   4   3   2   1

Contents

9/665

Foreword

When my friends ask me, "Where do I go to find workable models for church planting?" I immediately respond, "Check out the Southern Baptists."

It is not just a coincidence that Southern Baptists have become America's largest Protestant denomination. Many smaller denominations have theology that is as evangelical and as respectable as the Southern Baptists'. Many have pulpiteers who can preach just as well. Many have an equal passion for souls. The difference is not in music, worship, church architecture, prayer, or even (contrary to the opinions of some Baptist leaders) Christian education. The major difference, in my opinion, is in church planting.

No other denomination in America has sustained the high priority profile for church planting that has characterized Southern Baptists decade after decade. And declaring the denominational priority for multiplying churches has been much more than mere rhetoric. The Southern Baptist Home Mission Board is the most highly sophisticated agency of its type in the nation, in many ways years ahead of most similar entities. Southern Baptists have not hesitated to invest massive amounts of money and to recruit the finest of their leaders so that the Home Mission Board could continue to keep them on the cutting edge.

The Home Mission Board vice-president currently responsible for overseeing the continued multiplication of Southern Baptist churches is Charles Chaney. I have known and admired Charles for years. Through serving as a pastor, he has gained a sense of the needs of ordinary people and how to meet them. As a church planter, he has learned the trade through practical experience. As a denominational executive in Illinois, he demonstrated that the most effective evangelistic methodology under heaven is to plant new churches. As a university president in Missouri, he mastered the application of administrative procedures. And now all this has come together in his key role as a foremost national church planting strategist.

Wouldn't you like to know what Charles Chaney knows about church planting? Well, here it is. For years I used *Church Planting at the End of the Twentieth Century* as a textbook for my church planting classes at Fuller Seminary. But, since church-planting technology is advancing so rapidly, I often wondered what I would do when it got out of date. Now I wonder no more, for this new revised and expanded edition incorporates the new advances.

Not only will you find such up-to-date information as modern market segmentation techniques and the VALS methodology for determining the exact kind of church that needs to be planted in a given community, but the book has become even more valuable and relevant with real live case studies. Chaney has asked several of his most qualified church planters to give us the how-tos, and they are thrilling stories indeed.

Put this all together, and we have a tremendous book.

Church Planting at the End of the Twentieth Century will make a formidable difference in your personal life and ministry, in your local church, in your denomination or fellowship, and most important of all, in accelerating the spread of the kingdom of God in our generation.

C. Peter Wagner
Fuller Theological Seminary
Pasadena, California

During the summer of 1954 a few laymen from First Baptist Church in Morganfield, Kentucky, conducted a tent meeting at the edge of their city, out toward the old C.C.C. camp. A number of adults were converted to Christ. Soon a "mission" was opened on the north side of that small county seat because those newly won to faith in Christ didn't feel comfortable at the "big church," their name for First Baptist. Bankers and county officials, people one had to call "mister," attended there. It made worship and opinion-sharing a threatening experience.

The mother church asked Jim and Carolyn Toler, Marlin Wood, Madlyn Jones, Sally Banks, Louise Jones, Nora Parish, and Bob and Norma Rich, lay leaders in that fellowship, to invest their lives in the new church. I was a first-year student at Southern Baptist Theological Seminary in Louisville and a veteran of three years as pastor of a small church in central Texas. First Baptist Church asked me to become pastor of the new congregation. Later Ed and Frances Walker and Joe and Lucille Farris came from the "big" church to join us. My wife and I moved on "the field" soon and remained there five years. The Northside Baptist Church of Morganfield was born, and our entire ministry was shaped by those dedicated lay leaders, that growing new church, and what God did among us during those years. That episode in our lives began my long romance with church planting.

Twelve years followed, first in a mission church near Fort Campbell, Kentucky, and then nine years in a new church in Palatine, Illinois, a suburb on Chicago's northwest side. In vastly different contexts we spent seventeen years in planting and developing new churches. During our years in suburban Chicago I became involved with the Chicago Metro Baptist Association, which, with the commitment of young churches like the one I served, was planting ten or more new congregations each year during the sixties. Preston Denton was the inspired leader of that little association of churches. He is among the most gifted church planters that American evangelical churches have produced in this century. The First Baptist Church of Palatine became and is one of the strongest Southern Baptist churches in the Great Lakes area, but my most significant achievements while there were in the new congregations we helped to start.

For nine years I directed a division of work for the Illinois Baptist State Association. The Church Extension Division existed principally to assist in the establishment of new churches. Most of the chapters that follow grew out of my study and work during those years.

For eight years I served Southwest Baptist University, first as dean of the Courts Redford School of Theology and then as president. During those years more than a hundred students and faculty were sent out each year on month-long missionary projects. They assisted in evangelism and church planting from Mexico to Canada. They went in teams of ten to fifteen, nearly always led by a faculty member and engaged in academic as well as practical Christian experience.

I presently serve as vice president of the Home Mission Board of the Southern Baptist Convention. In partnership with forty-one state conventions, I give leadership to Southern Baptists' effort to plant churches among every people group in the U.S. and Canada. We believe that church planting is the most effective way to evangelize any people, and only by the multiplication of churches can any nation be thoroughly evangelized. Our goal is 50,000 congregations by A.D. 2000. Not including Canada, the convention by 1990 had crossed the 43,600 mark in total congregations (both churches and church-type missions). My involvement in starting and growing new churches has almost spanned my lifetime.

Remarkably, Southern Baptist churches have started 3.3 new congregations a day for the past ten years. Not all these new starts have survived through the decade. In addition, the convention loses about 235 churches each year from various forms of attrition. Our goal is 15,000 new starts for the 1990s—that is four new congregations started for every day of the year, for ten years.

These churches will be planted in every segment of American society. Looking at our present pace, I expect by the end of the century that the Southern Baptist Convention will be composed of more than 10,000 ethnic congregations and 4,000 congregations in predominantly black communities, something quite different than it was in 1900.

The privilege I have in being a part of what God is doing within this part of the Body of Christ fills me with awe and gratitude. Making disciples and gathering churches is the greatest romance in the world.

Dr. Arthur F. Glasser, then Dean, and the late Dean Emeritus Donald A. McGavran of the School of World Missions, Fuller Theological Seminary, invited me to give the annual lectures on church growth at the School of World Missions in 1979. That opportunity made it possible for me to get much of this material together in a manageable form. The faculty, staff, and student body at Fuller were gracious hosts during the time these lectures were delivered.

I have spoken on these subjects many times to different groups. Chapter seven was first given at the invitation of F. Jack Redford at a church extension seminar in Louisville, Kentucky. Some of the material in chapter two was first shared with home mission executives and directors of evangelism serving ecclesiastical bodies in the National Association of Evangelicals. Material in both these chapters was first published in the fall 1978 issue of *Search.*

The work of Eugene Gibson, Charles Wade, Joseph Rainey, Clarence Hopson, Rick Warren, Donald Sharp, and Claude Tears are featured in these chapters. I appreciate their friendship and cooperation.

I have had several collaborators in the preparation of this revised edition. David Putman, Carol Childress, Larry Wartsbaugh, Larry Martin, and Gordon Lawrence are all young, gifted, well trained, committed, and exciting church-planting professionals who give me stimulation and hope. They are representatives of an army of young men and women I have found in city and countryside across this continent who are completely dedicated to see the Church of Jesus Christ planted in every segment of North American society. Encountering these people is the single most important discovery I made since moving out of Christian higher education and into my more specific life's work: making disciples and gathering them into churches or training others to do the same.

In the chapters that follow I have used the word *Church* to refer to the church as the Body of Christ and *church* to refer to a local congregation. I have never used *Church* to refer to a large ecclesiastical body except in a title like "the United Methodist Church." Ethnicity is, of course, a significant factor in the Anglo-American and Afro-American communities. I have used *ethnic* in this book, however, to refer to those peoples, no matter what their racial derivation, who speak a "heart" language other than English or who identify themselves as belonging to a culture distinct from the two major cultures of North America.

Good things always happen to me. I've always been blessed with administrative assistants, executive secretaries, secretaries, and editors that take a deep interest in what I do and who make me look good. Jenny Nethery has, on her own time, typed, corrected, changed, and reworked this entire book. Margaret Dempsey has edited several of these chapters, including all the new ones. She spent hours putting chapter 6 together from papers prepared by three very creative people.

My wife, as always, has encouraged and helped, even though this work has come in a period of her life when she has lived with severe pain almost every day.

It is my prayer that this book be useful to the Church-at-large over the next few years.

June 4, 1991
Atlanta, Georgia

Acknowledgments

Grateful acknowledgment is given to the following publishers for permission to quote copyrighted material from the titles listed below:

Broadman Press, Nashville, Tennessee, for permission to quote from Talmadge R. Amberson, *The Birth of Churches*, 1979; William O. Carver, *The Glory of God in the Christian Calling*, 1949; Duke K. McCall, editor, *What Is the Church?* 1958; Wayne McDill, *Making Friends for Christ*, 1979; F. Jack Redford, *Planting New Churches*, 1979; and C. Kirk Hadaway, et al, *Home Cell Groups and House Churches*, 1987.

Abingdon Press, Nashville, Tennessee, for permission to quote from Robert L. Wilson and James H. Davis, *The Church and the Racially Changing Community*, 1966.

CBS, Inc., New York, New York, for permission to quote K. Livgren, "Dust in the Wind."

Christianity Today, Inc., Wheaton, Illinois, for permission to quote from the June 27, 1980, issue of *Christianity Today*.

Harper and Row, Publishers, New York, for permission to quote from Ezra Earl Jones, *Strategies for New Churches*, 1976.

Home Mission Board, Southern Baptist Convention, for permission to quote from B. Carlisle Driggers, *The Church in the Changing Community: Crisis or Opportunity*, 1977; and Jere Allen and George W. Bullard, Jr., *Shaping the Future of the Church in the Changing Community*, 1980.

Baker Book House, Grand Rapids, for permission to quote from Dean S. Gilliland, *Pauline Theology and Mission Pastor,* 1983; David Hesselgrave, *Planting Churches Cross-Culturally,* 1980.

Orbis Books, Mary Knoll, New York, for permission to quote from Louis Luzbetak, *The Church and Cultures,* 1988.

Probus Publishing Co., Chicago, Illinois, for permission to quote *Market Segmentation,* 1987.

Warner Books, New York, New York, for permission to quote Arnold Mitchell, *The Nine American Lifestyles,* 1983.

Dryden Press, Chicago, Illinois, for permission to quote James F. Engel and Roger D. Blackwell, *Consumer Behavior,* 4th ed., 1982.

Moody Press, Chicago, Illinois, for permission to quote from Melvin Hodges, *Build My Church,* 1957.

Princeton Religion Research Center for permission to quote from the June 1979 issue of *Emerging Trends.*

United Methodist Publishing House, Nashville, Tennessee, for permission to quote from the May 1979 issue of *The Circuit Rider.*

William B. Eerdman's Publishers, Grand Rapids, Michigan, for permission to quote from Donald A. McGavran, *Understanding Church Growth,* 1970.

World Wide Publications, Minneapolis, Minnesota, for permission to quote from J. D. Douglas, editor, *Let the Earth Hear His Voice,* 1975.

Macmillan Publishing Company, Inc., New York, for permission to quote from Michael Novak, *The Rise of the Unmeltable Ethnics,* paperback edition, 1973.

Zondervan Publishing House, Grand Rapids, Michigan, for permission to quote from Harold Lindsell, *An Evangelical Theology of Missions,* 1970; James F. Engel and Wilbert Norton, *What's Gone Wrong with the Harvest?* 1975.

Uncopyrighted materials in the form of graduate theses, research papers, and lectures have also contributed much to this book. I want to express appreciation for all of these sources and mention some that I have used extensively:

Donald A. McGavran, "Church Growth in America through Planting New Congregations," the closing address of the consultation on evangelism and church growth, October 1976, Kansas City, Missouri; Clay Price and Phillip Jones, "A Study in the Relationship of Church Size and Church Age to Number of Baptisms and Baptismal Rates"; B. Carlisle Driggers, compiler, "Churches in Racially Changing Communities," mimeographed proceedings of the National Leadership Conference, Department of Cooperative Ministries with National Baptists, Home Mission Board, Southern Baptist Convention.

Daniel R. Sanchez, "A Five Year Plan of Growth for the Ministry of the Baptist Convention of New York in the Area of Evangelism," published doctoral dissertation, Fuller Theological Seminary, Pasadena, California; George W. Bullard, Jr., "An Analysis of Change in Selected Southern Baptist Churches in Metropolitan Transitional Communities," unpublished Th.M. dissertation, Southern Baptist Theological Seminary, Louisville, Kentucky.

C. Kirk Hadaway, "A Compilation of Southern Baptist Churches and Resident Members Located in Standard Metropolitan Statistical Areas 1978"; and Language Missions Department, Home Mission Board, SBC, "America's Ethnicity."

Clay L. Price, "A Brief Study of the North Central States 1980 to 1988"; Phillip B. Jones and Richard C. Stanley, "HMB Environmental Indicators," 1990.

1

Biblical Pillars for Church Planting

The grand object
is to plant
and multiply
self-reliant,
efficient churches,
composed wholly
of native converts,
each church complete
in itself,
with pastor
of the same race
with people.

Rufus Anderson, 1869

Several years ago, some friends and I spent a week at what was then called the Garden Grove Community Church, now the Crystal Cathedral. We attended Robert H. Schuller's Institute for Successful Church Leadership. One morning we spent some time with Dr. Schuller in his office. It was a memorable few minutes. One of the things he said went something like this: "One of the primary reasons that we have been successful here is that we have learned to ask the right questions. Asking right questions has priority over getting right answers. If you do not ask right questions you cannot get right answers. You may not get right answers if you ask the right questions, but there is no possible way—except chance— to get right answers without them." That made a lot of sense to me.

In 1977, I had attended a conference, along with about a hundred leaders from various state and national Southern Baptist Convention (SBC) agencies, concerned primarily with church growth problems. For a couple of days, we addressed ourselves to three questions.

1. *How can we greatly accelerate the beginning of new churches all across America?*
2. *How can we penetrate ethnic America with the gospel of Christ?*
3. *How can we stimulate vitality among churches that have plateaued in growth or are in numerical decline?*

I am convinced that those continue to be the right questions. They are questions we must ask in the 1990s in order to get right answers.

When we asked the question about plateaued and declining churches, we focused on the greatest immediate problem that Southern Baptists and most evangelicals face today. Two questions baffle us. First, why do churches—whose people have Bibles in their hand and the Holy Spirit indwelling them, planted among thousands of responsive people—fail to grow? The second question grows out of the first: How can this pattern be changed?

When we formulated the question about penetrating ethnic America, we identified the major targets for missionary strategy and action in this country. The arena in which we work is a cultural and social complexity. Only recently—and always reluctantly—has this fact been perceived again by denominational leaders. If we do not discover how to penetrate ethnic America, we will miss America.

When we asked the question about greatly multiplying the number of churches, we were addressing a question that is at the heart of the missionary task of the Church. We focused on the crucial, specific activity upon which the evangelization of America—in all of its cultural and social complexity—depends. America will not be won to Christ by existing churches, even if they should suddenly become vibrantly and evangelistically alive. Nor will the United States (Canada could also be included) be won to Christ by establishing more churches like the vast majority of those we now have—churches that are predominantly white, or predominantly black, whose members usually speak an easily identifiable American English dialect, and who exhibit (whether white or black) middle-class tastes or magnify middle-class aspirations.

We live in a pluralistic, multiethnic, multicultural, diverse, perverse, openly pagan, secular society. Most church leaders are willing to affirm that fact, but few as yet are ready to face its implications for strategy. The United States has always been composed of such a mixture.

The dominant culture in America during its early history was shaped by one type of Protestantism—the New England variety—and the missionary dream was to impose that cultural pattern on the entire nation and the world. This cultural imperialism was oppressive to many other Protestants, to the most recent immigrants of that period, whether Protestant or Roman Catholic, and to the sectarians.[1]

America today is not a Christian nation but a mission field. The churches here should identify themselves with the young churches of the world and give attention to multiplying congregations among all the social and cultural segments of society.[2] In every population unit—whether census tract, city, county, or state—there are pockets of unchurched people. In some population units these pockets are huge. In no community are nine-tenths of the population dedicated disciples of Jesus Christ. In most of the communities we have surveyed less than 20 percent of the population meet for worship on a given Sunday. I believe the field is wide open to Southern Baptists, Methodists, Pentecostals, Lutherans, or any other denomination that will take finding the lost seriously.

This small book is addressed primarily to the question of accelerating the beginning of new churches. It will become very clear as you read this book that I write not only from the viewpoint of a practitioner, but also from the perspective of a Southern Baptist. I write primarily out of my own experience. My research, and especially my illustrations, reflect that experience. However, I have a deep conviction that what I write is germane to all Christian denominations. I believe I am writing about the whole North American scene. Conversations with other denominational leaders convince me that all ecclesiastical groups in America are experiencing much the same thing. They face almost identical situations. They have many of the same problems and opportunities.

In this first chapter I want to examine with you the biblical foundations upon which I structure my own concern for church planting. This will be a very personal statement from a practitioner. It will explore this question: What are the theological pillars upon which I insist that churches must be multiplied in every segment of society?

THE NATURE AND PURPOSE OF THE CHURCH

The first biblical pillar upon which I base my conviction that churches should be multiplied is the nature and purpose of the Church itself.

THE NATURE OF THE CHURCH I will not attempt a treatise on the nature of the Church, but I do want to look briefly at three common designations of the Church in the New Testament and what they say about the purpose of the Church, as these designations provide a foundation for aggressive church planting.

The *ekklesia* is the *laos* or people of God. I come from a tradition that has had a very strong emphasis on the local church. In fact, Southern Baptists as a whole have been so shaped by the Landmark movement, which began about 1860, that you cannot really understand us without some comprehension of Landmark principles.[3] Many SBC leaders and influential teachers have insisted that the word *ekklesia* in the New Testament always refers to a local church. A classic statement of this position was written by

B. H. Carroll, the founder of Southwestern Baptist Theological Seminary.[4]

The common Greek word *ekklesia* referred to a local assembly convened for some specific purpose. However, the use of the word by early Christians was informed and conditioned by its use in the Septuagint. There, *ekklesia* was used to refer to the congregation of Israel. It therefore had reference to the people of God. Peter spoke about the Church when he wrote:

You are a chosen race, a royal priesthood, a holy nation, a people for God's own possession, that you may proclaim the excellencies of Him who has called you out of darkness into His marvelous light; for you once were not a people, but now you are the people of God; you had not received mercy, but now you have received mercy. (1 Peter 2:9-10)

Paul, too, spoke of the Church:

For the grace of God has appeared, bringing salvation to all men, instructing us to deny ungodliness and worldly desires and to live sensibly, righteously and godly in the present age, looking for the blessed hope and the appearing of the glory of our great God and Savior, Christ Jesus; who gave Himself for us, that He might redeem us from every lawless deed and purify for Himself a people for His own possession, zealous for good deeds. (Titus 2:11-14)

The people that Christ has purified for his own possession are the *ekklesia* of God, and the Church is gathered from "all men." James referred to the conversion of Cornelius as the way "God first concerned Himself about taking from among the Gentiles a people for His name" (Acts 15:14). It is the Father's concern that a people be gathered for himself from all the multiplied clans and families of man. If the Church, the people of God, is to be composed of persons from all the ethnic groupings of mankind, then local congregations must be planted among all of these peoples.

The *ekklesia* is also the *soma* or "Body" of Christ. The Church is the present physical manifestation of Jesus Christ the Lord in the world. William O. Carver, a noted missiologist and New Testament scholar of the first part of this century, was bolder than most. He insisted that the Church is the continuing incarnation of Christ in the world. "The Church," he said, "is the extension of his [Christ's] incarnation. A local church is the manifestation of Christ in its community."[5] Carver spoke of the Church as "so intimately and so essentially related to the Christ and to his meaning in history as to constitute his growing self-realization in the process of accomplishing the ends of his incarnation. The Church is his growing Body, that in it he is himself growing into maturity."[6]

To my thinking, Roland Allen was on target when he said that what we ultimately seek in our efforts to bring the nations to faith in Christ is not converts, the multiplication of congregations, or the Christianization of the social order, but a manifestation of the character and glory of Christ.[7] We seek, when we address the gospel to any people, to manifest the universality, the love and mercy, the glory and power of Christ. This goal is possible because he is the hand that fills out the glove of every culture of mankind. He is the only one who can bring any culture to a true golden age. And though Allen would say that the ultimate mission of the Church is not identical with the growth of churches, he would also insist that the manifestation of Christ is achieved through and in the multiplication of congregations. When we plant churches among any people, we make it possible for the character and beauty of Jesus to become incarnate in that culture. That is how the Church "which is His body, [becomes] the fulness of Him who fills all in all" (Ephesians 1:23).

Through the process of church planting, the Body of

Christ is brought to its fullness. Ephesians 2:11-22, rather than being a bulwark against efforts to plant congregations among all the cultural groupings of mankind, supports church planting in all the tribes and families of men. This seminal paragraph describes the purpose of God in redemption from the point of view of corporate experience. It speaks of peoples, not individuals. Through his cross, Jesus has broken down the wall that divided Jewish peoples from Gentile peoples. The imagery found in this passage is surely the temple in Jerusalem. The walls that separated the Gentiles from the holy place have been destroyed. All the ethnic groupings of the world now have equal access to the Father.

So then you are no longer strangers and aliens, but you are fellow citizens with the saints, and are of God's household, having been built upon the foundation of the apostles and prophets, Christ Jesus Himself being the corner stone. . . in whom you also [as an ethnic group in Christ, not as an individual] are being built together into a dwelling of God in the Spirit. (Ephesians 2:19-20, 22)

I especially like W. O. Carver's paraphrase of these verses.

You are to think of yourselves, in each race group, as a structure built upon the eternal foundation of God's purposes . . . Christ Jesus Himself being the chief cornerstone in the entire structure that God is building in human history. This structure of a redeemed humanity is a vast, complex but unitary structure in which every distinct building, as one race group after another is redeemed, being harmoniously worked in with the rest into the comprehensive architectural plan of the Great Builder, makes a growing addition toward a temple sanctified in the Lord unto God's glory, thus a temple into which you, in your part, are in the process of being constructed. The great objective is to provide a place of habitation for God, who in his Spirit dwells in this new humanity.[8]

If it is true that Jesus Christ did, with his blood, purchase for God men from every tribe and tongue and people and nation, and has made them to be a kingdom and priests to our God, and if they are to reign on the earth (Revelation 5:9-10), then we should get busy gathering into churches those who say yes to the gospel proclamation.

Finally, the *ekklesia* is the *koinonia* or "fellowship" of the Spirit. In fact, the point could be made that the Holy Spirit himself does not just create *koinonia*—the commonality that is ours in Christ—but that he is himself that *koinonia.* Indeed, it is the Holy Spirit who makes the Church the living Body of Christ. It is the gift of the Spirit himself who implants new life in the believer. He is both the sent and the sending Spirit. He stirs in the hearts of saints a great desire to share with others what they have discovered in Christ. It is he who enables us to see in others the need that only he can supply. He enables us effectively to pass on to others what we have received. It is he who pushes the Church farther and farther into the ethnic world. When churches are planted among every segment of society, it is he who unifies us in Christ Jesus. In the Spirit we are all submerged into one body and all made to drink of that same Spirit (1 Corinthians 12:13). It is the Holy Spirit, not a superculture; it is the Holy Spirit, not a sacred, common language; it is the Holy Spirit, not a common organizational structure that makes the Church one. When churches are planted in the diverse and sometimes antagonistic cultures of mankind, it is the Holy Spirit who makes those human societies into something else—into real manifestations of the Lord Jesus Christ in the world. It was the Holy Spirit who said, "Set apart for Me Barnabas and Saul for the work to which I have called them" (Acts 13:2). Consequently, these men gave themselves to church planting.

If it is the Holy Spirit who gives new life to believers, and if it is the Holy Spirit who makes a church a growing, living organism, and if it is he who is the common ingredient among all Christians, then church planting is at the heart of the mission of the Church. For when churches are planted, the essential nature of the Church, the *koinonia* of the Holy Spirit, is actualized in the world.

THE PURPOSE OF THE CHURCH Melvin Hodges has said that the Church has a threefold purpose: to evangelize, to edify, and to be God's treasure in the world.[9] If one accepts that simple statement—and I do—it is easy to perceive a threefold ministry for the Church: (1) a ministry to the world of men—to evangelize; (2) a ministry to the body of Christ—to build up; and (3) a ministry to God—to exalt him, to praise and adore him, to be his heritage among the sons of men.

In church planting, we are primarily concerned with the ministry directed toward the world. How shall we fulfill that purpose? Let me remind you if that purpose is not fulfilled, the Church cannot adequately fulfill the other two purposes.

The big question is: How shall the Good News of Jesus Christ be carried effectively to all nations, tribes, clans, and families of men? Certainly, gifted, anointed men and women will have to cross barriers as pioneers to communicate the message to each of these peoples. But the ultimate method is to plant churches in each of those clans, tribes, and families. Only by seeing that the Church becomes indigenous to every segment of society, to every culture and language of man, can we be reasonably sure that the gospel will effectively touch all the clans of man.

THE NATURE AND CONDITION OF CONTEMPORARY MAN
A second pillar upon which I base my conviction that churches should be multiplied is the nature and condition of contemporary man.

MAN AS FALLEN   Man is not as God made him! I'm grateful and glad that the Bible bears witness to this principle. That truth gives Christians an authentic answer to the pervasive despair that has overcome modern man. Man in his present state is not as God created him. This world is not as God made it. Man is fallen. We are part of a cosmic rebellion. Our sin has shoved the entire universe into tilt. Our world, this created *cosmos,* is in the bondage of decay. This is the consistent witness of Holy Scripture.

There are far-reaching missionary and evangelistic implications in Francis Schaeffer's often-repeated assertion that the prevailing worldview locks contemporary man into unrelieved futility and meaninglessness. According to this assertion, modern man—at least Western man—perceives a universe of natural cause and effect, but a universe that is closed. There can be no intervention from without or within. The universe is a machine, and man is a robot, inexorably chained to his destiny without any possibility of deliverance.[10]

This perception is demonstrated in many ways. In the 1970s, the musical group Kansas had a song on the charts that is still heard with some regularity. It describes modern despair explicitly.

I close my eyes/Only for a moment and the moment's gone.
All my dreams pass before my eyes—a curiosity.
Dust in the wind,/All we are is dust in the wind.
Same old song,/Just a drop of water in the endless sea,/
All we do crumbles to the ground, Though we refuse to see,/
Dust in the wind,/All we are is dust in the wind./
Don't hang on./Nothing lasts forever but the earth and sky./
It slips away, and all your money won't another minute buy./
Dust in the wind./All we are is dust in the wind./
Dust in the wind./Everything is dust in the wind.[11]

This is not the biblical view of fallen man. The biblical view of man says man indeed is fallen; he is guilty. He is not as God created him, but he can be saved from his despair and restored to the purpose for which he was made.

This is what makes the news about Jesus Christ Good News. Fallen man not only can be rescued, but he can also be restored to his original purpose.

God had a purpose in creation. This universe and man were not created—as "Green Pastures" suggested— just because the Eternal Father was bored. God always intended to have a big family. His plan was to bring many sons to glory (Hebrews 2:10). Jesus Christ is to be "the first-born among many brethren" (Romans 8:29). Man was made in the beginning to be in God's family and, being made in his image, to share his life. But man was not just made to be in God's family; he was also created to express God's character, to be like God. God wanted not only many children, but also mature sons and daughters. And this is not all. Man was made to have dominion over the earth and its creatures (Genesis 1:26-27) and, eventually, to reign with Christ over God's entire creation (Revelation 5:10). This was God's original purpose for man. The Good News about Jesus Christ is that man not only can be rescued from that fallen state, but also can be restored to the ultimate purpose for which he was made.

As an illustration, imagine that you received a letter a few weeks ago from Australia saying that a very wealthy eccentric—of whom you knew nothing—had died and made you his sole heir. His estate was waiting for you to come and claim it. He had left 600,000 acres of Australia's best ranch land, a forty-room modern mansion, a sea-going yacht, and $100 million after taxes, just to keep it all running. Suppose that you invite me to go along with you to claim your heritage. The two of us are on board an ocean liner crossing the Pacific. It is three hundred miles to the nearest island. Suddenly, there is a swell in the sea. The ocean liner is pitched like a leaf in a rain-swept gutter. You lose your footing and are washed overboard.

Our conversation might go something like this:

"Are you all right?" I would yell down to you.

"Help!" would be your reply.

"Can you swim?

"Listen," I would shout in my most helpful and authoritative voice, "the closest island is three hundred miles due north. You had better swim that way. By the way, I would advise you to use the breaststroke."

That may be good advice, but it is bad news! Good news is, "Hang on! Someone is coming to get you." The result would be that you would not only be rescued from the sea, but you would also be returned to the ship and put back on the road to your destiny.

That is the kind of Good News that the gospel is: You can be not only rescued but also restored to that high purpose for which God made you in the beginning. That is the gospel and part of the foundation upon which we make disciples and multiply churches.

MAN AS SOCIAL BEING That man is fallen is not all we need to say, of course. What I have said is just an effort to portray something of the hope for fallen man from the biblical viewpoint. We must also speak to the cultural condition of humanity. Man's sin alienated him from God, from himself, from his neighbor, and even from nature. But he remains a social being. He exists in social structures. He speaks and hears, he thinks and dreams, within and by means of particular cultural forms.

It is impossible to communicate with him except through his own cultural channels. To deny that is to deny the reality of the human condition. The great formative missionary task, as I have already indicated, is to penetrate these social and cultural communities with the Good News. Our goal is not to tear down and destroy the structure of culture, but to seek an incarnation of Christ in each and every particular culture, to see the character and beauty of Jesus manifested in each distinct cultural world.

That goal is only achieved when the Church, which is Christ's body, is growing into his fullness among each people.

Let me make an observation about the growth of churches and denominations as it is related to cultural, socio-economic, and racial patterns. I will speak of my own larger ecclesiastical fellowship—the Southern Baptist Convention. The particular genius for growth that Southern Baptists have exhibited in the American South since about 1880 has been grounded in their ability to penetrate the various social groupings that were found there—except, of course, the large black community—and to plant churches in those various social groupings. We probably penetrated these groups without a conscious effort to do so, but it did happen.

Currently, many Convention leaders recognize this truth. But something else has happened. The South has become increasingly cosmopolitan and pluralistic. Also, during the last fifty years, Southern Baptists have exploded outside the boundaries of the Old South and Southwest into the complexities of northern and western social patterns. Deliberate, detailed strategies have been set in place to penetrate each and every social and cultural community—black, white, and ethnic. Now 5,600 congregations have been planted in the ethnic populations of the nation and 1,500 have been added to the fellowship in predominately black communities, most of them planted since 1960. The black communities of America that are experiencing so much violent crime in the 1990s are very responsive to evangelism and ministry. Black Southern Baptist leaders are expecting 4,000 total congregations by A.D. 2000. No denominational group in America can be faithful to God without commitment to and integrity in reaching all the peoples that make up America.

Let me respond briefly to two criticisms of this kind of missionary philosophy that I often hear. The first usually comes from those who take pride in traditionalism, holding great respect and appreciation for the past, especially the immediate past. The second comes from those who pride themselves on openness, modernity, and justice. Both, I believe, beg the point.

The first criticism has to do with the way the gospel is packaged. To aim the message at particular groups on the basis of culture is, say the critics, to dilute the message, to manipulate the hearers, or both. I am very concerned that the basic message about Jesus Christ not be watered down. I hold that the fundamental biblical tenets are given and authoritative. But we must not confuse the basic message with the cultural wrappings. There may still be a few SBC churches in northern Illinois or the Detroit area whose message is wrapped and delivered just as it was forty years ago in northern Alabama, but if these churches were offering their message in Alabama today, no one would be buying. The same misuse of cultural wrappings of the gospel also still lingers in some of the great immigrant churches from northern Europe that arrived in America more than a hundred years ago.

Adapting the message to the cultural condition of the hearer is not unbiblical. New Testament—specifically Pauline—missionary and evangelistic strategy was avowedly customer-centered:

For though I am free from all men, I have made myself a slave to all, that I might win the more. And to the Jews I became as a Jew, that I might win Jews; to those who are under the Law, as under the Law, though not being myself under the Law, that I might win those who are under the Law; to those who are without law, as without law, though not being without the law of God but under the law of Christ, that I might win those who are without law. To the weak I became weak, that I might win the weak; I have become all things to all men, that I may by all means save some. (1 Corinthians 9:19-22)

Nor is all this crass "manipulation," which is one of today's code words used to castigate aggressive efforts to persuade men to believe in Jesus Christ. Paul wrote in another place to the same people:

We have renounced the things hidden because of shame, not walking in craftiness or adulterating the word of God, but by the manifestation of truth commending ourselves to every man's conscience in the sight of God. (2 Corinthians 4:2)

Our concern must be with preserving biblical truth, not cultural tinsel. But we must be sure that the biblical truth is communicated so that it addresses people as they are and where they are.

The second criticism, of course, is with the homogeneous unit principle. Many responsible Christian leaders see those three words and then read them as R-A-C-I-S-M. The question we often hear is, Should not Christians be willing to love and receive into their fellowship all kinds of people? The answer is, of course, yes! Every church should aggressively offer Christ and welcome to full church membership every person within its geographical area who believes in him. But when we come to the matter of church growth—effective evangelism and the multiplication of churches—that is not the question. It is wrong to impose the sophistication or the culture of a mature Christian on a man before he becomes a Christian. He should not be forced to mix in intimate fellowship with those with whom he is uncomfortable in order for him to become a disciple of Jesus.

When we address the question of missionary and evangelistic obedience to Christ, the right question is, How will the non-Christians most readily receive Christ? My answer is, Plant congregations in every segment of society, so that men and women can find Christ among their peers without having to give up or renounce cultural distinctives that have structured a meaningful life for them in the world. Let the mature Christian cross the barriers to the unbeliever, not force the unbeliever to cross the barriers to come to Christ.

The social mosaic that describes the cultural condition of fallen man becomes, in the Bible, the vehicle through which God works man's redemption. I was instructed and encouraged when I discovered in Psalm 86 that it is God who has made the various ethnic groupings of mankind. Cultural diversity is not a punishment for sin to be overcome by the Cross. God himself made the nations and has decreed that all are to come and worship him (Psalm 86:9). The socioeconomic and cultural divisions of mankind are the occasion for the multiplication of churches and the building of the dwelling place of God in the Spirit.

THE NATURE AND CHARACTER OF THE TRIUNE GOD

A third pillar upon which we base our conviction that churches should be multiplied is the nature and character of God himself. Many say that the missionary and evangelistic task of the Church is grounded in the command of Christ. I believe that the footing of the missionary character of the Church is more profound than the commands of Christ that are preserved for us in Holy Scripture.

Our Lord's commission to the Church contains six distinct biblical statements. They are extremely significant and instructive. But should a group of people on a deserted island find a copy of the epistles of the New Testament, consequently be conveyed to Christ, and have no written account of the commands of Christ, these people would still have an inner awareness that other men needed to know Christ. They would sense with intuitive conviction that they who had been found of him were under a divine mandate to find others. This is true because to know Christ is to know the Father and to have received the

Spirit. The missionary task of the Church has its origin in the nature of the Triune God.[12]

THE PURPOSE OF THE FATHER Church planting is an essential, integral part of the mission of the Church, and the entire missionary task rises out of the ultimate intention of the Father. W. O. Carver expressed it romantically eighty years ago, "The origin of missions is ultimately to be found in the heart of God."[13] The Church and the planting of churches are no trivial afterthought. They were in God's purpose, to use a phrase of Spurgeon's, when this world was in the mind of God, like an oak tree is in the cup of an acorn. It is his purpose that all of creation experience redemption and reconciliation in Christ (Colossians 1:20) and be set free from its slavery to corruption into the freedom of the glory of the children of God (Romans 8:21). That hope waits on the revealing of the sons of God (Romans 8:19). According to God's purpose, Abraham was called, and the nation of Israel was chosen. It was the intention of the Father that his own Son should become flesh and be delivered up to death by the predetermined plan and foreknowledge of God (Acts 2:23). It was God's purpose to raise him from the dead. It is also God's purpose that the Church of Jesus Christ take this message of redemption and reconciliation to every people and tribe on the face of the globe.

THE LORDSHIP OF CHRIST Church planting is also grounded in the lordship of Jesus Christ. God has made him both Lord and Christ (Acts 2:36). He is seated at the right hand of God in heavenly places. He is far above all other rulers and authorities and power. He is made head over all things to the Church (Ephesians 1:20-23). All authority and power has been given to him (Matthew 28:18). God highly exalted him, and bestowed on him the name which is above every name, that at the name of Jesus every knee should bow, of those who are in heaven, and on earth, and under the earth, and that every tongue should confess that Jesus Christ is Lord, to the glory of God the Father (Philippians 2:9-11).

Jesus Christ is Lord! The nations have been given to him for a heritage (Psalm 2:8). Our task is to claim for him what is his. The decisive battle has been fought. The invader and usurper have been defeated. The final outcome is sure. Christ must reign until all things are put under his feet (1 Corinthians 15:25). The kingdom of God came to this age in the life, death, and resurrection of Christ. Jesus erected and then empowered his Church. The Church is the instrument of the kingdom of God, which works through the Church. It is the community of the kingdom of God. It presses the battle against satanic evil in the world and controls the keys that open the door to eternal life. Local congregations are intended to be outposts of the kingdom, where the doors to the kingdom are swung wide and where spiritual warfare is carried on.[14] Church planting is an expression of the concern that the way into the Kingdom be opened for all men, for every tribe and subtribe of humanity. It is part of the process of actualizing the lordship of Christ in the world.

THE MINISTRY OF THE SPIRIT Finally, church planting is grounded in the ministry of the Holy Spirit. "Methods alone, even correct methods, will not produce a New Testament church. The mechanics of proper procedure must be accompanied by the dynamics of apostolic power."[15] "New churches are born . . . because the Holy Spirit of God is still at work in . . . [the] world. Indeed, apart from the work of the Holy Spirit there would be no new churches."[16] The Bible punctuates the truth of these statements. Church planting is precisely the work of the Spirit. For, as I have said earlier, it is he who creates community; he is the commonality of the Church and the churches. It is in and through churches that the Spirit performs his ministry. The history of missions in its totality is the history of the work of the Spirit of God.[17]

Church planting is grounded in the ministry of the Spirit in at least four ways. First, the Holy Spirit indwells the gathered congregation as well as the body of the believer. His indwelling presence makes a church a living organism. He is, therefore, absolutely essential to the birth of a church. A crowd of people, meeting in one place, even to worship the true and living God, is not by the act of gathering constituted as a church. Even if the Word is preached and the sacraments observed, these alone do not transform a group of believers into a body in Christ. That is uniquely the work of the Holy Spirit.

Second, the Holy Spirit instructs churches. This is just what happened at Antioch in Acts 13. The Holy Spirit gave clear directions. "Set apart for Me Barnabas and Saul for the work to which I have called them" (Acts 13:2). It is the Holy Spirit that moves upon a congregation and calls individuals from that congregation to a ministry of church planting.

The last phrase leads into the third way that church planting is grounded in the ministry of the Spirit. The Holy Spirit endows churches. Through the gifts given by the Holy Spirit a church is enabled to function properly and effectively. It is time we gave up our identification of the Twelve as the only apostles and recognize the apostolic gift as still present in the Church. When a church becomes committed to church planting, God invariably raises up believers who are endowed with this gift and who prove very productive in church planting.

Finally, the Holy Spirit empowers churches. He mediates the power of the Lord Christ to his people. Anyone who has been involved in trying to gather a church out of the pagan pools of American society can testify to the absolute necessity of the direct intervention of the Holy Spirit in this work. The Spirit was poured out after Christ was exalted to the right hand of God. He is the dynamic force of vital Christian life. New churches will never be planted until those charged with gathering them learn to appropriate the power available through the Holy Spirit. "The Spirit of God," John R. Mott wrote eighty years ago, "is the great missioner [he could have said 'church planter'] and . . . only as He dominates the work and workers can we hope for success."[18] Church planting is grounded in the ministry of the Spirit because the essential ministries of the Holy Spirit are essential to the church planting process.

How shall I conclude this? I believe it is important to ask the right questions. I also believe it is important to operate from a strong biblical base. I have a deep conviction that God wants us to multiply churches in every segment of society in these last years of the twentieth century—both in America and around the world.

2

Biblical Guidelines for Church Planting

Paul was not
the only preacher of
Christianity
in the Gentile world
of that day . . .
but he outstripped
all others as a
pioneer missionary
and planter of churches,
and nothing can detract
from his achievement
as the Gentiles' apostle
par excellence.

F. F. Bruce, 1977

The significance of the Bible for contemporary church planting is not exhausted by a discussion of the grounds for a church planting strategy. In church planting, for many, the question is not *why* but *how*. Does the Bible provide practical guidelines that can help us obey the command of Jesus and emulate the example of the early church to gather new disciples into congregations?

The most seminal and extensive passage in the Bible for pragmatic church planting is Acts 16. More is known of Paul's work in Philippi than in any other city—even Ephesus. This chapter will identify and apply some first-century church-planting axioms to the current North American arena.

The bedrock principles employed by Paul and his team are transcultural. Even though they arise from events of a specific time, in a specific place, and in a culture that has passed away, they can serve us today. Therefore, these guidelines, though I have applied them here to the multi-ethnic, multicultural mosaic of North American society, can be extrapolated and used in any region, among all people groups, and by any group of disciples.

THE PHILIPPIAN LETTER AND ACTS 16

My interest in Acts 16 was aroused during an eighteen-month period when I studied Paul's letter to the saints in Philippi. For almost a year I read Paul's letter every day and Acts 16–18 over and over again. In that process I came to some very clear convictions about the Philippian correspondence.

First, Philippians is essentially a missionary tract. The major theme of the book is not "joy" or "rejoice in Christ," as many commentators have alleged. Rather, its major thrust concerns "the furtherance of the gospel." Philippians is a letter written by the leader of a church planting team to thank a group of Christians who had recently, as at other times, sent financial support for the team and its work (Philippians 4:10-19).

Second, I became convinced that the letter was not written to *the* church in Philippi, but to the believers in several churches. The salutation identifies the recipients as "the saints in Christ Jesus at Philippi, together with the overseers [bishops] and deacons" (Philippians. 1:1; NIV). The churches of the New Testament often had a plural eldership. However, the account of events in Acts 16, references to "the churches of Macedonia" in Paul's Corinthian letters, and evidence from social research about the eastern part of the Roman Empire in Paul's era suggest that several congregations ultimately were planted in Philippi and its surrounding territory. Paul was writing to all believers in Philippi. Perhaps the letter was circulated among all the churches of Macedonia.[1] They all had an astounding record of giving (2 Corinthians 8:1-5). Most of these churches, whether in this city or across the province, were household churches ministering to distinct social and geographical segments within the entire region.

Finally, I came to the conviction that Acts 16 is a gold mine of workable truth. These axiomatic guidelines can direct us now two thousand years later as we work in vastly different places and cultures. The principles of attitude and behavior that guided Paul, Silas, Timothy, and Luke can be practiced successfully today by persons with vastly different gifts and abilities.

I. FORM YOUR CHURCH PLANTING TEAM ON THE BASIS OF YOUR STRATEGY

[Paul] came to Derbe and then to Lystra, where a disciple named Timothy lived, whose mother was a Jewess and a believer, but whose father was a Greek. The brothers at Lystra and Iconium spoke well of him. Paul wanted to take him along on the journey, so he circumcised him because of the Jews who lived in that area, for they all knew that his father was a Greek. As they traveled from town to town, they delivered the decisions reached by the apostles and elders in Jerusalem for the people to obey. So the churches were strengthened in the faith and grew daily in numbers. (Acts 16:1-5; NIV)

The first two paragraphs of Acts 16 tell a wonderful but strange story. Paul and Silas visited the churches established in the early years of Paul's ministry. Located in Syria and Cilicia, near Tarsus, Paul's ancestral home (Acts 15:41), these churches were probably a result of the early ministry of Paul and the extension ministry of the Antioch church. After crossing the mountains out of Cilicia, they came to Derbe, in the district of Pisidia, and began to retrace the route of the earlier journey of Paul and Barnabas.

At Lystra, a new member, the young man Timothy, was added to this team. Though his mother was a Jewess, Timothy had never been circumcised. When Paul had Timothy undergo that rite, Paul revealed that his basic strategy had not changed since his first missionary journey. He intended to go first to the Jewish synagogues, where he would find people familiar with the Jewish scriptures and who worshiped the God of Israel.

Paul's strategy was to offer the gospel first to the Hellenistic Jews who were scattered across the Roman Empire and
who worshiped weekly in synagogues. Both Paul and Silas
were Hellenistic Jews as well as Roman citizens. Through
their communication to Greek-speaking kinsmen, they hoped
not only to evangelize Israel but also to develop a bridge to
the Greek-speaking ethnic groups that occupied what is mod-
ern-day Turkey. Paul's insistence that Silas, rather than John
Mark, form a part of the missionary team on the second journey, may have been based on his effort to match personnel
with strategy, as much as dissatisfaction with John Mark's
previous behavior. John Mark probably suffered a case of first-
century culture shock when he arrived among the uninhib-
ited and culturally diverse peoples in Pamphylia (Acts 13:13).

Paul saw Timothy as one who was indeed a Hellenistic
Jew—but more. Paul's home was not far away in the district
of Cicilia. Timothy was a native son of Galatia and culturally
much closer to people in the province of Bithynia and Asia.
Paul deliberately manned his team in order to execute his
strategy in the most effective manner.

This principle is applicable today: if ability, character, and
spiritual vitality are the same, always choose a leader or team
member who is the shortest cultural distance from the people
you are attempting to evangelize. Whether the team is a mar-
ried couple or a dozen highly skilled professionals, it is good
to have as few significant cultural or social barriers as possible
for the team to cross. In fact, if character, calling, and spiritual vitality are equal, cultural identity is to be preferred to
natural ability and technical or academic knowledge.

Cultural, ethnic, and linguistic realities only illustrate how
this principle can be applied today. If your goal is to plant
a church in a large, responsive population and the new congregation has the potential to reach several thousand, your
church planter should have ample large-church experience in
his background. The manning of your church-planting team
should follow your strategy. One primary reason churches
remain small, when surrounded by winnable people, is

because the vision of the local church held by the leaders is that of a small church. The leaders have not been part of a larger church. They do not know how the larger church functions. If your goal is to plant a congregation with megachurch potential, it is often better to look for a church planter who has been on the staff or been a vital member of a growing larger church. Only the most gifted and visionary leaders, whose lives have been spent in small churches, can plant and develop large, multicongregational churches.

II. GO WHERE THE SPIRIT DIRECTS, BUT GO!

Paul and his companions traveled throughout the region of Phrygia and Galatia, having been kept by the Holy Spirit from preaching the word in the province of Asia. When they came to the border of Mysia, they tried to enter Bithynia, but the Spirit of Jesus would not allow them to. So they passed by Mysia and went down to Troas. During the night Paul had a vision of a man of Macedonia standing and begging him, "Come over to Macedonia and help us." After Paul had seen the vision, we got ready at once to leave for Macedonia, concluding that God had called us to preach the gospel to them. (Acts 16:6-10; NIV)

Paul and his team were determined to move into new territory. The team delivered the report from the Jerusalem conference (Acts 15:23-29) and encouraged the churches. After spending some time with the churches in southern Galatia, they moved through the narrow, mountainous region of Pamphylia and attempted to go into Asia. In some unknown manner, Paul and his team were forbidden by the Holy Spirit to establish at the time a beachhead in the Roman province of Asia. It is clear from hindsight that the Holy Spirit had another strategy for the evangelization of Roman Asia. Paul's Ephesian ministry was yet to come. Undaunted, they moved north toward Bithynia, but they were hindered by the Spirit of Jesus. In utter frustration they moved on west, past the small district of Mysia, to the port city of Troas.

What shall we make of this strange account? Had Paul been running before the Lord, pushing stubbornly ahead without consulting the Father? Had he been mistaken about the will of God?

Several lessons can be learned from this story. First, the situation makes it clear that, in the divine intention, the Holy Spirit is the executive director of the expansion of the church. Paul, of course, would have embraced this axiom, but in these events the truth was strongly reinforced. Second, in the sovereign purpose of God, not all peoples are equally responsive to the gospel message at all times. Paul sometimes spoke of an "open door" that had been presented to him in a particular place. Third, we should direct our major resources and efforts toward responsive peoples. Fourth, those who would see disciples made and churches planted should spend time with God, seeking the direction and blessing of the Holy Spirit on church-planting endeavors.

Another lesson to be learned from this paragraph is extremely important to those who plant churches. A. T. Robertson said, "Two rebuffs on the same trip would have discouraged some men. Paul was not allowed to go west into Asia, nor north into Bithynia, but he had no notion of going home in disgust."[2] Plans, even for the greatest church planter in history, seldom operated just as they were intended to operate. If anything can go wrong, it will. Doors will not open. Helpers will turn back or fall by the wayside. Things *never* happen just as the church planter or missionary strategist anticipates.

When plans fall through, that does not mean that we fold our tents and go home. It means that we push on until we find either the open door or the open heart. We should be sure that we are led by the Holy Spirit; we should go as he commands. But when trouble, calamity, or discouragement come, we must not quit.

If untoward and capricious events can keep us from the church-planting task, churches will never be planted. Therefore, there should be a clear sense of call and direction to a church-planting ministry that will supersede all the disastrous and unpredictable events that often plague efforts to launch new churches.

These specific implications for those who would see churches established come out of Paul's search:

1. *The church planter without a specific call will probably not succeed.*
2. *That call should focus in a burden, special interest, or concern for a region, people, or community.*
3. *The church planter should undertake the task fully alerted to the inevitability of hardship and disappointment.*

III. TAKE TIME TO GET ACQUAINTED WITH YOUR COMMUNITY

From Troas we put out to sea and sailed straight for Samothrace, and the next day on to Neapolis. From there we traveled to Philippi, a Roman colony and the leading city of that district of Macedonia. And we stayed there several days. (Acts 16:11-12; NIV)

Paul and his team did not rush into their redemptive ministries. No ready-made program was put into operation. Tried and true methods were held in abeyance. Several days were invested to find out everything possible about Philippi. They found out that there was only a small Jewish community, not large enough for a synagogue. They discovered that some God-fearing women met regularly to pray, an evidence of spiritual hunger. They attempted to discover needs that waited to be met.

Research is never out of place; it should be employed continually. Today's technology enables us to gain incredible understandings of target areas for new churches. Demographic information provides irreplaceable knowledge about the size, economic status, age, gender, and other social characteristics of large and small population areas. Geographical information can tell us much about the history, environment, and physical situations of persons. Psychographic assessments indicate, in general terms, the values, life-styles, and attitudes of groups within population areas. Ethnographic studies open windows of understanding about cultural and racial distinctions and commonalities. Market segmentation (geodemographics) provides insight into the habits and hungers of groups. The computer can make all of this information immediately available.

Nothing replaces personal observation and involvement with individuals in the discovery of felt needs, attitudes, life-styles, and values. Before we attempt to plant a church, we need to find out where people hurt and bring Jesus and his message to bear at those points of need. The absence of hard data should never keep the church planter from responding to obvious need.

IV. USE THE BRIDGES OF CULTURE IF YOU CAN

On the Sabbath we went outside the city gate to the river, where we expected to find a place of prayer. We sat down and began to speak to the women who had gathered there. (Acts 16:13; NIV)

Reference has already been made to the basic approach that Paul and Barnabas had devised for gaining a foothold in the Roman world. Paul and Silas continued that strategy. It was essentially the same strategy that Korean evangelicals have used to gather churches around the world where Koreans have immigrated. It was the basic approach of German and Swedish Baptists in America in the nineteenth century. It was the basic strategy that Southern Baptists used in the early efforts to burst out of the bounds of the traditional South.

While Paul and Silas could not use the synagogue approach in Philippi, they used the fundamental principle. They discovered that a group met regularly for prayer. Though we have no evidence that Lydia was a Jewess, she was a worshiper of the God of Israel. She met with a group "on the Sabbath."

Paul used the bridge of culture, whether strong or weak, to accomplish his objectives when possible.

Ideas and ideals travel through the networks of culture and by the vehicles of culture. The gospel of Jesus Christ is a system of ideas and ideals. It cannot be communicated except along cultural paths and highways. When a cultural common denominator was available, Paul took advantage of that vehicle for the progress of the gospel. The church planter today should do the same.

V. LOOK FOR PEOPLE WHO ARE PRAYING: TAKE ADVANTAGE OF SPIRITUAL HUNGER

We sat down and began to speak to the women who had gathered there. One of those listening was a woman named Lydia, a dealer in purple cloth from the city of Thyatira, who was a worshiper of God. The Lord opened her heart to respond to Paul's message. (Acts 16:13-14; NIV)

The Holy Spirit always precedes us when we go where he directs. He is already at work in the hearts and minds of individuals and events of history. He uses, for his purposes, the mishaps and evils of life. The church planter can count on that with confidence. The example of Paul and Silas should guide us. They looked for people who were praying. They attempted to find individuals in whom God was directly at work, people who were already seeking him.

The principle has special application to North America today. A spiritual fallout occurred after the sixties, and the brief spiritual awakening that is called the Jesus movement was thwarted in most of the churches. Many small groups gathering for spiritual succor have been meeting since the late seventies. One researcher identified 125 independent "house" churches in Houston. Most, in his opinion, were floundering for want of direction. The rejection of materialism by many counterculture people in the seventies and eighties and the disinterest by many "baby boomers" in the formalism and sophistication of existing churches provide an open door for church planters today. This door is ajar to those who will adapt the form through which the gospel is communicated to these groups without compromising the content of the gospel message. One contributor to church decline during the last generation in North America is the opposite: altering the content of the message and holding on to old forms of liturgy and methodology.

North America is a continent with many responsive peoples. There are those who are listening and searching. Not all peoples in North America are equally responsive. Some groups resist the message of Christ. Significant subgroups in the North American black communities have been receptive for a generation. Numerous ethnic groups are exceedingly receptive to Christ. Suburbanites are usually receptive. Many other people groups are open to the good news about Jesus. Church planters must look for those people and take advantage of spiritual hunger.

VI. DELIVER A SIMPLE, CLEAR, AND SPECIFIC MESSAGE, ADAPTED TO THE SITUATION

We [Paul and his companions] sat down and began to speak to the women who had gathered there. . . . When she and the members of her household were baptized, she invited us to her

home. "If you consider me a believer in the Lord," she said,
"come and stay at my house." And she persuaded us. (Acts
16:13, 15; NIV)

Two accounts of individual and household conversion
appear in this chapter. The circumstances of both are radically different. Paul's message to Lydia was certainly not in
a formal setting. No pulpit existed for the riverside prayer
meeting. The message of salvation delivered to the jailer
occurred while the apostles were still in civil bondage. It was
adapted to the particular place and hour (Acts 16:29-34).
Paul spoke the Good News clearly and simply to those before
him, aiming at understanding on the part of his hearers.
The basic message was the same, but the articulation of it
depended on the time, the place, and especially the audience
he addressed. More detailed exposition and explanation evidently followed for the extended families, friends, and servants of these two individuals (Acts 16:15, 32). However,
these details were certainly not complicated or mysterious.

When one reads through Acts 16 and thinks through the
full and detailed scenario in which these events happened,
some conclusions are obvious. First, the message was personal. It focused on an individual and those in his or her immediate circle of influence. The message was not general but
specific. It answered the questions, What must I do to be
saved? What must my family do to be saved?

The message of Paul and Silas was also positive. Their
words did not have primary focus on what is forbidden to
Christ's disciples. Rather, their message focused on Jesus
Christ the Lord and a positive faith in him. We know from
Paul's other preaching that repentance was integral to his
message. However, the devout, God-seeking Lydia and the
desperate jailer were already convinced of their need for
something new. Paul and Silas responded with a positive
simple message about how to find the living God and how
to find salvation. They, with their families and friends,
were told how to find life.

Finally, the message of Paul and Silas was persuasive. Whatever is meant by the phrase "the Lord opened her heart to respond to Paul's message" (Acts 16:14; NIV), it included baptism. The result of speaking the "word of the Lord" to the jailer and his household was the same (Acts 16:32). Paul and Silas persuaded these people to openly identify themselves as disciples of Jesus Christ. They called for a decision and for the action that would make that decision concrete and permanent: water baptism.

The implications of this axiom for church planters are far-reaching. The message delivered today must *not* be garbled or confused, but clear; it must *not* be complicated or dense, but simple; and it must *not* be compromised or truncated, but made specific. The message of Christ should center in Christ Jesus as Lord and ask for commitment in the details of life.

VII. RECOGNIZE AND USE THE *OIKOS*

One of those listening was a woman named Lydia, a dealer in purple cloth from the city of Thyatira, who was a worshiper of God. The Lord opened her heart to respond to Paul's message. When she *and the members of her household* were baptized, she invited us to her home. "If you consider me a believer in the Lord," she said, "come and stay at my house." And she persuaded us (Acts 16:14-15; NIV).

"They replied, 'Believe in the Lord Jesus, and you will be saved—you and your *household.*' Then they spoke the word of the Lord to him and to *all the others in his house*" (Acts 16:31-32; NIV; italics mine). The words *home, house,* and *household* are translated from the same Greek word, *oikos.* That word clearly is used in two ways in the New Testament. It sometimes refers to the facility where a person lives. More often it refers to the family. The reference is not to the nuclear family of American society, i.e., father, mother, and children, but to the larger family system that often lived together in Roman society. In fact, it was often larger than the kinship family, including servants, friends, and associates, as well as relatives.[3]

The "household" concept first appears in the account of the growth of the church in Jerusalem. The new believers met daily in the temple courts where, I believe, they carried on their work of personal and mass evangelism. The activity of Peter and John in early days supports this contention (Acts 3-4). They also worshiped together within households, inviting acquaintances and friends to join them (Acts 2:46-47). The Lord was at work among them, and these household congregations enlarged daily. Peter returned to such a group when he was miraculously released from prison (Acts 12:12-14).

The precise nature of the *oikos* can be discovered in the account of Cornelius's conversion. Peter arrived at the centurion's home to find a gathering of Cornelius's "relatives and close friends" (Acts 10:24). When Peter reported on the visit to the "apostles and brothers" in Jerusalem, he recounted that Cornelius had been told by an angel that Peter would bring him a message by which he and his entire *oikos* could be saved (Acts 11:14). One's *oikos* is the constellation of relatives, associates, and close friends with whom an individual enjoys a very close relationship.

When Paul and his church planting team arrived in Philippi, they had long before recognized the significance of the *oikos*. They already looked beyond individuals to households. The early Christians were able to penetrate extended families and acquaintance networks, evangelizing them out to the edges.

Sociologists assert that the *oikos* is a transcultural structure found in every society. The contemporary church planter learns to recognize and use the *oikos* in the development of core groups and as natural growth centers for the new congregation.

VIII. EXPECT, ENCOURAGE, AND ACCEPT THE SUPPORT OF NEW BELIEVERS; THE RESOURCES ARE IN THE HARVEST

And when she and her household had been baptized, she urged us, saying, "If you have judged me to be faithful to the Lord, come into my house and stay." And she prevailed upon us. (Acts 16:15)

The gospel believed produces generosity. The stewardship of material things is a basic discipline of the Christian life. Don't be surprised when new believers want to join in supporting the new congregation.

Sometimes—as here—the generosity may be in "kind" instead of in cash. Sometimes—as was probably not the case with Lydia—the support may be at a level lower than the church planter would *like* to receive. However, when such help is offered, it should be received with joy and put immediately into the work. True gifts should never, as a rule, be rejected.

In the last century, probably with the passing of the frontier, an erroneous rule-of-thumb has been developed that says, "In church planting you do everything for the target people and do not expect the target people to do anything for themselves." In the New Testament, the opposite was true. In fact, one of the laws of the harvest (to which the church's task is likened) says, "The resources are in the harvest." "In the harvest," where the church planter is sent to labor, the resources will be found for the new congregation's future. Angels of mercy and bearers of the Father's bounty, never to be seen again, may appear to bring help. More often, in the process of reaping, individuals will be converted to Christ, leaders will be discovered, and believers will receive the gifts to perform those ministries necessary for the future effectiveness of the new church.

The church planter should look at those people who are

brought to Christ for participation both in the ministry and support of the work.

New believers should be used at once in the spiritual ministry of sharing their faith and meeting human need. The principles of the stewardship of material things should be included in the "all things" that they are taught to obey. The practice of listening to God should be developed in new believers, encouraging them to be obedient in sharing life's blessings. The biblical virtue of hospitality should be taught. However, the church planter should watch for the moving of the indwelling Spirit in the lives of new believers, prompting them to freely give as they have freely received. When that prompting is obeyed, it should be encouraged and accepted.

IX. DO NOT DISCOUNT THE PLACE AND EFFECTIVENESS OF WOMEN IN CHURCH PLANTING

We . . . began to speak to the women who had gathered there. One of those listening was a woman named Lydia. . . . The Lord opened her heart to respond to Paul's message. When she and the members of her household were baptized, she invited us to her home. (Acts 16:13-15; NIV)

Pastor Willie Simmons, of the Greater Cornerstone Baptist Church in Los Angeles, is fond of saying that Paul saw a vision of a man of Macedonia begging Paul to come over to Macedonia and help. When Paul arrived, he didn't find the man of his vision but a few women who were praying. Those women were, evidently, extremely significant in the growth of churches in Philippi and throughout Macedonia.

In almost every culture, women tend to respond more readily to the message of Jesus Christ than men and, thus, can become a significant factor in the planting of churches in the culture. Women have throughout church history been the first foundation stones of an expanding Christian movement. The pattern continues today.

However, early responsiveness is only one, and perhaps the least important, of the contributions that women have made and do make to church planting. Women often provide both the material and human resources necessary for beginning new churches. They provide open homes, and they open doors to extended families and larger circles of association and friendship through which the gospel travels.

This was certainly the case with Lydia of Thyatira. She and her household provided home and headquarters for the missionary team. Evidently the compound in which she and her immediate or extended family lived provided the meeting place for the new congregation. When Paul and Silas were to be later released from prison, and before they departed from Philippi, they met with the church in Lydia's house (Acts 16:40).

While I would deny biblical grounds for women to serve as the principle leader of a church, the *role* usually called "pastor" today, I do affirm that many women today have the shepherding or pastor *gift* and can and should lead small groups and congregations within the larger church. In fact, some women have the apostolic gift; they are extremely effective in making disciples and gathering new congregations, of doing that pioneering and most essential role in church planting.[4]

A biblical example of a woman who probably had this gift is Priscilla. Along with her husband, she is often described in the Bible as having a church meeting in her house (Romans 16:3; 1 Corinthians 16:19). Delores Thomas, who recently retired from years of labor in Maine, was instrumental in starting new congregations in that state during her years of service. She moved to Maine in 1962 with her husband, who was a pastoral missionary, sent by their denomination to be the pastor of one church and to start several others. After his death in 1976, Mrs. Thomas continued their work starting new congregations.

She gathered the nucleus of new congregations, helped
to find and orient pastors for the new congregations, and
provided advice and support for young pastors coming
to serve the new churches. She is one of many women
who have served and are serving my denomination in the
church-planting task. Do not discount the effectiveness
of women in all aspects of new church development.

X. DON'T NEGLECT INTENTIONAL, INTENSIVE PRAYER

*Once when we were going to the place of prayer . . . (Acts
16:16; NIV)*

Evidently, over time, Paul and his team continued to
participate in the Sabbath morning prayer service. They
may have continued because this was a place where spiritu-
ally awakened and searching people gathered. They may
have continued to find people prepared by the Holy Spirit
to receive the Word of God.

However, knowing of the significance Paul placed on
intercessory prayer, it is likely that he, Luke, and other
team members habitually went to the place of prayer to
pray. He testified that he had received grace from God "to
be a minister of Christ Jesus to the Gentiles, ministering as
a priest the gospel of God, that my offering of the Gentiles
might become acceptable, sanctified by the Holy Spirit"
(Romans 15:15-16). The "ministry of the priest" is the
ministry of intercession.

Prayer and intercession were as much a part of his ministry in church planting as were proclamation and evangelism. He often encouraged his correspondents to engage in
intercessory prayer for the ministry of his church planting
team. "Now I urge you," he wrote to the Roman Christians, "to strive together with me in your prayers to God
for me" (Romans 15:30). In the Ephesian letter he urged

believers to pray on his behalf that "utterance may be given to me in the opening of my mouth, to make known with boldness the . . . gospel, for which I am an ambassador in chains; that in proclaiming it I may speak boldly, as I ought to speak" (Ephesians 6:19-20). To the Colossians he said: "Devote yourselves to prayer . . . praying at the same time for us as well, that God may open up to us a door for the word, so that we may speak forth the mystery of Christ" (Colossians 4:2-3).

Early in his ministry he urged the Thessalonians to pray for him and his team, "that the word of the Lord may spread rapidly and be glorified, just as it did also with you" (2 Thessalonians 3:1).

If prayer for boldness, open doors, and rapid progress for the work was necessary in Paul's case, it is certainly necessary for the church planter today. Not only does a network of prayer support need to be developed for every new work, but the habit of daily, intentional intercession to God is required. Church planting is spiritual warfare and requires the use of spiritual weapons (Ephesians 6:18ff.; 2 Corinthians 10:3-6).

XI. EXPECT DEMONIC, CARNAL, AND WORLDLY OPPOSITION TO CHURCH PLANTING

Once when we were going to the place of prayer, we were met by a slave girl who had a spirit by which she predicted the future. She earned a great deal of money for her owners by fortune-telling. This girl followed Paul and the rest of us, shouting, "These men are servants of the Most High God, who are telling you the way to be saved." She kept this up for many days. Finally Paul became so troubled that he turned around and said to the spirit, "In the name of Jesus Christ I command you to come out of her!" At that moment the spirit left her. When the owners of the slave girl realized that their hope of making money was gone, they seized Paul and Silas and

dragged them into the marketplace to face the authorities.
(Acts 16:16-19; NIV)

Church planters often are surprised when they get into trouble. They assume that, if they go in obedience to the call of God to plant a church, everything will work great. The opposite is true. Everything that can go wrong will go wrong in church planting.

We live and serve in a fallen universe; we are fallen creatures and work with fallen creatures. Satan and his evil spirits are alive and on the attack. Carnal human beings still act according to their common nature. World systems still stand in opposition to the full sway of God's kingdom. *We should expect opposition.*

The old cliché that Christians can expect opposition from the "world, the flesh, and the devil" was turned around in Paul's experience. The first opposition he experienced was demonic.

A girl with a spirit "of divination" began following Paul and team members around the city. At inopportune times, she would bear testimony to who they were. "These men are bond-servants of the Most High God, who are proclaiming to you the way of salvation" (Acts 16:17). She disrupted their work, annoyed them personally, and cast a shadow of doubt about their integrity.

You do not want some people to give witness to you and your work. This woman was such a person. Demonic powers were at work through her, hindering the work of Christ. After a time, Paul turned, spoke to the spirit, and set the girl free from her bondage.

The exorcism aroused the greed and anger of the girl's masters. Instead of rejoicing at her freedom from a demonic spirit, they objected to their loss of revenue. She was a cash-producing commodity, valued only for her ability to generate income for their use. Carnality in its most vicious and vitriolic form had been unleashed.

The slave masters soon brought charges against the

apostles before the magistrates. With amazing speed, worldly power produced opposition against the work of making disciples and gathering churches.

This pattern, not always in this sequence, but in essence and substance identical, is repeated over and over again in church planting.

Church planting is, it must be said again, spiritual warfare. It is the process of reclaiming for Christ what rightfully belongs to him. In church planting, new outposts of the kingdom of God are erected in what has been enemy territory. Colonies of righteousness are planted in regions of darkness. One is foolish not to anticipate that the evil empire will strike back. Counterattack will take place.

Valued workers will fall by the wayside. Those living near the meeting place of the new congregation will complain about increased traffic or blocked driveways. Heretofore-forgotten city ordinances will be discovered to keep the new congregation from going forward. Pastors of nearby churches will feel threatened. Gangs will vandalize cars, steal equipment, or harass believers. Opposition will develop.

The principle to be gleaned from Acts 16 is that such opposition should not surprise the church planter. It goes with the territory. It should not create dismay, discouragement, or defeat. Without panic, opposition should be recognized for what it is. Through prayer, good counsel, the application of scriptural principles, and wisdom from above, the opposition should be met head-on. Solutions should be found. Correction should be made, if needed. Demonic attack should be resisted with spiritual weapons. The church planting work should go on.

XII. HANDLE ADVERSITY, DISAPPOINTMENT, AND PAIN WITH COURAGE AND HOPE

And when they had brought them to the chief magistrates, they said, "These men are throwing our city into confusion,

being Jews, and are proclaiming customs which it is not law-
ful for us to accept or to observe, being Romans." And the
crowd rose up together against them, and the chief magistrates
tore their robes off them, and proceeded to order them to be
beaten with rods. And when they had inflicted many blows
upon them, they threw them into prison, commanding the
jailer to guard them securely; and he, having received such a
command, threw them into the inner prison, and fastened
their feet in the stocks. But about midnight Paul and Silas
were praying and singing hymns of praise to God, and the pris-
oners were listening to them. (Acts 16:20-25)

The events that followed the act of deliverance were cata-
clysmic for Paul and Silas. In a brief span of time they were
arrested, charged with sedition, tried in a biased court on
trumped-up charges, beaten severely, and thrown into
prison. Such experience has often been the fate of pioneers
in church planting.

The mark of greatness in Paul and Silas was not that
they were persecuted. Thousands of believers have been
persecuted since Jesus returned to heaven. The key to the
greatness and effectiveness of Paul and Silas was their bear-
ing under violence and injustice. How did they react when
they were reviled, defiled, and demeaned?

When avaricious, carnal men and hostile authorities
came down on Paul and Silas, they were violated, disappointed, physically hurt, and in jail. All these things happened. Yet at midnight these apostles were praying and
singing hymns of praise to God.

They were practicing what they preached. "We . . . exult
in our tribulations" (Romans 5:3), Paul was later to write the
Romans. They were practicing what Jesus preached: "Blessed
are you when men . . . persecute you . . . on account of Me.
Rejoice, and be glad . . . for so they persecuted the prophets
who were before you" (Matthew 5:11-12).

What would most modern disciples have done? We
would have complained and whined. "Why would you let

this happen to me, God?" or "Where is my lawyer?" would be the question on our lips.

Paul and Silas were so sincere and real, everyone else in the jail was listening to them.

Unchurched people pay more attention to the way we handle adversity, to the manner in which we respond to disappointment, and to the reaction we make to pain in our lives than they do to what we preach and sing. How believers react to suffering and calamity makes more of an impact on unbelievers than anything else in the Christian life.

How the church planter responds when disappointment comes, when dreams and plans crumble beneath him, is of crucial importance in the church planting process. The attitude toward heartbreak and pain affects both unchurched persons and new believers. The church planting principle is to be ready always to handle adversity and tragedy with confidence and hope.

If the church planter is thrown into jail, it does not necessarily mean the new church will fail. In fact, God often uses adversity to cause a group of believers to come together as one body in Christ. If injustice, pain, and disappointment come to the church planter, it does not necessarily mean that God will not enable the church planter to do what he called him or her to do. In fact, as in this case, the Father may use the troubles as his method of helping the church planter accomplish the mission.

A basic skill for the church planter is the ability to deal with travail and tribulation in a manner that will honor Christ and build Christian strength in new believers.

XIII. EXPECT AN INTERVENTION FROM GOD

And he [the jailer] called for lights and rushed in and, trembling with fear, he fell down before Paul and Silas, and after he brought them out, he said, "Sirs, what must I do to be saved?" (Acts 16:29-30)

Churches cannot be planted through transfer growth alone. Starting new churches is directly related to conversion growth. Thank God, it is the Lord who adds to his church. The Holy Spirit convicts men and women of sin, convinces them that they should repent and turn to Christ, and does the work of regeneration. Without this divine activity and intervention, no true church planting would take place.

As pioneer church planters through the centuries have penetrated new areas and begun to make disciples of new people groups, they often have been accompanied by miraculous signs. Paul wrote the Corinthian Christians that "the signs of a true apostle were performed among you with all perseverance, by signs and wonders and miracles" (2 Corinthians 12:12). Apostles were the premiere pioneer church planters.

Whether or not the manifestation of the Holy Spirit in beginning new churches comes under the category of a sign or wonder is beside the point. In truth, God intervenes if a church is being successfully planted with wonderful provisions of resources, with the sacrificial commitment of time, natural talent, and learned skills, and with both routine and dramatic cases of regeneration.

When tribulations, disappointment, and discouragement come to the church planter, he or she should rejoice. Increased difficulty often means that God is about to do something great in and through the church planter's life. Therefore, the church leader who is being faithful to God can look for God to break into that situation. It may not be an earthquake, but it is, in fact, the living God breaking into history again, revealing himself to men and women and making them members of his family.

Church planters can count on God's intervention if they are faithful to share the message in the power and at the direction of the Holy Spirit.

XIV. TAKE EVERY OPPORTUNITY TO SHARE THE MESSAGE. LOOK ON EVERYONE AS A PROSPECT.

The jailer woke up, and when he saw the prison doors open, he drew his sword and was about to kill himself because he thought the prisoners had escaped. But Paul shouted, "Don't harm yourself! We are all here!" The jailer called for lights, rushed in and fell trembling before Paul and Silas. He then brought them out and asked, "Sirs, what must I do to be saved?" (Acts 16:27-30; NIV)

Philippi was a Roman colony (Acts 16:12). It was populated with a large segment of retired personnel from the Roman army. These people constituted, in all probability, a distinct people group in the city, quite different from the native Greeks who populated Macedonia. Lydia and her family were Greek-speaking Asians, another significant group in the city.

Retired Roman military personnel were not known for their cultural finesse or noble character. The jailer, in all probability, was one of those persons. Not in the first century and not in the twenty-first century would he and his *oikos* have been the most desirable prospects for a new church.

For Paul and Silas these facts were not factors for consideration. The jailer was a man made in God's image for whom Christ had died. He had been prepared by the Holy Spirit, by what means we do not know, to be concerned about his salvation. The church planters saw him as one of the lost sheep that the Eternal Father wants his church to find.

The jailer may have been a student or a disillusioned devotee of Mithraism. He may have been in one of the other mystery cults that thrived in the Roman Empire during the first century. Many older commentators suggest this possibility. He may have already attended to the preaching of Paul and his team. However it was done, the Holy Spirit had prepared the jailer's heart. He was ready to ask life's ultimate question.

Paul and Silas jumped at the opportunity to share the message of Christ with a seeking soul.

Sensitivity to both spiritual hunger and Spirit-given opportunity and the rejection of anything like selective evangelism must be the mark of those who plant churches from the perspective of the kingdom of God.

Paul's response to the jailer was in sync with his theology of the church. The church and, thus, those who made up the visible churches were the new people of God. God was gathering them from every culture. The gospel was, for Paul, God's power to save "everyone who believes: first for the Jew, then for the Gentile" (Romans 1:16; NIV). He wrote later to Titus that in Christ the "grace of God that brings salvation has appeared to all men" (Titus 2:11; NIV). "This spiritual fellowship of believers in Christ had no racial or religious limitations."[5]

XV. COUNT ON LONG HOURS AND HARD WORK IN CHURCH PLANTING

About midnight Paul and Silas . . . spoke the word of the Lord to him and to all the others in his house. At that hour of the night the jailer took them and washed their wounds; then immediately he and all his family were baptized. . . . When it was daylight, the magistrates . . . escorted them from the prison. . . . They went to Lydia's house, where they met with the brothers. . . . Then they left. (Acts 16:25-40; NIV)

This long report (Acts 16:25-40) of a day in the life of Paul and Silas is revealing. From their imprisonment to their ultimate departure from the city was probably a thirty-six-hour period. It was thirty-six hours without rest and of incredible stress. It was a time of depressive lows and ecstatic highs, of conflict, of frustration and pain, and of wonderful achievement. We might conclude that this was not a *normal* day. Perhaps not. However, can we say it was really *abnormal?* Paul wrote to the Corinthians, while defending his apostleship:

Are they servants of Christ? (I speak as if insane) I more so; in far more labors, in far more imprisonments, beaten times without number. . . . I have been on frequent journeys, in dangers from rivers . . . from robbers . . . in the city . . . in the wilderness . . . among false brethren; I have been in labor and hardship, through many sleepless nights, in hunger and thirst, often without food, in cold and exposure. Apart from such external things, there is the daily pressure upon me of concern for all the churches. (2 Corinthians 11:23-28)

Church planting is no task for the fainthearted or the lazy. Hard work, long hours, disrupted schedules, and significant risk are required. A forty-hour work week will seldom suffice to plant a church. Church planters get up early and go to bed late. They often have tremendous pressures laid on them. The physical, psychological, and spiritual needs of individuals and families are constant drains on energy and resources. The lack of spiritual maturity in new and old believers and the demands of a growing, new organization take their toll. A dearth of adequate leadership in new congregations often has a negative impact on the church planter. The load is often heavy. Dedication expressed in the investment of time, physical energy, and spiritual warfare is required.

XVI. BE WILLING TO EAT WITH THOSE YOU WIN TO CHRIST

And he took them that very hour of the night and washed their wounds, and immediately he was baptized, he and all his household. And he brought them into his house and set food before them, and rejoiced greatly, having believed in God with his whole household. (Acts 16:33-34)

What Paul and Silas were willing to do in reference to Lydia and her household, they were willing to do with the Philippian jailer. He and his household welcomed Paul and

Silas into their home; they ministered to Paul and Silas with deeds of kindness. In the words "that very hour of the night and washed their wounds" is the evidence of a changed heart and a reformed life.

Perhaps the jailer took Paul and Silas to a pool, perhaps to a Roman bath. Probably he had a water storage tank or a fountain with a large catch basin in the courtyard before the jail. Wherever it was, the jailer and his extended family washed the apostles' wounds beside some water supply, and in the same pool the jailer and his household were baptized.

The jailer then took the prisoners into his home for food and rest. The apostles welcomed the opportunity to eat and fellowship with this new group of believers.

To break bread with new believers, to accept their food in their cultural setting, and to step across barriers of culture are important acts for the church planter. Often the evangelist or church planter stands aloof from the people to be reached. Contemporary expositors and teachers often criticize the Jewish Christians for refusing to eat with the Gentiles. However, many Christian workers will not accept offers of food and hospitality from new believers. They imagine it to be unclean, ill-cooked, or something exotic they dare not touch.

The sharing of food in almost any culture is a sign of acceptance, hospitality, and generosity. The church planter should be willing to eat with new believers in their homes and to have the new disciples into his or her home.

XVII. CLAIM YOUR HUMAN AND CIVIL RIGHTS WHEN NECESSARY, BUT NOT TOO QUICKLY

Now when day came, the chief magistrates sent their police-men, saying, "Release those men." And the jailer reported these words to Paul, saying, "The chief magistrates have sent to release you. Now therefore, come out and go in peace." But Paul said to them, "They have beaten us in public without trial, men who are Romans, and have thrown us into prison;

and now are they sending us away secretly? No indeed! But let them come themselves and bring us out." And the policemen reported these words to the chief magistrates. And they were afraid when they heard that they were Romans, and they came and appealed to them, and when they had brought them out, they kept begging them to leave the city. (Acts 16:35-39)

Conflict with civil authorities and offended individuals is inevitable in church planting. A new church may be seen as a threat by other believers in other churches in the community. Law enforcement persons often have prejudices against newcomers who say they plan to "build a new church." Community residents may perceive witnessing efforts as invasions of privacy. Religious leaders act against proselytism, perceived or real.

Humility and a spirit of servanthood are the characteristics most needed in these times. Threats of legal retaliation, arrogance, offensive assertiveness, and anger are never the best options.

However, when basic human and legal rights are violated and evidence of intended malice is present, it may be time for church planters to stand their ground, expose the injustice, and demand their rights.

Evidently, this was the approach of Paul and Silas. They claimed their rights as Roman citizens only after the fact of mistreatment, injustice, and suffering. This was to have been Paul's approach on other occasions. He did not move into a city and demand special treatment because of his Roman citizenship.

XVIII. TRUST NEW BELIEVERS WITH THE GOSPEL AND TO THE HOLY SPIRIT

And they went out of the prison and entered the house of Lydia, and when they saw the brethren, they encouraged them and departed. (Acts 16:40)

Paul often left his newly won converts to function on their own. His time in each city was extremely limited, even in Corinth and Ephesus. His common practice seems all but impossible to achieve today. In some North American communities it takes up to ten years for a church to become self-supporting, self-propagating, and self-governing. Some congregations, in responsive fields, never achieve these basic criteria for an indigenous church. They continue to be subsidized by the parent church or a supporting agency.

Many factors contribute to their situation. Often sponsoring churches fail to distinguish between a dependent satellite and a pre-independent satellite. Both are legitimate methods for reaching a city or county in the totality of its diverse social segmentation.

Some satellites are located in communities that, because of economic problems and significant physical need, will always require dependent relationships to the parenting churches. Other satellites will be able to function much more effectively if they can eventually become independently organized. Only by independent organization will indigenous leadership develop and the congregation turn in dependent faith to God rather than live in dependence on its supporting agencies.

Paul's solution was to trust the new congregation and its indigenous leaders to the Holy Spirit. Some of his team members often remained behind to complete the instruction and organization of the new congregations. Paul or some of his team visited the new congregations with some regularity. He attempted to address the problems that arose in the young churches. Consequently, we have much of our New Testament. However, his overall method was to trust the new believers with the gospel and to the Holy Spirit.

The situation in North America today is vastly different than in the Roman Empire of the first century. However, the principle of turning leadership and spiritual ministry over to new believers is irreplaceable. This axiom holds true in the development of both dependent and pre-independent satellites.

Roland Allen, the seminal missiologist of the first half of this century whose influence is pervasive today, was sure that this lack of trust in new believers contributed to the anemic character of many churches on the mission field.[6] Melvin Hodges, one of the human architects of the great growth of the Assemblies of God in Latin America, followed Allen at this point. What he said about church planting overseas can be transliterated to the North American scene today:

A church that must depend on foreigners for its workers, that must call for additional missionaries to extend the work . . . is not an indigenous church. It is a hot-house plant that must have an artificial atmosphere and receive special care to keep alive. . . . Surely the weak thing we have produced is not what Jesus meant when He said, "I will build my church and the gates of hell shall not prevail against it."[7]

XIX. HAVE AS YOUR GOAL THE PLANTING OF A CHURCH

Paul was not satisfied just to announce the good news about Jesus Christ. He was not content just to see individuals or, indeed, entire households "believe on the Lord Jesus Christ" and be "saved." Paul was intent on creating a community or family of faith in which believers could be nurtured and from which they could bear witness by word and deed to the unbelieving world. His goal was to see a manifestation of the household or family of God in a localized and contextualized setting. His role was to lay the foundations, to plant the new *ekklesia* of God. Others would build on the foundation or, to use his other metaphor, water the organism he had planted, and God would cause the growth (1 Corinthians 3:5-9).

William O. Carver insisted that the Church, as the Body of Christ composed of all the redeemed, is the continuing incarnation of Christ in the world. He called that concept "the boldest, most awesome" idea in Paul's thought.[8] Commenting on Ephesians 2:19-22, Carver said,

The several buildings included in this figure of speech are the various race groups. Jews were first, then Samaritans, next Romans, Greeks at Antioch, and so one racial group after another, as the gospel was reaching out for all races. A great structure, like the Temple in Jerusalem . . . consists of many units, each unit with a relative completeness and beauty and utility. If the whole is an architectural success, each separate unit must be fitted harmoniously into adjacent structures and into the total scheme.[9]

In discussion about the relationship between the Church and the churches, Carver asserted that in Paul's thought it was understood that "the Church is represented locally in an organized, functioning church." The New Testament nowhere treats the local church as part of an organized, catholic, or worldwide institutional church. "The Christian movement is one Church, but the churches are not under or in one church in any outward, institutional sense."[10]

Roland Allen had much the same understanding. He insisted that the way unity was achieved in the Church was by regarding each local church as part of the yet incomplete body of Christ. "New churches established in the (Roman) provinces (were) regarded equally with the first (church in Jerusalem) as parts of a still incomplete whole which must grow up by degrees into its completeness."[11] Dean Gilliland has described this understanding of Paul's intention graphically (see Figure 1). "All these true churches, of which Jerusalem was one, together reveal the growing total body that is also the church."[12]

Paul was intent on planting these local churches, which, while part of the Body of Christ, were manifestations of the risen, reigning Lord Christ in the local community of people.

FIGURE 1. **Paul's View of the Church and the Churches**

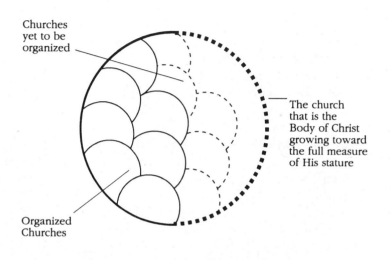

Churches
yet to be
organized

The church
that is the
Body of Christ
growing toward
the full measure
of His stature

Organized
Churches

Adapted from Dean S. Gilliland, *Pauline Theology & Mission Practice* (Grand Rapids, Mich.: Baker Book House, 1983) p. 211.

XX. HAVE AS YOUR GOAL THE PLANTING OF SEVERAL CHURCHES

The result of the labors of Paul and his missionary team in Philippi was the formation of at least two congregations. Their work with Lydia and her household, it might be said, resulted in the constitution of the Riverside Church, meeting in a public "place of prayer" and in the homes of Lydia and her friends and associates. The conversion of the jailer, continuing in the same vein, led to the formation of the Jail Street Church.

While these statements are somewhat tongue-in-cheek, I am very serious about the concept. This is surely what happened. Paul and Silas left Philippi, but Luke and Timothy remained to instruct the new believers from the jail keeper's household as well as to continue to encourage the congregation in Lydia's house.

"The house church emerged in the New Testament era and continued as the most pervasive form of church structure until the time of Constantine."[13] This structure has reappeared with almost every renewal movement that has emerged in Christian history for two thousand years. Paul Yonggi Cho reported that he received the idea for the cell-group system in the Yoido Full-Gospel Church in Seoul from reading Acts.

He noted that there were two types of meetings in the early church. The disciples met regularly at the temple, but they also met in houses.[14] Dean Gilliland insists that the most important feature of the early Christian movement was "the multitude of small units, each of which met together, working out its new life in sharing blessings and working through problems."

It is a mistake to consider any of the urban churches that Paul established as large, single-unit congregations. Each unit was, rather, composed of people who identified themselves with Jesus Christ and shared common cultural and social identities. In fact, Gilliland suggests that this trait is "the key to the contextual quality of Paul's churches."[15]

This guideline demands more faithfulness in North America today than ever before. Social distinctives and cultural diversity have become both more prevalent and more important than at any time in history. "One church for one city" is a strategy of decline and death for any denominational group or any local church.

We now have learned that churches have life cycles. Unless they have a significant renewal and redirection every other generation, they grow old and die. One reason is the mobility in North American societies. Communities change; the members of a church will move and continue to meet in their old community. They are unable to see or reach the new residents. If the church will not change and redirect its life-style and ministry, another church is required.

Ethnic and racial diversity demands that churches be culturally in sync. Churches get sick. Divisions disrupt their fellowships. Doctrinal error erodes their effectiveness. Entrenched leadership holds them back. When these things happen, members need other fellowships to which they can move. Further, as James Engel and Wilbert Norton said years ago, one demonstrated principle of church growth is that the only way for a Christian movement to make gains in a given society is by the multiplication of new churches. "Multiplication of new congregations of believers, then, is the normal and expected output of a healthy body."[16]

A salient lesson we can learn today from the experience of Paul and his team in Philippi is that our vision should be expanded. Our dream should include effective churches for every distinct people group in a city as well as every geographical area. The dominant cultural group in any city or county of significant size will require multiple churches before it can be thoroughly and effectively evangelized.

3

Developing a Regional Strategy in Church Planting

The multiplication of
soundly Christian churches
throughout all segments of society,
throughout all homogeneous units,
till every people, every ethnic unit
is seeded with churches
is . . . a procedure
well pleasing to God.

Donald A. McGavran, 1980

For most of this century, and especially
during the 1960s and 1970s, Christian leaders deprecated
the need for new churches in America. In an age that
emphasized social action and ecumenical interest, the
romance was with church mergers, not church planting,
and with the application of the gospel to the various issues
and systems of society, not the gathering of churches in the
various segments of society.

This pattern characterized most evangelicals as well as
councilor Protestants.

"Church extension" became a loaded phrase, more closely
related in the minds of many to denominational empire-
building than to the mission of the Church of Jesus Christ.
"Church planting," a more biblical and acceptable term, has
now come into use. "Church planting" is used in these chapters to refer to those things one existing Christian fellowship
does to share its faith in Jesus Christ with another community of people and to form them into a new congregation
of responsible disciples of Jesus Christ.[1] The fellowship of
Christians may be members of a local church or agents of a

missionary board, society, or association. Church planting is preeminently an apostolic task, and it is central to the mission of the Church.

Space and time do not allow documentation of the need for new churches in America.[2] There are 80 million people in the United States who do not claim to have an allegiance to any Christian group. There are only six other nations that have a total population larger than 80 million. This makes America one of the great mission fields of the world. It is absurd to think that those 80 million, plus another 90 million who are affiliated with Christian churches but are nonresident or inactive, are going to be adequately discipled by existing churches. Most of the 80 million are socially and culturally removed from the homogeneous units in which the majority of existing churches are established. New churches must be planted if these peoples are to be brought to personal faith in Christ and responsible membership in his church.

At least two major problems hinder the various denominational bodies in America from taking the church-planting task seriously. First, there is often no national or regional strategy for church planting to which the group is committed. What is done is piecemeal and projected on the basis of communities of people already won to faith in Christ and committed to a certain theological or doctrinal position. Seldom is a strategy designed to plant churches in the large unchurched communities of people in the U.S. and Canada.

Second, there is no climate within local churches for them to become actively involved in extension and bridging growth.[3] Local churches resist the idea of planting daughter churches in another city (or town) or another section of their city among people in essentially the same homogeneous groups as their own. Further, many local churches do not get excited about planting daughter churches among people who are a significant cultural or racial distance from themselves.

This chapter is addressed to the first of these problems. Confident that our experience in Illinois will continue to be of interest to many other denominational groups, especially to those ecclesiastical leaders responsible for new church development, this chapter is a report on what the churches of the Illinois Baptist State Association (IBSA) did from March 1973 through December 1976. During that period, 100 new church-type congregations were added to our fellowship. This chapter will also describe the planning procedure of the North Central States Mission Thrust, a thirteen-year effort to double the number of Southern Baptist churches in a seven-state area around the western Great Lakes from 1977 through 1990. The thirteen-year period has elapsed. The effort has been continued. However, an opportunity for evaluation has arrived.

CHURCH PLANTING IN ILLINOIS

THE HERITAGE OF ILLINOIS BAPTISTS The Illinois Baptist State Association (IBSA) is a convention of approximately 1,000 congregations in Illinois, with about 235,000 members, created, according to the 1969 constitution, to "assist in establishing and developing Baptist churches." When the IBSA was formed in 1907 by 226 churches that had withdrawn from the Illinois State Baptist Convention, its constitution stated: "The leading objects of this Association shall be the planting and supporting of Baptist churches in the State of Illinois." Except for one church in Zion founded in 1917, four or five little churches around the Calumet Harbor begun in the thirties and forties, and about fifty churches immediately west and south of Springfield, almost all of the IBSA churches were located in the southern one-third of the state. This situation continued for about forty years. Messengers of IBSA churches were seated at the Southern Baptist Convention in 1910.

By the end of World War II, there were 573 churches. After 1945, churches began to be planted at various places in central and northern Illinois, and in 1950 an intensive and deliberate effort was begun to start new churches all over the state. Between 1945 and 1970, there was a net increase of 312 churches. Many more than that were established, but attrition in rural southern Illinois held the net increase down.

In addition to the Illinois churches, about seventy-five new churches were planted in Indiana, Minnesota, and Wisconsin. Membership during that same twenty-five year period increased from 89,000 to 191,000.

The missionary method during this period was much the same as that used in the formative years of the Baptist General Conference, the Evangelical Free Church of America, and the missionary team sent out from the church in Antioch during the first century. The plan was to find a couple of families from "down home"—people who said "y'all" and ate cornbread—get them in a Bible study, let them invite their friends and extended family members, and then watch the Lord save some and reclaim others. Soon twenty-five to fifty members would become a nucleus for forming a church. Invariably, some of the families reached for Christ would be from a nearby town or a different community in the city. So, the new, baby congregation—enthusiastic and excited—would start a "mission" in that place, in the home of a family from their fellowship. The process would start all over again. In this manner, the Harvey Missionary Baptist Church of Harvey, Illinois, became the mother church to about twenty congregations. The Larkin Avenue Baptist Church in Elgin sponsored ten new churches in the first ten years of its existence.

Who led these churches? Laymen and men who had felt an inward call to preach. These latter had been licensed or ordained; they were with or without formal training. But they moved to one of these communities and "made tents." Actually, very few were really tentmakers! However, many were carpenters, schoolteachers, and factory workers. Even today 50 percent of the pastors in Illinois continue to be bivocational.

By 1965, most of those clusters of similar-culture prospects had already been found and penetrated. The formation of new churches leveled off. IBSA had a net increase of only thirty-five churches between 1965 and 1972. This situation demanded a new missionary strategy.

A NEW MISSIONARY STRATEGY In March, 1973 the board of directors of IBSA authorized a three-year program (1974–1976) called *ExtendNow to All of Illinois.* It was designed to mobilize all IBSA churches in a united, voluntary effort to extend their ministry and witness to all parts (places) and all populations (peoples) in the state.

This action grew out of a strong conviction that pervaded the fellowship, that Christians are under divine orders not only to offer Jesus Christ to all men, but also to plant evangelistic churches in every nook and corner of this land. During the previous quarter century, as I noted earlier, there had been the growing realization that this meant not only a church in every place, but multiple churches where there are significant racial, socioeconomic, or cultural distinction in the populace.

The particular objectives and goals of *ExtendNow* were based on information gathered in a study of 1970 Census data related to the number and location of IBSA churches and the number of resident members in those churches.

With the assistance of the Planning Section of the Home Mission Board in Atlanta, a formula was devised by which we could, through the use of a computer, determine a Geographical Extension Index (GEI) for every place in Illinois that would indicate probable need for new churches.

In addition to a realistic estimate of the need for new churches in a community, we also wanted to know something about the demographic, socioeconomic, and ethnic character of each community. We therefore wrote a computer program that not only gave the GEI, but also provided information on each community in reference to:

1. *Number of IBSA churches*
2. *Number of IBSA resident members*
3. *Total population*

4. *Percent change in population 1960–1970*
5. *Percent nonwhite population*
6. *Percent ethnic population*
7. *Percent non-English speaking in the home*
8. *Percent single, separated, or divorced*
9. *Percent 65 or over*
10. *Percent owner-occupied housing under $15,000*
11. *Percent owner-occupied housing over $35,000*
12. *Percent of housing rented*
13. *Percent of those living in multiple family units*
14. *Percent of families with income above $15,000*
15. *Percent of families under federal poverty level*
16. *Percent in professional occupations*
17. *Percent in labor occupations.*

With this data we had a good preliminary profile on each place. We then gathered all of this information from six perspectives:

1. *Total population*
2. *Total population of each of the 102 counties in the state*
3. *Total rural population of each county*
4. *Total urban population of each county*
5. *Every city in Illinois with 2,500 or more population*
6. *Each of the 76 distinct communities in Chicago.*

This provided an excellent factual base on which to develop a statewide strategy.

The formula for discovering the GEI was as following:

$$\text{G.E.I.} = 1/3 \left[\frac{2(P70)}{C71} + \frac{(P70)}{M71} \right]$$

where: P = population in each place
C = number of churches in each place
M = number of members in each place

The GEI is a score given to each place on the basis of the ratio of IBSA churches in 1971 (C71) to the population in 1970 (P70) and the ratio of IBSA resident members in 1971 (M71) to the population in 1970. Each of these ratios was given an arbitrary value.

Arbitrary Value for Population per Church Ratio	*Arbitrary Value for Population per Member Ratio*
1, if 1:1999 or less	1, if 1:19 or less
2, if 1:2000–3999	2, if 1:29–39
3, if 1:4000–5999	3, if 1:40–59
4, if 1:6000–7999	4, if 1:60–79
5, if 1:8000–9999	5, if 1:80–99
6, if 1:10000–11999	6, if 1:100–119
7, if 1:12000–13999	7, if 1:120–139
8, if 1:14000–15999	8, if 1:140–159
9, if 1:16000–17999	9, if 1:160–179
10, if 1:18000 or more, or if no churches located in the areas	10, if 1:180 or more, or if no members are located in the area

Because we felt that the presence of a church was of more relative importance than the number of church members, we doubled the value of the church-to-population ratio. Since the uppermost arbitrary value was ten for each ratio, we divided the sum of the two ratios by three, which resulted in a GEI for each place between one and ten.

CHURCH PLANTING NEEDS IN ILLINOIS The results of this survey were overwhelming. Although the IBSA was second only to United Methodists among Protestants in number of churches and members in Illinois, we found that there were many places and many population pockets we were overlooking.

1. Twenty-six counties—all in northern Illinois—had great church extension needs (GEI of 10.0). Twenty additional counties had large enough ratios of IBSA Christians and churches to pull the GEI below 7.0.

2. We found 110 small cities (2,500–10,000) had no IBSA church. Sixty-six other small cities had only one church with less than 200 members.

3. Fifty-one medium cities (10,000–50,000) had no IBSA church. Sixty other medium cities had only one IBSA church, which had less than 300 members.

4. Six large cities (50,000–150,000) had no IBSA church. Seven other large cities had only one or two IBSA churches, which had an average membership of 150.

5. Thirty IBSA churches existed in the city of Chicago in 1971, but those were located in only 19 of the 76 communities. There were 57 significant "cities" inside Chicago in which we had no organized work.

6. The survey revealed a varied ethnic population of 2,000,000, growing rapidly, especially among Spanish-speaking groups. We had barely begun to penetrate those different ethnic populations.

7. We discovered a black community in Illinois of 1,400,000 in which we had no strategy for evangelism or church planting.

8. We discovered 159 towns (1,000–2,500) and 256 villages (500–1,000) in which we had no organized witness.

9. It was obvious that the Chicago Standard Metropolitan Statistical Area (SMSA) demanded our great effort and resources. It had 62.8 percent of the population of the state and only 15 percent of our churches. Sixty-one of the small cities, and all fifty-seven of the Chicago communities where we had no organized witness, were in this SMSA. The bulk of the ethnic and black communities were located there.

We adopted a strategy with five overarching objectives and fifteen distinct goals. One of those goals was to add 100 churches or church-type congregations to our fellowship by 1976. We set out to do a more detailed profile of every place in Illinois with a population of more than five hundred. Only in this way could we discover if there was an adequate evangelistic witness in these various places. This was a long process that we did not totally complete. We did profile hundreds of places. We found an inadequate witness to Christ characteristic of most communities. In some towns as few as 13 percent of the population were in a church on a given Sunday. If all the alleged church members were to go to church on a given Sunday, more than twice the number of available seats would be required. In many places there was competition among various churches. But the competition was for the middle- or upper middle-class families. Few efforts were being made to reach the "poor folks" except by Pentecostals, a few Holiness churches, and some Baptists.

As I have already indicated, in forty-four months we counted exactly 100 new churches or church-type congregations. Of that 100, 12 either failed or did not follow through with official affiliation with IBSA or one of the thirty-four local associations within our state. At the end of the period, 9 might legitimately have been called "Bible fellowships," not having reached the full phase of "mission" or "chapel" status. The net increase was 79. Eighteen of those were in the black communities of Illinois, and 28 were in eleven different language culture groups.

CHURCH PLANTING PRINCIPLES

The question is, of course, how did we do this? My answer is: Any and every way we could! It was accomplished through a broad involvement of local churches, an extensive use of volunteers, the efforts of a few catalytic missionaries, the ministries of many bivocational preachers, the allocation of limited supportive funds, and the efforts of a very small number of fully salaried church planters. We were doctrinaire about the insignificance of permanent sites and buildings for new churches. We were unashamed of small churches and unafraid of failure. We seriously attempted to maintain broad prayer support for the entire effort. And all the time we trained, encouraged, evangelized, propagandized, baptized, and prophesied wherever we were. In short, church planting takes dedication, spelled *W-O-R-K.*

Let me give a word of explanation about some of these factors.

1. Missionary responsibility, in our view, did not rest in the Church Extension Division of IBSA, the Home Mission Board of the Southern Baptist Convention (SBC), or with any board or society organized for missionary purposes. It belonged to the local church. We took that very seriously. We began no new work without local church sponsorship of some kind. To start a hundred new churches, we had far more than a hundred sponsoring churches involved to some degree. Missionary responsibility was diffused to the grassroots.

2. All but about ten IBSA churches were affiliated with a local association of churches, such as the Chicago Metropolitan Baptist Association, Oak Park. There was no organic or organizational relationship between IBSA and these local associations. Twenty-three had full-time directors of missions. Some of these men served in areas where new churches were most needed, and they were catalytic agents in church planting. IBSA also had five men located over the state who served in a catalytic capacity, in addition to a director of a Language Missions Department and a director of a Missions Department. My immediate subordinates and I attempted to be directly or indirectly involved in starting a new church each year.

3. Volunteers were used by the hundreds to cultivate new church communities. Youth choir groups, mission groups, individual adults, and college and seminary students who gave a summer or semester all played a part. They came mostly at their own expense and without remuneration.

Several youth choirs, after one or two weeks in a community, were able to leave in existence a new Bible fellowship or, on occasion, a new congregation. Missionary partnerships between local associations in southern Illinois and those in northern Illinois were formed, so that the resources of each were shared to meet various mission goals—primarily through volunteers.

4. Many of the baby churches were nurtured and developed by lay preachers or by men who experienced God's call to preach after they already had families and careers. Some had theological training, and some did not. They worked at various vocations and "bootlegged" the gospel. Such a man would lead a new church part-time until it grew beyond him, or until it could assume his support and that of his family. A few continued to be bivocational pastors of large churches with multiple staffs. This method was effective in many small towns in Illinois, where the mainline denominations had consolidated or withdrawn, leaving a vacuum for an evangelistic witness, and in the ethnic and black communities. A school for training lay preachers was conducted among the Spanish-speaking and another for providing college credit in Bible and religious education courses for lay persons and pastors without theological training.

Most of the new churches that will begin in Illinois during the balance of this century, I believe, will be led by men like these, rather than those with more professional ministerial training. Availability is far more important than capability.

5. Monetary support of new churches and missions is minimal, when all things are considered. When men were placed on Church Pastoral Aid (C.P.A.), only rarely did IBSA contribute as much as $500 per month. Under that program, a man gave full time to his work, and the new church and the sponsoring church or chapel provided the remainder of the salary. The aid decreased over no more than five years. The goal was full support by the new church. Most churches achieved this self-support in less

than five years. Language Pastoral Assistance (L.P.A.) was more lenient, but we moved rapidly toward self-support with the same general guidelines for both C.P.A. and L.P.A. Total subsidy support over forty-four months was about $650,000. This included new churches as well as those already receiving C.P.A. and L.P.A. before *ExtendNow* began.

The Home Mission Board (HMB), SBC, worked in Illinois in a cooperative arrangement through the Church Extension Division, IBSA, now called the Missions Division. We cooperated in budget and program planning. The HMB participated at a 60/40 ratio in the total IBSA missions budget, including staff salaries. In 1976, that total budget was $443,000. Besides dollar participation, HMB personnel provided valuable assistance in placing, training, and recruiting volunteers and staff. The HMB, however, only participated in about $450,000 of the forty-four months' subsidy. The remainder was given in Illinois.

6. The total subsidy for forty-four months included a small number of fully salaried church planters. These were men with experience or training whom we located in strategic communities and provided a livable salary. They usually went to a community to begin from scratch. Ultimately thirteen such men served during the forty-four-month period: three in ethnic communities, two in black communities, and eight in white, English-speaking communities. These men accounted for 14 percent of the new units we began.

7. The availability of a permanent building or building site was never a prerequisite or determinative to beginning a new church. Our watchwords were: "Get the people and you can get a place." "God's people, led by God's man, can produce the facilities that are needed." We were able, late in the process, to provide some seed money for a down payment on property, but that was not a feature of *ExtendNow*.

8. Numbers of small churches that needed to grow did not keep us from beginning other new churches. IBSA had

a full division of Church Development. We were convicted that churches always begin small. If you multiply churches in your fellowship, you must expect to have small churches around.

Nor did the fear of failure deter us. Some new churches did not survive, and some existed only a few years. We held doggedly to principles of local church autonomy. Some new churches decided not to affiliate with us. We regretted this, of course, but held no strings that would compel affiliation.

9. We saw the whole effort of church planting as a spiritual ministry done effectively only in the power of the Holy Spirit. We therefore prayed much and enlisted and trained others to pray much. The IBSA staff members preached often, witnessed, and did soul-winning in all kinds of places. In other ways we invested our lives personally in these budding new congregations. We, with many others, planted and watered, but we counted on God to give the increase.

CHURCH PLANTING IN SEVEN
NORTH CENTRAL STATES

This method of identifying church-planting needs on a more scientific basis was picked up in 1973 by the executive directors and missions directors of the SBC state conventions in Ohio, Michigan, Indiana, and Illinois, in a joint planning effort. Because the SBC churches in these four midwestern states shared many similar problems, these men had been meeting each January for several years for fellowship and discussion of common needs. When the results of the survey in Illinois were shared, a decision was made to join together in a significant step forward—especially in church planting—in these Great Lakes states.

The North Central States Mission Thrust (NCSMT) had three purposes: (1) to double the number of churches, missions, and organized ministries in the region by 1990; (2) to focus the attention of SBC on the region for a significant period of time—1977–1990; and (3) to assist in turning the resources of all SBC agencies to meet priority mission needs in the region.

The Iowa and Minnesota-Wisconsin Fellowships of Southern Baptist churches soon joined with the four state conventions. The base date for counting was made October 1, 1973. At that time, there were 1,738 churches in the seven-state area, and 180 church-type chapels that had not yet become independently organized churches. The first target date has been reached. The NCSMT has been extended to A.D. 2000 to coincide with the national denomination's century-end emphasis, called Bold Mission Thrust.

Two questions need to be answered: How was this regional strategy developed? and What have been the results?

First, what steps were taken to develop the NCSMT strategy?

DEVELOPING A PLANNING BASE First, a common planning base for the seven states was developed. The Planning Section of the Home Mission Board helped build a data-gathering model—much like the one used in Illinois. It was adjusted because of the much larger population and number of places in the seven-state area. The model was designed to delineate communities of people in the north central states (NCS) that were in need of a church, a church-type mission, or a special ministry to certain groups of people.

The model was developed on three assumptions:

1. The model had to be flexible enough to consider the presence of existing SBC units of work, both large and small, and the diversity and distribution of the population.

2. The model had to be built on the same geographical base as the existing church and population data. The most compatible base consisted of places and county boundaries grouped into appropriate population categories. We gathered data as follows:

Counties, Total Population	*623 Counties*
Places of 1,000,000 or more	2 Places
Places of 500,000–1,000,000	4 Places
Places of 250,000–500,000	5 Places
Places of 100,000–250,000	21 Places
Places of 50,000–100,000	61 Places
Places of 25,000–50,000	140 Places
Places of 10,000–25,000	346 Places
Places of 5,000–10,000	409 Places
Places of 2,500–5,000	546 Places
Counties, Rural Population	*623 Counties*

3. Since the major unit of work was that of churches, the model had to be built on a base which would show the need for new churches by a single geographical index score. To help indicate the need for special types of churches and to reflect the need for special ministries, support data was gathered alongside the geographical index score when it reached a certain predetermined point for a specific condition. This support data included racial, cultural, social, economic, and housing data.

The geographical indicators included the number of SBC churches in each place, the number of resident members in these churches, and the total population of each place. The support indicators that helped understand the social character of each place and identify the need for social or cross-cultural ministries were as follows:

1. *Percentage net change in population, 1960–70, if 25 percent or above.*

2. *Percentage of total population, nonwhite, if 20 percent or above.*
3. *Percentage of total population, ethnic, if 20 percent or above.*
4. *Percentage of total population with mother-tongue other than English, if 20 percent or above.*
5. *Percentage of population 14 years or over, single, separated, widowed, or divorced, if 15 percent or above.*
6. *Percentage of population 65 years and over, if 15 percent or above.*
7. *Percentage of occupied housing units renter occupied, if 40 percent or above.*
8. *Percentage of housing units not single-unit structures, if 40 percent or above.*
9. *Percentage of families with income over $15,000, if 30 percent or above.*
10. *Percentage of families under poverty level, if 15 percent or above.*
11. *Percentage of employed persons 16 years and over in professional and administrative professions, if 30 percent or above.*
12. *Percentage of employed persons 16 years and over in laborer occupations, if 25 percent or above.*

The data-gathering model was a formula much like the one developed for Illinois. It was limited in that it only pointed to possible trends and above-average possibilities that might call for new units of work. It looked like this:

$$\text{Geographical Extension Index (G.E.I.)} = 1/3 \left[2\left(\frac{P70}{C73}\right)_{av_1} \left(\frac{P70}{M73}\right)_{av_2} \right]$$

where: P = population of each place
C = number of churches in each place
M = number of church members in each place
av = arbitrary value assigned to various ratios

DATA FINDINGS What conclusions were drawn from this statistical look at the area?

1. *The north central states (NCS) were crucial for a national strategy.* The seven states that compose this region are a vital part of the great agricultural belt across the Great Plains, but 75 percent of the population lived in urban areas. These states contained the second largest metropolitan cluster in America; only that along the northeastern seaboard was larger. The population in the NCS in 1970 was 46,881,877, or 23 percent of the population of the nation. Almost one out of four people who lived in the U.S. lived in these seven states.

2. *The region had tremendous church-planting needs.* Twenty percent of the 47 million population lived in eleven cities of over 250,000. Among the almost 10 million people in these cities Southern Baptists had only 124 churches in 1972. That amounts to a ratio of more than 100,000 people for each SBC church. This would be approximately the same ratio as if there had been only 62 SBC churches in all of Atlanta, Birmingham, Dallas, Houston, Louisville, Memphis, Miami, New Orleans, and Oklahoma City combined!

There were 21 cities with a population between 100,000 and 250,000—a total population of over 3 million. There were 109 SBC churches in these cities— a ratio of one to 30,000. This would be comparable to a situation where there would be only 109 SBC churches for all of Kentucky!

There were 201 cities in the NCS with a population between 25,000 and 100,000. They had a combined population of over 9 million with 231 SBC churches— a ratio of one to 40,000. This would be equivalent to having only 121 SBC churches in Tennessee and Georgia combined, or to having one church for Jackson, Tennessee.

Finally, there were 3,301 small cities in the NCS with populations ranging between 2,500 and 25,000. The total population of these cities was 10 million—almost identical to the total of the 11 very large cities. There were 337 SBC churches in these cities—a ratio of one to 18,000.

In the survey we identified every place in the NCS with a population above 2,500, as well as doing a study of the total population and rural population by counties. There were 1,534 cities with a population in excess of 2,500 in these seven states; 1,014 had a GEI of 10.0. There were 623 counties in the seven-state area; 418 had a GEI of 10.0. This did not take into account the large number of places with GEI of 7.0 to 9.9. These also had significant church-planting needs.

There were, of course, other Baptists and other evangelical Christians in the NCS. There were many strong, evangelistic churches in this region. This is also true where Southern Baptists are strongest. In fact, there were more evangelical churches per 1,000 population where Southern Baptists are strongest than in these seven states. We did a comparison between two cities in Illinois of approximately the same size—Marion and Buffalo Grove, Illinois. Marion is in southern Illinois, where Southern Baptists have been strong all of this century. In this city of 10,000 there were five SBC churches, one American Baptist, one Freewill Baptist, one National Baptist, one American Baptist Association, and one General Baptist. There were also two Methodist, one Presbyterian, five Pentecostal, one Catholic, one Episcopal, one Lutheran, one Reformed Latter Day Saints, one Jehovah's Witness, etc.—thirty-two churches in all. Buffalo Grove, in suburban Chicago, was atypical in that it had two small Baptist churches—one affiliated with the North American Baptist General Conference and one with the General Association of Regular Baptists. In addition, it had one Catholic, one United Church of Christ, one Methodist church, and a Jewish synagogue. If all the Southern Baptists in Marion were removed, there would still have been more Baptists and other evangelicals there than in Buffalo Grove. This was the typical pattern.

As you can imagine, this information was highly motivational. It also provided each state convention with a data base upon which to do planning during this significant planning period. It was helpful in identifying geographical, socioeconomic, and cultural communities that might be ripe for church-planting ministries.

Another way was discovered to look at the region. Using information gathered from ninety-two different denominational groups in America, the Planning Section of the Home Mission Board fed into the computer the basic information about numbers of churches and resident members for each county in the United States. They were then able to develop an Evangelism Index and Church Index for each county. Using this data, we were able to compare the situation of Southern Baptists in the seven north central states with Southern Baptists in seven south central states (Alabama, Arkansas, Kentucky, Louisiana, Mississippi, Missouri, and Tennessee). Here is what we discovered:

	NCS	SCS
Total Population	46,881,877	23,044,572
SBC Churches	1,782	14,115
SBC Members	420,913	5,439,390
Other Baptist Churches	7,569	8,762
Other Baptist Members	2,421,504	2,242,000
Other Evangelical Churches	10,115	6,605
Other Protestant Churches	24,599	16,617
Other Protestant Members	9,773,108	3,628,462
Catholic Churches	6,471	2,129
Catholic Members	12,646,463	2,794,191
Sectarian Congregations	762	386
Sectarian Members	180,966	100,576
Non-Christian Congregations	403	157
Non-Christian Members	640,586	138,894
Unaffiliated with any group	17,782,878	7,607,925
Language Population	6,204,208	974,005
HMB Estimate of Lost	32,007,057	12,627,133
Proportion of Lost/Population	68.3%	54.8%

Do you see the contrast? There were twice as many people in the NCS as in the SCS, but there were eight times as many SBC churches and ten times as many SBC members in the SCS. There were as many other Baptists in the SCS, with one-half the population, as in the NCS, and twice as many other Baptists per 1,000 population. More evangelical churches of other stripes were in the NCS. In ratio to population, however, the NCS had one evangelical church other than Baptist for each 4,635 people. In the SCS there was one evangelical church other than Baptist for each 3,489 people. Over six times as many ethnic people are in the NCS. It became a common, spontaneous, unofficial goal among NCS leaders to have as many SBC churches and members in the NCS as in the SCS. The North Central State Missions Thrust was designed to be only a little step in that direction. The realization of that goal waits for the twenty-first century.

USE OF DATA How was this information used?

1. Each state developed its own strategy. There was no organic relationship among the state conventions or between the state conventions and the SBC agencies. Everything was done on a cooperative, voluntary basis.

2. There was some cooperative emphasis planning as well as use of common promotional procedures. This was very low-key.

3. One meeting was held each year for the training and inspiration of specifically invited leaders from each of the NCS. This meeting is now conducted once every three years.

4. A combined effort was made to enlist associational leaders in the planning process and to insure the commitment of the small ecclesiastical bodies to the overall project.

5. Working together, the leaders were able to pull more resources into the seven-state area and to arouse interest and commitment within the laity. In Illinois

$1,000,000 was raised in four years for the salaries of pastors of new churches, above and beyond everything else. This was done by a lay task force in each of the district associations.

The second major question we must answer is: What have been the results? Reports and evaluations were made annually. At certain times, special evaluations were made to provide information for course corrections. By April 1, 1979, six years, six months after the base date, there were 1,984 SBC churches and 342 church-type chapels in the seven-state area. On December 16, 1979, the 2,000th SBC church within the NCS was organized in Milford, Michigan.

In 1989, Clay L. Price made a thorough study of the NCSMT for the leadership of the seven conventions.[4] It was based on statistical information in the SBC's Uniform Church Letter from churches in the North Central States. Not all churches report every year, since the process is voluntary. Using data from 1980 to 1988, the study showed that growth had continued at a rate greater than in the SBC as a whole, but not at the rate anticipated.

On October 1, 1988, fifteen years after the base count, 2,119 SBC churches and 357 church-type missions were functioning in the seven-state area, a total of 2,476 congregations. This was a net increase of 558 congregations or 29 percent rather than a 100 percent increase as intended. Membership had jumped in that period from 494,934 in 1973 to 546,804 in 1988, or 32.5 percent.

In the Uniform Church Letter a different method for reporting church-type missions was adopted in 1990. This actually contributed to a decline in total congregations from 1988 (see Figure 1). The new totals are probably more exact. They do make comparison with 1973 and 1990 statistics not absolutely precise. However, the

FIGURE 1. Churches and Church-Type Missions North Central States 1973–1990[5]

	Convention/ Fellowship	IL	IN	IA	MI	MN/ WI	OH	TOTALS
1973	Total Churchs	870	243	26	170	40	389	1,738
	Total Missions	39	24	15	22	4	76	180
	Total Congregations	909	267	41	192	44	465	1,918
1980	Total Churchs	909	272	59	190	67	450	1,947
	Total Missions	67	25	15	26	15	67	215
	Total Congregations	976	297	74	216	82	517	2,162
1990	Total Churchs	936	304	63	236	89	512	2,141
	Total Missions	59	49	13	55	25	61	262
	Total Congregations	995	353	76	292	114	573	2,402

obvious response is that the thirteen-year effort came far short of its announced goals.

At least six observations should be made, however.

1. The growth in the NCS exceeded the growth in the SBC in number of churches in this period. Across the SBC growth increased only 9 percent. In the NCS the increase in churches was 23 percent. Membership in the SBC grew by 17 percent during the period; in the NCS membership growth was 33.2 percent.

2. The goals as related to congregations were more than achieved in two of the regional conventions. Southern Baptists in Minnesota/Wisconsin and in Iowa more than doubled in number of churches (see Figure 1). Total membership in Minnesota/Wisconsin increased by 11,322, or a whopping 868.2 percent. Iowa's total membership increased by 4,853, a little over 225 percent.

3. Illinois, the state that needed to show the largest numeri-

cal gain if the goals were to be reached, actually had a net increase of only 86 congregations. Indiana had the same net increase, beginning from a much smaller base. Michigan, in the throes of severe recession and a declining population during this period, had a net increase of 100 congregations. Ohio had a net increase of 184 total congregations.

4. Several factors contributed to the failure to reach the goals. Leadership change took a severe toll. All regional conventions had one or more changes in the executive director's office during the period, except Michigan and Minnesota/Wisconsin. New leaders did not always or immediately share the vision of the NCSMT. Further, the population growth in the area was plateaued during these years. Iowa and Michigan both had population declines between 1980 and 1990. Finally, the entire region was hard hit by recession. Economic stagnation and decline began earlier and lasted longer in these states, during this period, than in most other regions of the nation.

5. This was a period of radical decline among mainline denominations in the United States and in this region. If there had not been a strong emphasis on church planting, Southern Baptists in this region would have declined also. The study by Clay Price of the eight-year period from 1980 to 1988 shows that in that period alone Southern Baptists dropped 174 churches through various forms of attrition.

The 174 churches dropped during these eight years averaged 110 members each. They represented 4 percent of the NCS's members, program enrollments, and giving in 1980. Between 1980 and 1988, 346 new churches were added. In 1988 these churches accounted for 16 percent of all the churches, 6 percent of total membership, 9 percent of Bible study enrollment, 15 percent of baptisms, and 9 percent of total receipts. "Without these new churches the North Central States would have experienced no growth in resident membership and severe drops in Sunday school enrollment and attendance."[6]

6. The ratio of SBC churches to population, except in

Illinois, declined during this period in every state.[7] Decline in this instance is a positive statistic. Looking at the entire region, at the beginning of the period there was one SBC church per 26,300 people in the NCS. In 1990 that ratio was one church to 23,104. In 1973, the SBC membership in the NCS was .88 percent of the total population. In 1990, Southern Baptists composed 1.1 percent of the population of the NCS. Southern Baptists have seen some growth in these seven states in relationship to population fluctuation.

Southern Baptists in the NCS failed to reach the goals established in 1977, even though they established their base count on October 1, 1973. However, the churches and conventions in the region have thwarted decline in the face of population stagnation and economic recession.

Southern Baptists have grown while several councilor and evangelical groups have experienced decline. Southern Baptists have been able to grow in the North Central States context, gaining in market share in the entire population.

INGREDIENTS OF A REGIONAL STRATEGY To talk directly about a regional strategy, I will have to come back to the strategy of the Illinois Baptist State Association. I would suggest the following twelve steps:

1. *Begin with the divine imperative.*
2. *Build on self-study. Know who you are and what you have been doing.*
3. *Know your region geographically, culturally, and ecclesiastically. Pinpoint areas where there is evidence of need for new churches.*
4. *Have clear objectives and specific goals.*
5. *Determine what factors in an area will dictate immediate priority consideration or continued priority consideration.*
6. *Identify and make advantageous use of homogeneous units.*
7. *Identify felt needs as a means of discovering areas of responsiveness.*

8. *Mobilize missionary staff, volunteers, and financial resources to meet felt needs.*

9. *Don't permit your missionary strategy or method to be dictated by real estate considerations. Renounce the "temple" complex in church planting.*

10. *Give central responsibility to volunteers. Let the laity find their gifts and ministries in church extension skills.*

11. *Make direct evangelism a major factor in your strategy.*

12. *Count on God to give a marvelous increase. "He gives to His beloved even in his sleep" (Psalm 127:2).*

4

Intentional Church Planting in the Megacity: A Boston Case Study

by Larry K. Martin
Director of Missions
Greater Boston Baptist Association, Massachusetts

Paul's strategy called for the planting of churches in the urban centers, and then, through the contagious witness of the converts, reaching the surrounding region.

Roger Greenway, 1973

Introduction: The only effective method for thoroughly evangelizing any extensive geographical area or significant people group is by planting indigenous congregations among that specific group or throughout the specific area. This strategy can be achieved today on the continent of North America because the peoples that compose the geopolitical nations of the continent are generally responsive. Many groups are exceedingly responsive.

The rise of the great city is one of the most important sociological developments of the nineteenth century. Urbanization has continued to sweep across the North American continent throughout the twentieth century. An unquestioned axiom of twentieth-century Christian historiography is that the Protestant churches (read in most cases, "white Protestant churches") have lost the cities of the continent.

My thesis is that the cities of North America need to be re-churched from an ethnolinguistic and socioeconomic/psychographic perspective. Further, this objective requires strategic planning for church planting on the part of larger ecclesiastical bodies.

The following is an account of the first seven years of the Greater Boston Baptist Association (hereafter referred to as the Boston Association), illustrating how intentional, grass-roots planning for evangelism, ministry, church development and growth, and church planting, in particular, can be done with extremely limited resources. Larry Martin, the leader of this association of churches, has told an informative and inspirational story.

Church planting is an irreplaceable strategy for reaching the modern North American city. The task can be enhanced with strategic planning by the denominational group, by visionary leadership and spiritual commitment, and if the blessing of God is on those who do the work. All ecclesiastical planning is ultimately ineffective without the power of the Holy Spirit opening doors, overcoming obstacles, and doing all along his work of regeneration. —Charles L. Chaney

Significant growth marked the years 1982 through 1989 in the churches and ministries of the Boston Association. In rapid succession, God has presented challenging opportunities to the young churches and association.

BACKGROUND AND EARLY HISTORY

The history of Southern Baptist work in Boston must be understood in the context of Southern Baptist beginnings in the Northeast. The nine northeastern states were unexplored territory for Southern Baptists until the early 1950s. Comity agreements between Northern Baptists and Southern Baptists, worked out in 1894 and updated in 1912, had marked the boundaries for each denomination's work. However, by 1942 the two groups agreed that nothing existed in either convention to prevent unlimited expansion if either chose to do so. By 1956, only four U.S. cities with more than one million in population had no Southern Baptist Convention work. Three of these were in the Northeast: New York City, Boston, and Philadelphia.

Organized Southern Baptist work began in the North-

east in the spring of 1957 when a group of transplanted
Southern Baptists held Sunday services in New York City.
In January 1958, meeting in the Hotel New Yorker, they
organized as the Manhattan Baptist Church of New York
City.

Work began in New England in 1958 when the United
States Air Force transferred the 509th Bomber Wing
Division from Roswell, N.M., to Pease Air Force Base in
Newington, N.H. In February 1960, a group of 125 con-
stituted as the first SBC church in New England—Screven
Memorial Baptist Church in Portsmouth, N.H. The
Northeastern Baptist Association organized in 1960 with
five churches and six chapels, Screven Memorial Baptist
Church being the only church in New England.

By October 1962, the number of congregations had
increased so that the Northeastern Association could dis-
solve and three new associations could form. The New
England Baptist Association functioned as an association
of the Baptist Convention of Maryland/Delaware until the
Baptist Convention of New England (hereafter, the New
England Convention) organized in November 1983.

Boston was the last major U.S. metropolitan area without an organized Southern Baptist association of churches.
In October 1982, the Boston Association formed with seventeen churches and chapels. This association is one of six
associations that cover the six New England states and
make up the BCNE.

Geographically, the Boston Association covers approximately five thousand square miles, an area roughly forty
miles east to west, one hundred miles north to south, and
extending sixty miles to the tip of Cape Cod. Also
included are many islands; the best known are Chap-
paquiddick, Martha's Vineyard, and Nantucket. The population of 4 million includes at least 3 million people who
do not know Jesus Christ as Savior and Lord.

In July 1983, Larry Martin came to serve with the association as its first executive director from a similar position

in Detroit. At that time, Ignatius Meimaris, language catalytic missionary, and Dan McClintock, campus minister at Harvard University, served as the associational staff.

DEVELOPMENT OF ASSOCIATIONAL STRATEGY

One of the greatest challenges facing the association in the early days was the development of a strategy indigenous to the churches, challenging enough to cover several years, and yet not so comprehensive as to overwhelm such a small group. In the fall of 1984, this process began as part of Mega Focus Cities, a process developed in the early 1980s by the Associational Missions Division of the Home Mission Board, SBC, to address the needs of the forty-four largest cities in the United States. Mega Focus Cities was designed to bring together national, state, and local leaders to discuss issues that might be addressed in a long-range strategy, and to form partnerships to achieve goals set out by the association. Local formulation and ownership of the strategy were key principles in the planning process.

Building an identity as an association and gathering information about how the association could minister effectively in its setting became foundational elements. In the fall of 1984, a twenty-minute multi-image presentation, "Boston: Yesterday, Today, and Tomorrow," was produced and shown at the associational annual meeting and then presented in most of the churches of the association. The presentation dealt with Boston in its historical and cultural settings and then looked at existing SBC churches and their dreams for the future. It helped Boston Southern Baptists feel a part of something greater than just their local churches' ministries. It also became the basis for gathering their dreams for the future work of the association. Those who viewed the presentation in the churches completed a response sheet that asked them to list their ministry or evangelism dreams, what would be necessary to make these dreams become reality, and what they would be willing to commit to these dreams. More than two hundred written responses gave valuable input from the grassroots membership of the local churches.

Identity and consensus-building continued with an overnight convocation/retreat in January 1985. Ninety-seven people attended, representing every church of the association except one. Except for Meimaris and Martin, no one present knew even half of those attending. For more than one-third of the people, this was their first denominational meeting. The convocation had three purposes: first, get to know each other; second, share what God was doing at present; and third, dream about what God wanted to do through the churches and association in the future. On Friday evening, after prayer and get-acquainted time, participants divided into groups of eight. The groups shared what God was doing in their lives, their churches, and their communities. On Saturday morning, participants returned to the same groups and, after other consensus-building activities, discussed what they believed God wanted to do in the coming months and years in their lives, their churches, and their communities. Following the retreat, written reports from each group became part of the information pool for strategy planning.

To better understand the demographic and sociological setting of the association, from the fall of 1984 through the spring of 1985, task groups studied population trends, social issues, church histories, and other area religious groups. A compilation of these studies became another important part of the information gathered in preparation for strategy planning.

Two other factors were extremely important in building a foundation for strategy planning. The first occurred in the spring of 1984 when twenty men from five churches spent a weekend in the south Bronx in New York City. They worked with pastor Sam Simpson and the Wake Eden and Bronx Baptist churches in rebuilding burned-out apartment buildings. This trip

produced several results. It helped build a strong relationship between SBC lay leaders in the two cities. In addition, Boston Association members saw firsthand what
could be done through the dreams of a single church
with limited resources in a difficult area. However, the
most important goal was more intangible. Leaders knew
their fledgling association would receive much help from
sister churches in other states. From the beginning, associational leaders wanted to set the pattern for the association to give as well as receive.

The other major factor in laying the foundation for
effective strategy planning was building a strong prayer
base as the most important component permeating the life
of the association. During the planning process, ten
churches conducted Prayer Seminars.

Leaders in the association had a strong commitment
to prayer not only as the foundation from which all
growth and ministry would flow, but also as an integral
part of the ongoing life of the association. From the
beginning, associational executive committee meetings
became prayer times. All of the business of the association between annual meetings is conducted at the executive committee meetings. However, typically not more
than ten minutes of the two-hour meetings have been
used for business. The remainder of the time has been
spent in hearing reports from the leaders of associational
programs and activities. The reporting has been done
with an attitude of thanksgiving to God for doors he has
opened and changes he has brought in the lives of individuals and churches. The meetings always close with an
intense prayer time related to needs freely shared by the
group. Most other associational meetings have been
marked by significant prayer times as well. Weekly associational staff meetings follow the same model.

With the foundational components of a sense of identity and unity, the commitment to giving as well as
receiving, the dreams of more than two hundred lay

people and one hundred other church leaders, the demographic data gathered by the task forces, and the prayer emphasis permeating the association, the association's leaders were ready to formulate a five-year strategy.

In late spring of 1985, twenty-five associational and church leaders met in an overnight retreat to develop priorities and goals for the years 1986 through 1990. These leaders represented the ethnic diversity of the Boston Association's membership. George Bullard served as consultant and leader through the process and has continued to serve in a consulting relationship with the Boston Association.

On Friday evening of the planning retreat, the data-gathering task forces shared their information, and the entire group talked about issues related to developing a strategy. Participants listed potential associational priorities.

On Saturday morning, participants formed three work groups with the assignment of selecting five priorities from the larger list of potential priorities as most important for the association for 1986 through 1990. When the work groups had finished, they sensed God had given a consensus. All three groups had listed identical priorities, and two of the three groups placed them in the same order. Foundational statements for the five priorities were:

1. *Prayer is the basis for all of the planning and work of the association.*
2. *Evangelism is an integral part of every priority area.*
3. *Local ownership of plans and personnel serving in the association is vital.*

The five priorities were:

1. *Church development*
2. *Planting new congregations*
3. *Student work*
4. *Christian ministry*
5. *Communications*

Church development emerged as the first priority since 60 percent of the congregations at that time were less than five years old. The group felt the need to develop these fledgling congregations and knew priority attention had to be given to this matter.

Church planting surfaced as second priority because of the overwhelming need for new congregations in the greater Boston area. Many of the 160 cities and towns comprising the greater Boston area had no evangelical church. Surveys conducted by church planters discovered the total attendance during a typical week at all places of worship in most towns to be less than 15 percent. Churches were committed to planting congregations as a natural part of their own growth. For example, Metropolitan Baptist Church in Cambridge was responsible for beginning twenty congregations in its first twenty-five years. Each of the twenty was planted directly by Metropolitan Baptist Church or by one of its "daughter" congregations. Metropolitan Baptist Church has never averaged more than a hundred in attendance. Bethel Haitian Church, Cambridge, was sponsored by Metropolitan Baptist Church. Before the group constituted as a church, pastor Gaspard Matheus had begun three other Haitian congregations. Similarly, New Meadows Chapel in Topsfield initiated work toward two new congregations before it was a fully constituted church.

Campus ministry was also urgent. Ninety campuses with more than 300,000 students are located in the area. At the time of the strategy planning, McClintock and one part-time volunteer were the only campus ministers. McClintock resigned in late 1985 to become a missionary to France.

The fourth priority of Christian ministry dealt with needs discovered by the Social Systems Task Group. Needs included housing for low-income families, food and clothing ministries for people living on the streets, and teaching English as a Second Language classes.

The fifth priority of communications had several

dimensions. The first was helping the members of the association's churches know who they are as evangelicals and as Southern Baptists. Eighty-five percent of the members of English-speaking congregations were native New Englanders. Many churches had no member with an SBC heritage. Most people were relatively new believers and had no evangelical background. A second need was to let other Boston-area churches know who Southern Baptists are. A third purpose was to tell Southern Baptists throughout the United States about the work of the Boston Association, especially in order to build prayer support for beginning congregations and other ministries.

RESULTS OF PLANNING STRATEGY

Growth occurred in each priority area from 1982 through 1990. The number of congregations tripled. Worship and Bible study attendance more than doubled. Participation in training opportunities and missionary education also doubled. The association's Educational Council took seriously the challenge to offer training and educational opportunities to all churches in the association. Leaders in the association were actively involved with leaders from twelve northeastern states in developing the Northeastern Baptist School of Ministry, which began in Northboro, Massachusetts, in 1989. They also began an Ethnic Leadership Development Center to train ethnic leaders.

Until 1989, campus ministries grew slowly. Rapid transition in leaders made growth and continuity difficult. In early 1989, however, associational lay leaders began praying intently for campus ministries. During the next six months, the number of campus ministers increased from two to ten; and the number of campuses served, from two to nine. Betsy Draper, who had served four years as volunteer minister at Massachusetts Institute of Technology, was appointed director of student ministries for the association.

E.S.L. classes began in several ethnic churches. Organized and led by Vicky Brunson, volunteer assistant ethnic ministries director, summer day camps for Indo-Chinese children began in 1986. By 1989, these camps, meeting five days a week for four weeks, reached four hundred children. During 1988 and 1989, more than sixty Cambodian children professed faith in Christ. A Cambodian church, the second in the GBBA, and a second Khmer Bible study began as a direct result of the camps.

Antioch Missionary Baptist Church, located in the Dorchester community of Boston, was the catalyst for building thirteen town houses adjacent to the church property for ownership by low income families. Leaders in the association assisted the Antioch church in working with Christians for Urban Justice, an interdenominational ministry, to build these homes. Later they helped form a Boston Habitat for Humanity affiliate.

Volunteers from several of the association's churches joined with more than one thousand volunteers from throughout greater Boston and several states to complete the Habitat houses. Volunteer Jim Pierce, who became GBBA director of lay ministries in 1988, served as construction foreman. Fifteen television reports on Boston stations featured the initial building week. Boston Mayor Raymond Flynn was involved personally with the project. Plans are under way to construct more houses as soon as additional land becomes available.

Metropolitan Baptist Church in Cambridge developed a Saturday community meals program for the homeless. During the first two years, attendance increased from 12 to 120 per week. The church installed showers and a washer and dryer for the homeless. They also began a clothing ministry. Metropolitan Baptist Church members, assisted by volunteers from other churches and students from campus ministries, plan and staff these programs. Several people served by the meals program began attending Sunday worship, made commitments to Christ, and became members of Metropolitan Baptist Church.

The GBBA made progress in the area of communications as well. The multi-image presentation "Boston: Yesterday, Today, and Tomorrow" helped create a sense of associational identity as it was shown in the churches. It also helped build a wide base of concern and prayer support as it was shown at various meetings in several states. A videotaped version was used extensively in small group and home settings. During 1989, a monthly prayer letter sent to individuals and churches in several states was begun. Each month the letter focuses on one area of associational ministry and identifies ten specific prayer requests.

A denominational grant made possible the purchase of video production equipment. Producing videotapes in the various languages used by GBBA churches augments the few available written materials. By 1989, six 10-minute segments in Greek were produced. The tapes, to be shown on television in Greece and Canada and on cable television in the United States, deal with family issues and conclude with an invitation to receive Christ. They are used to train lay people in Greek-speaking churches. Ignatius Meimaris and John Hionides, pastor of the Hellenic Gospel Church (SBC) in Newton, Massachusetts, are featured on the tapes.

Videotapes also have been produced in Spanish. In 1989, Raphael Hernandez began work toward planting three Hispanic churches simultaneously using videotaped home Bible study materials. While he leads one study in person, two other studies are conducted using the videotapes.

Growth in lay ministries occurred through beginning a monthly Friends of Evangelism meeting in which lay people from several churches meet to listen, encourage, pray, and share concerning their ministry in the marketplace. The strategy plan makes evangelism an integral part of every priority area. Through church development programs, church members and leaders receive training in evangelistic methods. New congregations begin with a commitment to share Christ with their communities. Church-planting leaders stress the importance of growing churches through reaching nonbelievers with the gospel, rather than just trying to enlist people who are already believers.

Evangelism is a vital part of campus ministries. Students and campus ministers regularly share Christ through small-group Bible studies, retreats, interpersonal contacts, and special events. Several students who have accepted Christ through campus ministries now are active members of newly established congregations. Christian ministries have provided several avenues for effectively presenting the gospel. E.S.L. classes, community meals programs for the homeless, Habitat for Humanity projects, and day camps for Southeast Asian children all have been bridges for leading people to personal faith in Christ.

Evangelism is also integral to the association's communications ministries. Videotapes produced in various languages effectively communicate the gospel for use on television, in church meetings, or in home studies. Through the leadership of the association's volunteer communications director, George Wakim, five churches now use cable television.

PRINCIPLES OF GROWTH

Several principles contribute to the growth of the Bostion Association.

A TEAM APPROACH The approach to church growth has been a team effort. None of the five priority areas stand alone. People involved directly in church planting are concerned deeply with church development. Campus ministers and students are involved with church planting and various aspects of Christian ministry. Staff and lay leaders in each priority area are concerned with communicating the overall associational goals and ministries.

Pastors and church leaders regularly cooperate and share resources with each other. Associational staff members in their weekly meetings routinely share information concerning potential resources with people serving in other priority areas.

USE OF VOLUNTEERS During the 1985 planning process, associational and church leaders shared dreams and goals that were far beyond associational financial and personnel resources. They began seriously praying that God would send additional staff to serve in the Boston area. During the next five years, the associational staff (including campus ministers) grew from four to twenty people. Seventeen of the twenty were volunteers, most with the SBC Home Mission Board's Mission Service Corps. Each priority had at least one volunteer overseeing it. During the five years, twenty-one long-term volunteers served in the GBBA. All served for at least one year; most served two or more. Two served more than four years each. Most were young adults who had just completed seminary.

As the number of volunteers serving in Boston Association grew, its leaders had to consider the need for housing. With the cost of living in Boston near the highest in the nation, volunteers as well as life-long residents had difficulty finding affordable places to live. In April 1989, with the help of a $50,000 grant from denominational agencies and $20,000 given by individuals and churches, the association purchased a seven-bedroom house for $255,000. Each volunteer pays monthly rent significantly lower than comparable area rent. These rents amortize the loan. The purchase of this house will have significant long-term impact for continued associational growth. A second house is anticipated within two years, donated by one of the churches.

As associational leaders faithfully shared across the country what God was doing in Boston and as they prayed for workers, God continued to send leaders to start congregations. By the fall of 1989, the churches had started fourteen additional congregations. Eight of these are ethnic congregations worshiping in five languages; six are English-speaking. Conversations were underway with three other prospective Anglo church planters.

These church planters came from varied backgrounds:

- An experienced Hispanic pastor who planned to begin Hispanic churches in three towns simultaneously.
- An experienced Anglo pastor who left an established congregation with a weekly attendance exceeding three hundred to come to the GBBA to develop a church from a nucleus of two families.
- A Connecticut church planter's son who came to the GBBA immediately after seminary graduation to begin a home Bible study.
- A man who had previously attended seminary and pastored ten years in the Boston area and then lived outside of New England several years before returning to develop a Bible study and church.
- An Anglo church planter who, having learned the Khmer language and begun one Boston-area Cambodian church, prepared to begin another Khmer Bible study.
- A bivocational church planter who developed a Bible study in the town where he is employed and lives—the town from which Adoniram and Ann Judson and Luther Rice, early foreign missionaries who became Baptists, set sail.
- Lay leaders who began a second Brazilian church although the mother church was without a pastor and both congregations would have to wait for one pastor to serve both groups.
- A nucleus for a Vietnamese congregation who prays for a pastor who speaks their language.

A POSITIVE APPROACH Telling the story of what God is doing through churches of the association and individuals has been important. From the beginning, associational leaders committed themselves to making regular personal contact with churches and individuals. They sought to facilitate fellowship between churches by sharing the stories of what God is doing in the local congregations. They used speaking opportunities outside New England to develop both a national prayer base and additional financial and personnel resources for the association.

Associational leaders also made a conscious decision to concentrate on telling the positive things God was doing. Over several preceding decades, New England and Greater Boston had received much negative publicity as the "graveyard of evangelism." New England had the reputation of defeating spiritual leaders. Many had left the area discouraged and broken. Associational leaders felt that negative news somehow has a life of its own; it will spread whether anyone consciously works at it or not. However, positive news often is not shared. They decided to share the positive things God was doing in the midst of the difficult New England environment.

Developing an effective communications system among GBBA churches has always been a challenge. The structure had to be appropriate to the association's diversity. From the early years, associational membership has been 60 percent ethnic, 30 percent Anglo, and 10 percent Black. Churches worship and teach in eleven languages. Half of the congregations worship in a language other than English. First Baptist Church of Chelsea illustrates the diversity of the GBBA. This congregation, which nearly disbanded in 1984, revived and, in five years, had grown to an average weekly attendance of 120. Those attending a typical Sunday service represent as many as seven languages and fourteen countries of origin.

From the beginning, GBBA leaders have depended primarily on verbal communication since most of GBBA congregations, by their traditions, depend more heavily on oral communication than on written material. Associational newsletters and letters from program leaders share basic information, but contact through telephone and in personal conversations is the primary vehicle for developing relationships and sharing information. Personal contact and relationships are extremely important in continuing unity in the association.

Stories of the victories and struggles of individual churches are shared in order to encourage other congregations and to build prayer support. A prime positive example is the Chatham Baptist Church, located on the elbow of Cape Cod. In 1977, church planters Ray and Carolyn Allen moved to Carver, south of Boston, to begin several Southern Baptist churches. At that time, there was not a single SBC congregation south of Boston. Ray began a Bible study, which became Faith Baptist Church, in Carver. He also began a Bible study in Marshfield. For a year, only one woman attended, but that was the beginning of Victory Baptist Church in Marshfield. In Chatham, an hour's drive from Carver, Ray found a group of women who had been meeting regularly for several years to pray for a Bible-teaching church to begin in their town. He began meeting with the women and soon started Sunday services. They held their first Sunday service from the back of a flatbed trailer in a shopping center parking lot. The weekly Bible studies grew to thirty people, and a recent seminary graduate was called as pastor.

The new congregation began to grow rapidly, quickly filling rented spaces. At one point, they met in the Grange Hall, which they learned had once been a Baptist church. However, the church had died sixty years earlier, and no Baptist church had existed in Chatham since. In 1982, the church formed a committee to search for land to purchase. When a realtor showed them a piece of property, which turned out not to be suitable for building, she asked, "What type of property would you like?"

They replied, "The four acres next door would be ideal, but we know we can't afford it." They estimated its value at that time at $100,000.

"Have you made an offer to purchase?" she asked.

"No, we know there is no need; we can't afford it."

"Let me make an offer for you—it won't hurt anything," she countered. "What would you like to offer?"

"Well, this sounds crazy, but we have $30,000—we would offer that."

When the realtor called the owner, who lived in New Hampshire, the man said the property was no longer for sale and he would have someone take down the "for sale" sign.

"Thanks for your time; I'll tell the group," the realtor replied.

Surprised, he responded, "You didn't mention a group, what group?"

"The Baptist church."

"I didn't know Chatham had a Baptist church," he countered.

"This is a new group just starting out, and this would be their first property," she said.

"Let me get back to you," the owner replied.

A couple of days later, he called the realtor and said, "I've talked with my sister. We'd be delighted to sell to a Baptist church."

When the realtor asked the price, he replied, "Oh, the $30,000 the church mentioned is fine. You can tell them they can pay as little down as they want and I'll carry them as long as they need at low interest."

He then added, "Now this is not a condition of sale, but please ask them if they'd mind somewhere out in the back of the property putting up a small marker in memory of my father. He was a Baptist preacher."

Through prayer, God led the committee to the son of a Baptist pastor sympathetic to their efforts. Within the next year, Chatham had constructed a 250-seat sanctuary and educational building with volunteer labor. By 1989, Chatham averaged 175 in weekly worship.

Leaders share church-planting stories such as Grace Baptist Church in Marlboro. In 1985, David Dean, pastor of First Baptist Church of Sudbury, asked for volunteers from the Sudbury congregation to become the nucleus for a new congregation in the neighboring town of Marlboro. With a population approaching forty thousand, Marlboro had very little evangelical witness. Mark Acuff, who had served for two years as a seminary intern at First Baptist, would be the pastor of the new congregation.

When the pastor gave the invitation for those wanting to begin the congregation in Marlboro, he expected three or four families. To his amazement, seven families volunteered. Over the next few weeks, several additional families joined the initial group. On a Sunday in October 1985, seventy people left the Sudbury congregation to help plant new congregations: fifty-five went to begin the congregation in Marlboro and fifteen to begin a congregation in Milford. At that time, First Baptist Sudbury had a Sunday morning attendance of approximately two hundred. That day one-third of the attendance, one-third of the deacons, one-third of the Sunday school teachers left—and took approximately 40 percent of the weekly offerings. The following week, First Baptist Sudbury voted to begin construction of a new worship auditorium costing approximately $500,000. It was humanly impossible, and the church knew it.

Over the next several months, the Sudbury congregation experienced a sense of loss. The pastor had not realized the full impact the families' leaving would have on him. However, neither he nor the congregation questioned that it was God's will or had second thoughts about beginning the congregation in Marlboro and helping begin the one in Milford.

During the spring of 1986, a new Greek congregation, begun through the efforts of Ignatius Meimaris, asked to meet in First Baptist's building. For the next two years, Greek worship and English Sunday school were held simultaneously. Then the groups reversed, and English worship and Greek Sunday school took place. The Greek congregation added enthusiasm to the Sudbury congregation when it was needed. The Greek congregation constituted as the Hellenic Gospel Church (SBC) in May 1990 and purchased the building formerly used by Newton Corner Baptist Church in Newton.

By January 1987, the new worship sanctuary was completed and ready for dedication. Still no one knew how First Baptist would afford the building payments. The construction loan was at 12.5 percent interest.

God worked through the death of a First Baptist member to address that need. A church deacon, who had become a believer only a few years earlier, died the week before the building dedication. At his memorial service, held on the Wednesday evening before the building dedication Sunday, many First Baptist members shared the impact this deacon's life had had on them. Some, who had been Christians for many years, told how the deacon had taught them to pray.

Several of the deacon's long-time friends visited First Baptist for the first time for the memorial service. One was a banker who, after seeing the new building and knowing of his friend's impact on the church, volunteered to secure a loan through his bank for $450,000 at 8.5 percent interest when the going rate was nearly 12 percent. God had worked in a most unusual way to provide long-term financing.

Grace Baptist Church at Marlboro grew from its nucleus of 55 to an average worship attendance of 175 by the fall of 1989. By September 1989, four Grace Baptist Church members were enrolled in seminary. None of the four had been believers four years earlier when the congregation began. In the fall of 1989, Grace Baptist Church voted unanimously to sponsor a new congregation in the nearby town of Ashland. Grace Baptist Church continues to meet in rented facilities.

INTERDENOMINATIONAL COOPERATION Interdenominational cooperation, especially among evangelical churches, has been an important factor in growth. Evangelical leaders share resources, build mutual prayer support, and occasionally sponsor joint training events. When a new SBC bivocational campus minister needed housing, Methodist friends provided permanent housing for the Baptist campus minister. Another family, who worships in an interdenominational church, provided a year's free housing for a volunteer couple.

Evangelicals also cooperate in occasional combined training events. After a young layman asked for an interdenominational church-planting seminar, a committee, under the auspices of the Evangelistic Association of New England, conducted the first one in March 1986. To everyone's delight, 145 people from twenty denominations attended the eight-hour seminar. The church-planting seminar has become an annual event with attendance most years exceeding 150 people from twenty denominations. In addition, the group produces a newsletter that gives general church-planting tips and provides specifics of what various groups are doing in church planting in New England.

Interdenominational prayer efforts have taken a variety of forms. In 1979, a group of three hundred ministers came together for three days in Sturbridge, Massachusetts, to pray for spiritual awakening throughout New England. A few small groups have continued praying as a result of that effort. Since 1984, Martin has been a part of a personal support group of five ministers from five denominations who meet monthly for two hours to share with and pray for each other. In 1985, this group began discussing the possibility of a regular area-wide ministers' prayer group to pray for spiritual awakening. Ninety people were invited to meet at Newton Corner Baptist Church to pray for three hours for spiritual awakening. Fifty-five ministers from eight denominations came. During the summer of 1989, an overnight prayer leaders' seminar drew more than 160 people from more than twenty denominations. Most of the participants represented prayer groups meeting on a regular basis.

The Evangelistic Association of New England sponsors a two-day congress each January. At the 1990 Congress, four thousand people spent one and a half hours praying in concert for spiritual awakening. Evangelical leaders regularly pray for each others' church-planting efforts.

A POSITIVE CLIMATE FOR CHURCH PLANTING   A key factor in the growth of the Boston Association is the positive climate for starting congregations established by the associational Missions Development Council. This group plans regular missions emphases to encourage churches to plant congregations. Churches start other churches. The denominational agencies are partners in helping find resources to enable the local churches to plant congregations.

Denominational leaders encourage congregations by conducting surveys to pinpoint communities where new churches seem to be needed. Surveys regarding the need for ethnic congregations are done by members of those ethnic groups. Surveys regarding new English-speaking congregations are accomplished by looking primarily for the presence or absence of other evangelical churches in particular areas.

The parent-child concept of church planting is the primary method used in church extension. Of thirty-two new congregations begun in the first seven years of the association, twenty-nine were planted with a parent-child approach.

DENOMINATIONAL PARTNERSHIP   Another major factor in the growth of the Boston Association is an effective denominational partnership. While strategy planning has been done by the association, denominational agencies have been strong partners. Both the state convention and the Home Missions Board emphasized the importance of local planning and have committed their personnel to assist the association and churches. Personnel from other denominational agencies also are involved in helping the association accomplish its goals.

CHALLENGES FOR THE FUTURE

By the fall of 1989, several challenges faced the GBBA. Simply maintaining the level of enthusiasm experienced during its first seven years would require concentrated effort. Much of this enthusiasm came from having new congregations composed primarily of new believers.

Some challenges naturally arose out of the rapid increase in the number of churches. Integrating those new congregations into the association and developing them as Southern Baptist churches in the New England context would remain a principal issue.

Dealing with few church-owned facilities remained primary. Of the forty-eight GBBA congregations, only twelve owned buildings. The other thirty-six met anywhere and at any time they could rent facilities. Each Sunday from 9:30 A.M. through 9:30 P.M., at least one GBBA congregation was in worship and Bible study. More than one congregation shared most of the buildings owned by the churches of the association. For example, four congregations held six worship services each Sunday at Newton Corner church. In the near future, the association may have fifty congregations that do not own buildings. A two-pronged plan emerged: Where possible, help congregations secure buildings in an extremely expensive and difficult market and help those without buildings develop a growth mentality without the necessity of owning property.

Realistically, most of the congregations probably will never own buildings. Thirty-two new congregations began between 1982 and 1989. Of the thirty-two, only one had bought property. In 1990, that church of fifty people built a 120-seat $450,000 church facility using volunteer labor.

In addition to high costs, zoning regulations challenged the patience of associational leaders. For example, since 1987, the association, in partnership with a Messianic Jewish congregation and a Mennonite congregation, had planned to build office and worship space jointly on a two-acre site in Needham. When the two congregations applied for a building permit, the town of Needham rejected the application on the basis of inadequate parking. The town building inspector asked for 157 parking spaces for a building seating 180 people for worship. When the town denied the churches permission to build and refused to negotiate further, the churches reluctantly filed suit in state superior court. After four years and at the time of this writing, they were still awaiting resolution of the matter.

SUMMARY

Challenges, enthusiasm, and growth for the GBBA marked the years 1982 through 1989. Associational leaders from the beginning consciously sought to follow this dictum:

If you want to make a lasting impact when you begin a work in a new area, take the time to learn where God is already working, then get in step with Him.

Four principles have been articulated about how God has worked in Boston:

1. Everything we attempt is humanly impossible.
2. God is accomplishing the humanly impossible.
3. God is working in such a way only he can get the credit.
4. Prayer is the basis of all that has been accomplished.

5

*Developing
Congregational
Strategy for
Church Planting*

*Church planting is
a task of the local church.
This is based on Scripture.
Also, it is a more practical,
efficient, and effective
way than any other system.*

F. Jack Redford, 1979

Jack Redford, late director of the Division
of Church Extension for Southern Baptists' Home Mission
Board, alleges that "church planting is primarily the task of
a local church." (I agree with him wholeheartedly.) He
insists that beginning new churches is a "normal and natural function for a church. If it does not take on this task, it
has become root bound."[1]

I have not traced the roots of this missionary conviction,
but it is deeply ingrained in the Southern Baptist mentality. Historically, it might be traced back to Shubal Stearns
and the Sandy Creek Church of North Carolina. That
church, constituted in 1754, was the first Separatist Baptist church in the South to survive for any length of time,
and it was the mother church to many congregations in
North Carolina, Virginia, and Georgia in the eighteenth
century. This church and the numerous churches and associations that were spawned from it provided much of the
spiritual heritage out of which Southern Baptist evangelistic enthusiasm has grown.[2]

I suspect, however, that the axiom that "church planting

is primarily the task of a local church" took its substance from Gospel Missionism, the missionary expression of the Landmark movement. This movement, which arose in the 1880s, threatened the life of the Southern Baptist Convention. Overseas, Gospel Missioners maintained that the missionaries should adopt the living conditions of the people where they served and that churches should be self-controlling and self-supporting from the beginning. In the homeland, the leaders of this movement objected to mission boards and insisted that the local church be the agency through which missionaries were sent and supported.

The Convention rejected Gospel Missionism, but the movement left an indelible mark on Southern Baptist missionary principles, especially in their formulation and application in America.

INTEREST AND DISINTEREST IN CHURCH PLANTING

Whatever may be the historical roots of the axiom among Southern Baptists that missionary responsibility lodges with the local church, that conviction is certainly not one that has been shared directly by leaders of most other denominations, nor is it reflected in denominational structures. Church planting, for most of the larger ecclesiastical bodies, is the responsibility of the national church, regional organizations, or home mission agencies.

This assessment is shared by many leaders of local churches. In fact, there has been and continues to be an aversion to church planting on the part of many pastors, elders, deacons, and other local church leaders. I am happy to report that for some local church leaders this attitude is changing. The last decade of the twentieth century has seen a rebirth of commitment to starting new churches. Nevertheless, the disinterest remains and is apparent even among pastors who would defend the principle of local church responsibility in church planting.

Many factors have contributed to this. The first one is related to interdenominational cooperation: The advocates of ecumenical cooperation have interpreted the multiplication of churches as a denial of the unity of the Church. Church planting is seen as obvious, irrefutable, empirical evidence of the schism of the body. The multiplication of monocultural churches in various geographical areas is viewed as a disgrace, for which we should be ashamed, or a transgression, from which we should turn in repentance.

Admittedly, the duplication of services and ministries has been a costly and confusing situation in overseas missions as well as in this country. For example, Brownwood, Texas, a small central Texas city, was the home for many years of Daniel Baker College (Methodist) and Howard Payne College (Baptist). About eighty miles farther west, in a little larger city—Abilene, Texas—there was McMurray College (Methodist), Hardin Simmons College (Baptist), and Abilene Christian College (Churches of Christ). With the exception of Daniel Baker, which no longer exists as a separate institution, all of these have become universities.

In spite of multiple examples of this kind of evidence, I believe that a monopoly is a dangerous pattern ecclesiastically and evangelistically, as well as commercially and politically. Comity agreements, in time, produce religious monopolies or establishments. At best, they produce a monopolizing attitude and an "establishment" mentality that is more interested in protecting turf and maintaining hegemony than aggressively discipling and developing churches among the various peoples of an area. Comity arrangements often crystallize certain missionary methods that become wooden and unproductive. They can result in an insensitivity to human need and deplete the evangelical passion for souls that should mark biblical Christianity.

A second factor that has produced an aversion to

church planting on the part of local church leaders and denominational leaders is related to technology. Modern transportation has greatly extended the effective radius of strong, exciting churches. People can travel farther, quicker. There is no need for new congregations, church leaders allege, when large, well-staffed, well-housed, full-programmed churches can be reached with no serious time problems. This whole philosophy is based on the idea, of course, that the community that a large church serves is a cultural monolith or that a culturally conglomerate church is the best kind of church and the only kind that should receive high visibility.

At the opposite pole lies a third factor that has contributed to the disinterest in church planting by local church leaders: Our frightful struggle with racism, Anglo-Saxon ethnocentrism, and the social exclusiveness of middle-class respectability over the past quarter century has idealized conglomerate churches. Missions and denominational leaders express pride in and give high marks to those churches that have racial, ethnic, and socioeconomic diversity within their fellowship. Evidence of cross-cultural inclusiveness seems much more significant to church leaders than successful evangelistic penetration of the various segments of society. Our denominational reward system, the way we "stroke" pastors and other local church leaders, has actually discouraged church planting.

A fourth factor that has contributed to the disinterest in church planting by the leaders of local churches has also contributed to a rebirth of interest in this apostolic task. A strong commitment to develop large and super-large churches exists today. The church growth movement has contributed to this development ever since it began to address itself to the North American situation. The focus on greatly growing churches, which often are described after they have become large churches, has contributed to the romance with megachurches.[3]

The age of the megachurch is just dawning in America.

The day that some churches, located in high populations, will have twenty thousand or more in attendance, probably in multiple services, is in our near future. However, research has shown that megachurches, by their nature, create satellites. Megachurches grow and develop by the creation of multiple congregations within their fellowships. They tend to be highly creative and responsive to felt need. They create cell groups and congregations designed to reach and nurture new people in the gospel. This discovery is already bringing balance to prevailing attitudes toward church planting.

Church leaders have discovered that church planting is essential to a growing denomination.[4] In 1990, a group of leaders from about forty denominations reported that those ecclesiastical bodies had plans to begin fifty-five thousand new congregations in the U.S. and Canada by A.D. 2000. More and more pastors are leading their churches to develop a strategy for satellite development.

Satellites come in two basic forms: dependent, those that will always have an organic relationship to the parent church, and pre-independent, those that will eventually move to independent organization. Local church leaders, especially those committed to significant growth within their own congregations, are discovering that satellites, whether dependent or pre-independent, become feeders to the parent church and that they are the best method by which to share Christ effectively with the various people groups that make up North American society.

I affirm the growth of large churches. Three things should be underscored. First, big churches always come from little churches. Even in a day when new churches are launched with an attendance of several hundred, this axiom is true. The greatest churches in North America have yet to be planted. Second, it needs to be said again and again that success in the numerical growth of a local church does not preclude involvement in planting daughter churches. Rather, it can be shown from Christian history and current local church experience that by the intentional creation of daughter congregations the growth of a central church can be significantly enhanced. Finally, the contribution made by small churches needs to be realistically assessed. I cannot speak about other denominational groups, but for Southern Baptists, smaller churches are more effective in evangelism than are the larger churches. In a report prepared in May 1978 entitled "A Study of the Relationship of Church Size and Church Age to Number of Baptisms and Baptism Rates," Clay Price and Phillip Jones of the Home Mission Board, SBC, found that "the younger the church and the smaller the church, the higher the baptism rate."[5] To bring statistics up to date, in 1990, Southern Baptist churches with less than a hundred resident members baptized two more people per hundred resident members than those churches with more than five hundred resident members. If the age of churches is considered, the churches under ten years of age with less than a hundred resident members are almost three times as effective in evangelism as the churches more than forty years of age with more than five hundred resident members. There is no basis for demeaning the small church when discussing evangelistic effectiveness.

Many other factors that have contributed to disinterest in church planting could be mentioned. The reasons for this lack of interest by the leaders of local churches are much more complex than I have described here. Such attitudes continue to exist. However, the tide has turned. Another spirit has arisen among some church leaders. The question I address is not, What holds us back? but, What can we do to move forward to a strategy for church planting in a local church? To respond to this question, I will describe briefly the strategies of two churches, one already well known for its growth over ten years and the second destined to become well known during the 1990s. Then I will make a few simple observations about how multiplication strategies can be developed in other churches.

SADDLEBACK COMMUNITY CHURCH, MISSION VIEJO, CALIFORNIA

The Saddleback Valley story is well known. Knowledge, however, tends to be from only one dimension. We know of Pastor Rick Warren and the Saddleback Valley Church as a case study in church planting, one that has been highly successful in penetrating the baby boomer generation. We know that since the first Sunday in January 1980, when Rick held his first Bible study, the church has grown so that ten years later it has passed five thousand in attendance in its several weekend worship services. We know that after its first twelve years, the church still had no permanent building. We know of the very clear strategy that was developed for reaching "Saddleback Sam." Thousands have heard Rick speak in church planting and church growth seminars. Hundreds have attended his own church growth seminar conducted annually in Mission Viejo.[6]

Very few people know of, or have paid attention to, the Saddleback Valley strategy for planting new churches. One denominational executive said, "Why would you want to hear Rick Warren at a church planting conference? He has only planted one church." Still others doubt the effectiveness of the new congregations that Saddleback Valley Church has sponsored. Another denominational leader said, "Rick Warren's methods cannot be duplicated. In fact, they have not been successful in southern California with other churches he and his church have tried to start."

From the beginning, the Saddleback Valley strategy included the multiplication of congregations. The stated goal was a church with twenty thousand in attendance by A.D. 2020 and one daughter congregation for each of the forty years in the process.[7] Amazingly, Saddleback Valley

Church is exceeding its goal. In 1990, the church had launched twenty new congregations.

None of those twenty congregations have yet had 5,000 in attendance. However, I visited ten of these daughter congregations in 1990 and found them all exceeding 150 in attendance. One Spanish-speaking church now exceeds 800 in attendance. Another congregation also has more than 600 in worship each week. Like their parent, these two churches had no permanent buildings in which to meet at that time. Plans are under way at Saddleback Valley to begin multiple congregations annually.

FIRST BAPTIST CHURCH, ARLINGTON, TEXAS

The First Baptist Church, Arlington, Texas, is located in a city of 261,000 between Dallas and Fort Worth, near Six Flags over Texas and the stadium of the Texas Rangers. Charles Wade has led this church as pastor since 1976. It is an older church with a wonderful history of starting daughter congregations. First Baptist is one of many Southern Baptist churches in the city of Arlington.

In 1986, the church launched Mission Arlington, a concerted effort to reach the whole city and specifically to pinpoint the more than three thousand multihousing properties in Arlington. Not one was being effectively reached by any church in the city.

The effort is led by Mrs. Robert (Tillie) Burgin, who became part of the church staff with the title "Minister of Missions." Their strategy attempts to meet human need, teach the Bible, and move toward house churches. The Bible studies and worship services are conducted within each multihousing property at 11:00 A.M. on Sunday morning. Each unit is an indigenous satellite unit (ISU) of the First Baptist Church.

At the time the program was launched, First Baptist averaged eleven hundred on Sunday morning in two worship services. By the end of 1991 there were 125 ISUs with two thousand in attendance. The First Baptist Church had increased its average attendance in downtown Arlington to nineteen hundred in Sunday school.[8]

Charles Wade works hard at keeping the two ministries tied together as the expression of one church. More than 200 workers, many raised up within the multihousing ministries and more than 150 from First Baptist, attend the early worship service of the central church. A workers' conference for reporting and training is conducted every Sunday afternoon. On special occasions, the ISU congregations are brought to the First Baptist for a celebration service. The strategy has enabled the church to minister to all socioeconomic and ethnic groups in the city, to address the whole city with the gospel, and to see hundreds of lives changed by an encounter with Jesus Christ. The growth of First Baptist has been enhanced by the effort.

OBSERVATIONS ABOUT STRATEGY

These two stories suggest some conditions essential to a bold and effective strategy for church planting on the part of a local church. My observations about these essential conditions will not be comprehensive, nor will they necessarily be in proper order.

1. I would stress the importance of a dynamic, creative leader who thinks big, who has a genuine compassion for people without Christ, and who has an overpowering commitment to obey Jesus Christ in his own life. I doubt that a church will ever develop a deliberate, long-range plan for church planting without a leader who is himself committed to such a strategy.

2. In order for a congregation to develop a strategy for planting churches, that congregation—or at least its principal leaders—must have assumed evangelistic responsibility for a significant geographical area. The burden of an entire city or county that needs to know Christ must be embraced.

A church-planting strategy grows out of this kind of vision and concern. Charles Wade and Tillie Burgin speak, with all sincerity, of reaching the city of Arlington for Christ. They have a plan to do it. Their plan does not exclude other Christians. In fact, they rejoice when other churches grow and when new congregations are started by sister churches. Other churches in the city have adopted this strategy. But that does not lessen their burden for Arlington.

3. Flexibility is another ingredient that is essential to a church-planting strategy. I have not seen a church more creative and flexible in methodology than Saddleback Valley. When they discover a felt need, they attempt to rise to the occasion and meet it. Operating ten years in rented facilities has required them to push creativity and flexibility to the limits. The first priority is to evangelize the area effectively and to incorporate the believers into a thriving congregation. When this requires a new congregation or special purpose ministries, the Saddleback Valley church is sensitive to this and has sufficient commitment to do it.

4. A transferable philosophy of ministry may be essential to developing an effective, long-range church-planting strategy. Thus far, the leadership of the Saddleback Valley Church seems to have been successful in passing on a philosophy and attitude that desires, expects, and counts on growth. The daughter churches are marked by the same concerns and commitments as Saddleback Valley. The model at First Baptist, Arlington, is providing a new paradigm in church planting that will enable established churches to reach thousands of persons they have not been able to reach before. The creation of dependent satellites to reach an entire city can become a major new method for the twenty-first century. If new churches are to be successfully planted by a mother church, this kind of transferable approach to the growth task must play an important part.

5. The congregation and its leaders need to have a single

commitment to direct evangelism done by the laity. This shapes its commitment to church planting and appears as a trait in the daughter churches as well. The evangelistic style of these two churches is quite different, but they are both engaged in direct evangelism.

6. Another essential is an unyielding commitment to the Word of God, not only in doctrine, but also in basic strategy, along with a firm belief in the direct leadership of the Holy Spirit. These have helped to shape the church-planting strategy of these two churches. These churches see church planting as a basic New Testament methodology for evangelistic faithfulness. They are more concerned that the Holy Spirit is leading to an area or to a homogeneous group for a new congregation than they are about the findings of a community survey. They look for a need and try to meet that need with Jesus Christ.

7. A positive, forward-looking attitude that is grounded in a wholesome faith in God is another essential. This is a contributing factor to the congregational strategy of these churches. It is no accident that Rick Warren calls his tape ministry An Encouraging Word.

8. A team approach to church planting needs to be fully explored, both by leaders of local churches and by denominational strategists. Most denominational approaches to church planting are conceived as beginning with a church planter and his family who will attempt to gather a nucleus of believers. Perhaps, however, the idea of a committed team, a team with a sense of calling from God and a dream that includes more than one new church, needs to be examined. In developing a church-planting strategy for a local church, it certainly has merit.

WHAT CAN YOU DO?

Let me suggest several things that you can do if you are a pastor, a lay leader in a congregation, or a seminarian who plans to become a pastor.

1. Accept personal evangelistic responsibility for all peoples. You probably think that I am being melodramatic or that I am asking you to become a megalomaniac. But Paul said in Romans, "I am under obligation both to Greeks and the barbarians, both to the wise and to the foolish." In Ephesians 3:8, he said, "To me, the very least of all saints, this grace was given, to preach to the Gentiles the unfathomable riches of Christ." Accept personal responsibility! You probably will not be successful in leading the church you serve to sustain a strategy for church planting if it is not the passion of your own life to reach all peoples that you can with the gospel of Christ.

2. Think bigger than the boundaries of your own congregation and in ways that will enable you to extend those boundaries. Dare to dream of an effective evangelistic strategy for a whole county, an entire city, or an entire urban region. Take a close look at the community where your own church is located. Who are the unchurched people there? How many of them are so distant from your church in terms of culture or socioeconomic factors or race that you must do more than use good growth methods to reach them effectively? Ask yourself how many of these you can realistically hope to reach only through a church-planting strategy. I doubt that you'll ever lead your church to have an enlarged vision that sees people groups, rather than just individuals, if you do not have that vision yourself.

3. Ask God for a deep conviction that he wants the lost found and that he wants to use his people to do the job. I'd like to stress this strongly. All committed Christians would agree with this doctrine, but often—and I struggle with this in my own life—we get so busy doing the "things" of our ministry that we neglect the obligations of the doctrine. We do not nurture this compassion. If you do not have a conviction that is so deep that you cannot get away from it, then ask God to give it to you.

If the most profound justification for church planting you can identify is the sociological axiom that the church is one of the necessary institutions of society, you are never going to lead a church through a sustained church-planting strategy. An evangelistic compassion for those without Jesus Christ must motivate you and your church.

4. Take time to create a climate for church planting in your congregation. I want to put the emphasis on *take time.* A later chapter will go into some detail about ways this can be done. However, I want to make one point here: A congregational strategy for church planting will not be born overnight.

5. Do not cling to traditional methods, no matter how "sanctified" they are, if they do not work. Major on effectiveness, not on efficiency. An effective congregational strategy for church planting demands flexibility.

6. Study principles and procedures of church planting yourself, and train your laity in those principles. Your key church-planting families should be raised up out of your own church.

7. Plan to stay long enough in the church where you are serving—or where you go to serve—to see the strategy through to the end. A congregational strategy for church-planting demands years—not months—of commitment.

I believe that church planting is very closely related to the apostolic gift. I fervently and regularly pray not only for Southern Baptists, but for all Christians—that God will raise up apostles, gifted men and women, who can gather churches. We desperately need them today in North America.

6

Harnessing Old and New Technology in Church Planting

by
Carol Childress, Program Information and Research Consultant
Baptist General Convention of Texas

Gordon Lawrence, Church Starter Strategist
South Metro Baptist Association
Georgia Baptist Convention

Larry L. Wartsbaugh, Director of Missions
Great Rivers and Northeast
Iowa Southern Baptist Associations

The Goal of the Great Commission
is the establishment of a church
of committed Christians
in every community,
every neighborhood, every class
and condition of people,
where everyone can hear
and see demonstrated
the gospel from his own intimates,
in his own tongue,
and has a reasonable opportunity
to become a disciple of Jesus Christ.

Donald A. McGavran, 1977

INTRODUCTION

Since this book was first published ten years ago, amazing technological development has taken place that makes the church-planting task far easier.

The correlation of census data with church and denominational data in church planting, described in the third chapter of this book, was new in the 1970s. Far more sophisticated and effective formulas for measuring the probable need for new churches have been developed.

Market segmentation from both a geodemographic and a psychographic perspective has come of age in the 1980s. It will be vastly more effective by the time the 1990s have passed.

As far as I know, this is the first effort to introduce market segmentation and make suggestions about its use in church planting.

The three authors are all practitioners, using demographic and psychographic material every week in their work as church-planting strategists—from three different perspectives. Carol Childress was program information and research consultant for the Baptist General Convention of Texas when this chapter was written. She now is on the staff of the Leadership Network, Tyler, Texas. She was involved daily in community and church assessment for purposes of church growth and church planting. Gordon Lawrence presently serves as a church starter strategist with the South Metro Baptist Association in suburban Atlanta, a very productive area for new church development. Larry Wartsbaugh is director of missions for the Great Rivers and Northeast Iowa Southern Baptist Associations. One of his principle responsibilities is to assist the churches of that association in church multiplication.

If nothing else, this chapter will stimulate your creativity as you think of ways the data at our fingertips today can be made of more practical use in the growth of the kingdom of Christ.

I. PLANTING CHURCHES IN CULTURAL CONTEXT

Every church, new or old, exists within the cultural context of its community. While a church is a living, spiritual organism, it is also a social institution that is shaped by its members' values, attitudes, beliefs, and life experiences. The extent to which a church reaches its community depends in large measure on how well it understands its cultural context and adapts both its message and ministries to the needs of the local population.

Contextualization can be defined as "the various processes by which a local church integrates the gospel message (the 'text') with its local culture (the 'context')."[1] The eternal, changeless message of the gospel is proclaimed according to the uniqueness of each community and the diversity of social and cultural groupings within the targeted population. "The gospel must be preached to human beings as human beings and where they happen to be at this particular point in time and place."[2]

Understanding the needs of people in its community should be one of the highest priorities for a new church. People will be reached more effectively for the kingdom when a new church understands and presents the gospel according to the motivations, aspirations, concerns, and needs of the people. When ministries and church programs are planned on this basis, people are more likely to respond to the church and the gospel.

Contextualization in the business world is reflected in market segmentation, the "process of partitioning markets into segments of potential customers with similar characteristics who are likely to exhibit similar purchase behavior."[3] Motivations, needs, demographics, perceptions, and life-styles are all considered in developing the most appropriate strategies to reach a particular market.

The concept of contextualization is not new, and it did not originate with the business world. Rather, its origins are in the Bible. Historically, God revealed himself to mankind in the context of individual cultures in both the Old and New Testaments. The ministry of Jesus and the missionary efforts of Paul can be understood more fully in light of their contextual approaches to dealing with people.

THE CONTEXTUAL APPROACH OF JESUS The incarnation, life, and ministry of Jesus Christ as recorded in the New Testament provide us the supreme example of biblical contextualization.

The incarnation, when "the Word became flesh, and dwelt among us . . . full of grace and truth," so beautifully described in John 1:14, is the most complete revelation of God to man. This intrusion of the Divine into the context of human history has meant the identification of Jesus with the needs, hurts, and hopes of men and women for almost two thousand years.

Jesus responded to the needs of people within their cultural contexts and adapted his approach uniquely to them.

He based his approach on his understanding of their values, attitudes, and life-styles, derived from personal observation, questions, and conversations. "He adapted his message to the circumstances—to the needs and backgrounds of those he encountered."[4]

The Synoptic Gospels contain the encounter of Jesus with the rich young ruler. The young man had wealth and a position of authority in the community. While he had social standing, he knew something was missing from his life. Even his adherence to the laws had not filled the vacuum in his life, and he was searching for the answer to the basic question asked by people. In responding to his inquiry, Jesus went beyond the obvious and moved directly to the center of the young man's value system. "Sell what you possess and give to the poor, and you will have treasure in heaven" (Luke 18:22, *our paraphrase*). Because he knew the social context of the young man's life and his value system, Jesus was able to address his deepest need.

John chapter 4 provides another example of the adaptive contextual approach of Jesus in ministering to people. His conversation with the Samaritan woman revealed his insight about her culture, religious beliefs, and personal life-style. Jesus' directed probing, moving from the woman's physical need of water to her ultimate spiritual need, is an example of the benefit of knowing as much as possible about an individual's needs and life-style and adapting the gospel presentation accordingly. His message was heard and accepted by this woman because his approach was based on sensitivity to her culture and life-style.

THE CONTEXTUAL APPROACH OF PAUL

The strategies employed by Paul in preaching the gospel and planting churches were based on his conviction to become "all things to all men," that by all means he might save some (1 Corinthians 9:22). While Paul's central message was always focused on Jesus Christ, he adapted his approach to the uniqueness of the people and cultural context in which he ministered.

In his first letter to the church at Corinth, "Paul mentions four groups to whom he deliberately adjusted his life-style and message presentation in order to gain their allegiance: Jews, those under the law, those outside the law, and the 'weak.'"[5] He was able to make the necessary adjustments in approach and strategy because he understood the culture, values, and life-styles of his target population.

Paul knew his audience at Mars Hill in Athens. Acts 17:16-34 tells us that he had observed both the city and the people before his remarks at the Areopagus. He knew that Athens was a city full of idols (v. 16) and divergent philosophies (v. 18). He "began his message with references to the 'unknown God,' a Greek poet, nature, and man as the creation of God."[6] He spoke to their life-styles, the image of their city, their perceptions of God, and their value systems.

Earlier in the same chapter, Paul used another approach in Thessalonica, speaking to a different audience in the synagogue. With his insight into the local culture and religious values, his message in this city focused on Jesus as the Christ. The same was true for his messages in Antioch (Acts 13) and Damascus (Acts 9).

CONTEXTUAL RESEARCH AND TODAY'S CHURCH

The 1980s might be called the "age of clustering." During this time, the triad of marketing, technology, and sociology joined forces to create powerful new tools of human analysis. Someone has coined the phrase "the paralysis of analysis" to describe the overwhelming nature of our analytical tendencies. George Barna, in an article entitled "The Analysis of Our Paralysis," defines ten illnesses in the churches of America. One of these is the lack of targeting the specific audience toward which our message is directed.

In the 1960s and 1970s mass marketing was in its heyday. The decade of the 1980s, however, has brought to the fore a major shift—to niche marketing and segmentation marketing. No longer does it work to proclaim a general message through a mass medium in the hope of reaching enough people to justify the effort. Secular marketers have shifted their emphasis to targeted marketing, seeking to personalize their message, sent by way of a selective medium that is likely to reach the most responsive audience. Yet, the Church has been slow to recognize and adopt this shift. We have largely ignored the increased return on investment achieved by targeting our message and our audience. This is especially important today because it is an expectation among the public. If we do not approach them with a specific, targeted message, other marketers will—with consequent rewards.[7]

But why should the church concern itself with the principle of secular marketing practices? The validity of that question lies in the practical definition of the term *marketing*. At its simplest, marketing is identifying needs and resources and finding creative ways to bring them together for mutual benefit. Should a church have a marketing plan? Is not the gospel the essential need for the lost, and is not the church the steward of the resource to meet that need?

The first real challenge for the church, then, is to identify the need of the community and the resources of the local fellowship. Ray Bakke enhances our understanding of the term "identifying our community." Using a theological term, he exhorts us to "exegete" our community as we do a passage of Scripture.[8] We do this first by locating the passage in context; next, interpreting the passage through the use of context; and, finally, applying the passage faithfully in context to meet present needs.

To provide a comprehensive tool of community exegesis for the local church, five primary factors may be involved: *geographics, demographics, geodemographics, psychographics,* and *ekklegraphics. Geographics* tell us where the people are located. *Demographics* tell us who the people are in terms of social characteristics. *Geodemographics,* a sophisticated combination of the first two, identify segments of the populace that tend to cluster in certain habitats and to follow certain behavioral patterns. *Psychographics* tell us how the people behave from a specific psychological and sociological perspective, focusing on common values and life-styles. *Ekklegraphics* tell us how a church or denomination is similar to or different from the neighboring community.

The church of the 1990s that reaches people will do so because it is "market-driven." It will be a church that responds to the needs and demands of its targeted population based on a thorough understanding of the area's demographics, attitudes, life-styles, and values. Its ministries and programs will be developed in response to the community rather than standardized programs that do not consider local needs. All church planning in the 1990s must be "outside-in" rather than the present "inside-out" if the planning is to reach unchurched people for Christ. The needs of the target group must determine ministry and programs, not the preferences, traditions, and habits of those inside the church.

CONTEXTUAL RESEARCH AND CHURCH PLANTING Understanding the needs, values, and life-styles of a target community can best be achieved by the church planter who approaches local research deliberately. The church planter should know as much as possible about the community's demographics, social structure, and culture before beginning the church.

Just as ample biblical evidence supports contextual approaches to evangelism and church planting, the Bible also provides a model of community or area research before beginning a work. The modern church planter should follow the example of the research team assembled by Moses in Numbers 13.

The information collected by that research team amounted to an analysis of the area to be claimed for God by the Hebrew children. They were to report on the kind of people who dwelt in Canaan and their number and strength. They were to report on the social and economic condition of the land, especially the cities, and they were to evaluate their potential for taking the land.

Thorough and relevant research on the community or area is a crucial step in beginning a church. Based on research results, appropriate evangelism strategies and ministries can be designed that take into consideration the community's demographics, culture, social structure, life-styles, and values. The church can then be planted biblically, according to the context of the local population.

The church planter, above all church leaders, should effectively use the technology available today. To adequately analyze and exegete the target community, however, a more detailed introduction to the analytical information available is needed.

II. AN INTRODUCTION OF DEMOGRAPHIC PROFILES AND MARKET SEGMENTATION

LIFE-STYLES—"THE NEW MICROCULTURE" It has been said, "Birds of a feather flock together." Not only do they flock together, but they share many creature eccentricities that we might call microcultures in the world of ornithology. But let's translate that into human terms. The human species is a product of sociology that demands acculturation. Usually when we think of cultures, we imagine language barriers and geographical zones of isolation. In missiological terms, the definition of a culture is a "people group," which consists of individuals with common behavioral patterns, popularly known as "life-styles."

The American public is infatuated with the notoriety of life-styles. After all, we've been putting labels on people since the dawn of time—the haves and have-nots, country bumpkins and city slickers, blue collars and white collars, rednecks and honkies, hippies and yippies.

According to the U.S. Bureau of Census, there are approximately 90 million households in the United States. Are we to believe that all of these households share one massive monolithic behavior pattern? Of course not. Should we then believe that all 90 million have distinctively different life-styles? Probably not. Our task, then, is to determine what patterns of commonality exist among us. In generations past, the United States has been popularly known as "the melting pot," a country in which the citizens blend together in mutual habitation. Charles Kuralt says that America is "some kind of alloy that cannot be melted."[9]

Three basic qualities of human nature make North America more like a stew pot than a melting pot. People are *tribal.*[10] Whether you focus on the Zulu clans of Africa or the Bohemian communities of Chicago, the root system of social identity will always be the ethnic, national, or family kinship that provides an adhesive quality. It is true that "blood is thicker than water."

People are *territorial.* The vernacular for the concept of territorialism is the term "turf protection." People not only live on the land. They become a part of the land, and their heritage is anchored in a sense of environmental ownership.

People are *hierarchical.* In the egalitarian society of the democratic west, we don't like to think in terms of a caste system composed of social strata or layers of citizenry. Yet, society always has a system of deference in which some individuals are "more equal" than others.

One of the paradigmatic shifts in American society during the past forty years has been the dissolution of the mass market and introduction of niche or specialized marketing. The fragmentation of the population has resulted in a new emphasis on segmentation that reflects the values and attitudes and shared life-styles of people more than common demographic information. These new life-style groupings have become in effect microcultures within the larger framework of contemporary American culture in the 1990s.

GEOGRAPHICS—"THE PHYSICAL TEMPLATE" The primary interpreter for community exegesis is the physical definition, commonly called the geographic survey. This physical profile of land boundaries is a "template" through which the demographic, psychographic, and ekklegraphic data can be interpreted.

The ZIP code is the unit of measure of the U.S. Postal Service for carrier route distribution. It has become the preferred unit of microgeography for the demographics industry because of the clear assignment of the five-digit ZIP codes for every property in the county. For many years, the census tract has been the standard means of county subdivision. In areas of sparse population, the census tract has deferred to county boundaries for legal purposes.

The block group or enumeration district is a geographic definition used by the U.S. Census Bureau to divide the county into quantifiable units for census workers during the decennial survey.

As indicated in Figure 1, these units of microgeography range in size from the 37,000 ZIP codes to 254,000 block groups. They range in average number of household units from 2,320 for ZIP codes to 340 for block groups. Given these boundaries from which we track the location and mobility of the populace, we can identify who lives within a specific geographic region.

FIGURE 1. **Microgeography**

Field	Units in Country	Average Households Per Unit
ZIP Code	37,000	2,320
Census Tract	68,000	1,270
Block Group	254,000	340

DEMOGRAPHICS—"THE ANATOMY OF THE INDIVIDUAL"
The decennial census is the cornerstone of information
related to the social and economic characteristics of
people and their communities. Due to the exhaustive
efforts of the U.S. Bureau of Census, we have public
records that track approximately six hundred components of information for most households in the United
States. These components can be broadly grouped
into three categories: population, housing, and household.

Population information includes people's age, sex,
race, ethnicity, education, occupation, and marital status, among other things. Housing information includes
the age of the dwelling, type of dwelling (single-family,
multifamily, etc.), and value and other characteristics
of the dwelling. Household information includes the
composition (family or nonfamily), as well as income
levels.

This information is an indispensable part of community
analysis, but it is incomplete without other data. What we
really want to know is this: What cultures are represented
among the populace? Are their modes of life-style oriented
toward survival or leisure? Do they have traditional values,
or are they eccentric and experimental in their notions of
daily living?

Why do we ask these questions? Because the local
church and the church-planting team need to know who
lives in their community so that they can know how to
minister to their needs.

GEODEMOGRAPHICS—"THE CLUSTERING OF THE
NATION" Advancements in computer technology have
allowed demographers to analyze certain social characteristics, quality of life factors, and other criteria. This
analysis, in combination with geographical factors, has
resulted in a series of geodemographic systems that can
augment the population of a given area. Six corporations

that specialize in this process are Claritas, Inc., and CACI Marketing Systems, both of Alexandria, Virginia; National Decision Systems of Encintas, California; Donnelley Marketing Information Series of Stamford, Connecticut; National Planning Data Corporation of Ithaca, New York; and Urban Decision Systems of Los Angeles, California.

Each of these companies has segmented the United States into social clusters ranging from forty to forty-eight groupings with trademarked "images" to classify each cluster. Claritas, Inc. introduced PRIZM (Potential Ratings Index for ZIP Markets) as its cluster system and uses "Furs and Station Wagons" as one example to describe 3.19 percent of the population who are educated, affluent professionals living in elite metro suburbs. Equifax (NDS) has a cluster system called MICRO. "Leave it to Beaver" is one image conveyed by NDS to imprint the picture of 1.9 percent of the population who live traditional nuclear family life-styles. CACI's cluster analysis is called ACORN, the acronym for "A Classification of Residential Neighborhoods." One example of ACORN's imagery is "Old Money," which targets .5 percent of the nation's neighborhoods as inhabited by wealthy, elite families whose inherited fortunes are distinct from those of the new breed of corporate entrepreneurs.

Each of these four data-vendors groups its clusters into approximately ten to twelve major categories, which provide subsets of economy, ranging from wealthy to welfare, and of environment, ranging from urban to rural. Each classification system has in common the targeting of "high concentrations of homogeneous characteristics."

Michael Weiss has immortalized this new social segmentation in his popular book *The Clustering of America*. Based on the PRIZM cluster system, Weiss credits Jonathan Robbin, the founder of Claritas, as a pioneer in this new dimension of demographics (see Figure 2).

FIGURE 2. **PRIZM Life-Style Clusters**

Nickname	Percentage of 1987 U.S. HHH's	Nickname	Percentage of 1987 U.S. HHH's
Blue Blood Estates	1.13	New Melting Pot	0.90
Money and Brains	0.94	Old Yankee Rows	1.59
Furs and Station Wagons	3.19	Emergent Minorities	1.72
Pools and Patios	3.42	Single City Blues	3.35
Two More Rungs	0.74		
Young Influential	2.86	Shotguns and Pickups	1.85
		Agri-Business	2.09
Young Suburbia	5.40	Grain Belt	1.24
Blue Chip Blues	6.04	Golden Ponds	5.25
Urban Gold Coast	0.48	Mines and Mills	2.84
Bohemian Mix	1.14	Norma Raeville	2.34
Black Enterprise	0.76	Small Town Downtown	2.44
New Beginnings	4.32		
		Back Country Folks	3.43
God's Country	2.71	Share Croppers	3.98
New Homesteaders	4.16	Tobacco Roads	1.22
Towns and Gowns	1.15	Hard Scrabble	1.50
Levittown, USA	3.05	Heavy Industry	2.73
Gray Power	2.94	Downtown Dixie Style	3.37
Rank and File	1.41	Hispanic Mix	1.88
Blue Collar Nursery	2.24		
Middle America	3.19		
Coalburg and Corntown	1.94		

In 1978, Robbin launched the PRIZM index, with the bold claim, "Tell me someone's ZIP code, and I can predict what they eat, drink, drive—even think."[11] Weiss observes: "Wonder Bread, that all-American white bread hawked by Howdy Doody and wrapped in balloon covered packages, is found predominantly in the pantries of small town clusters like Back-Country Folks and Middle America. They are also among the nation's biggest purchasers of packaged luncheon meats."[12]

For many demographers, a life-style clustering system is more an art than a science. Some people swear by this new system of segmentation. Others swear at it. For many, it is still a leap of faith. For others, it opens the

door into new vistas of understanding the social mecha-
nism of our western culture. The primary motivation for
life-style analysis is not sociological but economic. Clustering is a means to an end for the advertising industry to
more accurately target the segment of society that will
most likely use its product. For this reason, the primary
validators of cluster analysis have become the private
enterprise media producers who provide research and
feedback for their clients. Among the electronic media
monitors are A. C. Nielsen and Arbitron, who are leaders
in broadcast measurement. Consumer market surveyors,
such as Simmons Market Research and Mediamark Research, poll thousands of households every year to determine product usage. National Family Opinion (NFO)
Research produces mail panel surveys that test both the
marketability and the attitude of its respondents. R. L.
Polk and Company matches new car registration to ZIP
codes, providing a data base for area-specific buyer tendencies.

An example of this consumer targeting is the two
urban communities of Buckhead and Bankhead located
within two miles of each other, bordering downtown
Atlanta. Buckhead is often called "yuppie-ville" because
of the elite stores, conspicuous consumerism, and high
concentrations of BMWs and upscale leisure activities.
Bankhead, reflecting much of the antithesis of elitism, is
a crime center of Atlanta. A high percentage of residents
receive public assistance; the housing would be labeled
survival, rather than comfort; and transportation consists
of buses or aging autos. The life-styles of these two independent communities are symbolic of the forty cluster
segmentation systems that can define and predict patterns of social behavior based on the location of residential neighborhoods.

PSYCHOGRAPHICS—"PUTTING FACES ON THE PLACES"
During the 1980s, social scientists began to emphasize

the term *segmentation* as a means of analyzing the national populace. The late Arnold Mitchell of SRI International, a Palo Alto, California, research firm, developed one such segmentation system. Mitchell's system, called VALS, the acronym for Values and Life-Styles, is a composite of the needs hierarchy of psychologist Abraham Maslow[13] and the mobility paths of sociologist David Reisman.[14]

In 1989, SRI released another psychologhraphic segmentation system. The VALS 2 system reflects changes in the consumer marketplace in the last decade. The primary interest of VALS 2 is consumer behavior and motivation.

VALS 2 looks at individuals from two perspectives: the perspective of *self-orientation* and that of *resources.* *Self-orientation* describes the attitudes and activities that help people reinforce, sustain, or modify their social identities. *Orientation* determines what in particular about the self or the world governs a person's activities in life. Three types of self-orientation people have been identified: principle, status, and action.

Resources, ranging from minimal to abundant, describes the ability of persons to act out their self-orientations in the practice of life. The ability to do so increases with education, energy level, health, intelligence, and income; it declines with extreme age, depression, physical or psychological impairment, and indifference to material possessions.

The resources dimension is a continuum. At the lower end people have minimal resources. They tend to be older, poor, undereducated, unemployed, in poor health, alienated, or apathetic. At the upper end people tend to have abundant resources. They tend to be wealthy, well-educated, self-confident, sophisticated, and energetic. Individuals in the middle range of resources show one orientation more than another. Persons at the extremes do not fall squarely within any of the self-orientation categories. VALS 2

FIGURE 3. **A Network of Segments**

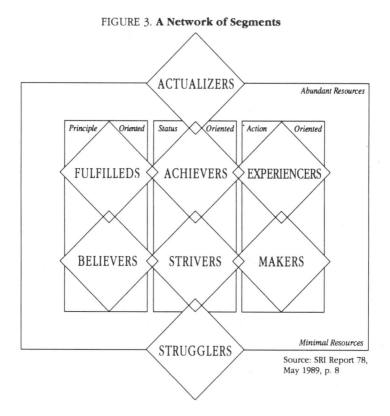

Source: SRI Report 78,
May 1989, p. 8

classifies individuals into eight interconnected segments of roughly the same size, as seen in Figure 3.

Actualizers—8 percent. The highest resource segment is the Actualizer, making up 8 percent of U.S. adult population. No single self-orientation prevails with this group. Because of abundant resources, they are sometimes guided by principle and sometimes by a desire to have an effect or make a change.

Strugglers—14 percent. Strugglers comprise 14 percent of the U.S. adult population and have the lowest level of resources of any group. They experience the world as pressing and difficult. Inadequate resources place them outside the realm of self-orientation, and they struggle to meet their immediate needs.

Principle-Oriented—27 percent. Principle-oriented people make decisions grounded in the realm of ideas, knowledge, and ideals. For some this orientation is revealed in intellectual curiosity or aesthetic interests. For others it is manifested in adherence to a code of conduct. The principle-oriented with the higher resources are called the *Fulfilled.* They make up 11 percent of the U.S. adult population. Those with fewer resources are called *Believers,* with 16 percent of the population.

Status-Oriented—26 percent. Status-oriented persons strive for a clear social position. They seek explicit responsibilities and rewards conferred by a valued social group. They make choices based on the expected reactions, concerns, and desires of these social groups. They tend to be conservative, favoring established, well-accepted products and services. The status-oriented with greater resources are *Achievers,* with 13 percent of the population. The lower resource group, called the *Strivers,* has 13 percent of the population.

Action-Oriented—25 percent. Action-oriented people base their choices on direct experience. Actions are valued for their impact on the physical world, for their pleasure or excitement, or for their effect on others. Social controls, which threaten to rule out experimentation and self-reliance, are resisted. Events are taken at face value rather than regarded as part of a larger plan or purpose. Choices are made that promise adventure, risk, and discovery. The action-oriented group consists of the *Experiencers,* 12 percent, and the *Makers,* 13 percent. *Experiencers* are usually young and single, consider themselves

FIGURE 4. **Psychological Characteristics of the VALS 2 Segments**

ACTUALIZERS
Optimistic
Self-confident
Involved
Outgoing
Growth-oriented
Active, take charge

FULFILLEDS	*ACHIEVERS*	*EXPERIENCERS*
Mature	Politically	Extroverted
Satisfied	moderate	Unconventional
Reflective	Goal-oriented	Active
Open-minded	Conventional	Enthusiastic
Self-assured	Respect authority,	Impetuous
Intrinsically	status quo	Energetic
motivated	Successful,	Savor offbeat, risky
Value order,	work-oriented,	Politically uncommitted,
knowledge,	family-oriented	uninformed
responsibility	In control	Like social activities
	Seek recognition	

BELIEVERS	*STRIVERS*	*MAKERS*
Traditional	Dissatisfied	Practical
Conforming	Unsure	Self-sufficient
Cautious	Alienated	Constructive
Moralistic	Impulsive	Committed
Settled	Approval-seeking	Satisfied
Family- and church-	Easily bored	Traditional
centered	Fascinated with	Active within narrow
	status, power	context
		Suspicious of
		new ideas

STRUGGLERS
Deprived
Feel powerless
Narrow focus on present
Averse to risk
Burdened
Conservative
Rely on organized
religion

iconoclasts, and often attack religious beliefs and institutions. *Makers,* however, are traditional, are oriented toward work and family, and value security, stability, and self-discipline.[15]

EKKLEGRAPHICS—"A PORTRAIT OF THE CHURCH"
Another factor must be considered if an existing church is
going to effectively identify with and minister to community residents based upon their needs. One of us suggests
the word *ekklegraphics* as a new term, describing a series of
general social profiles for the local church. Just as individuals have common social characteristics, so these same individuals, when assembling together as the body of Christ in
one locale, bring with them certain social patterns that
define, attract, and repel other individuals of differing life-
styles. Ekklegraphics, then, become the church's counter-
part for geographic, demographic, and psychographic
information. An ekklegraphic survey of a total church
might reveal that 85 percent of residents in the surrounding three-mile radius are age fifty or more, while the youth
program struggles, guilt-laden, to keep up with the growing adult population of the church. Another indicator in
the ekklegraphic survey that could significantly impact the
church's ministry is the knowledge that 60 percent of the
households in the church field live on multihousing properties, and only 25 percent of church families reflect that
life-style. The church should actively seek to discover, and
cannot long ignore, the overwhelming implications of this
kind of membership profile and its consequent ministry
potential.

This kind of information can only be gathered if a
church has already been planted. Its primary value is to aid
in the growth of that congregation. However, it does have
implications for church planting.

If ekklegraphic data reveal numbers of people or people
groups that are a significant socioeconomic, cultural, or
racial distance from the existing church, then the development of multiple congregations related to the existing congregation may be required. Only by starting congregations
that have social or cultural correspondence to the various
groups will the existing church be able to thoroughly evangelize those groups.

The development of demographic and psychographic data bases and the new, immediate access to this and other information through the computer provide a rich resource and ready advantage to the church planter. Its availability to the church-planting strategist, as well as the church planter, requires the acquisition of a new field of information and new skills in the application of readily available data to the task at hand.

III. UTILIZING DEMOGRAPHICS AND PSYCHOGRAPHICS IN CHURCH PLANTING

When church and denominational leaders understand this demographic and psychographic information, they can apply that material appropriately.

MORE ABOUT DEMOGRAPHIC PROFILES Demographic information is, as has been said, primarily raw census data, categorized and refined for certain purposes. One can examine census data for an area at a library reference room. The full range of information is shown for each census tract separately, as well as for total cities and counties. Maps are also available that show the tract boundaries, making the data readily discernible.

This basic census information provides the primary data base for demographic data vendors such as CACI, NDS, and others. The data vendors supplement the material, however, with current updates and future estimated projections. Great pains are taken to be sure the information is reliable and accurate. These data vendors usually have computer software systems that allow demographic profiles to be determined for census block groups, tracts, ZIP codes, cities, counties, states, or other regular geographical boundaries, as well as for radii around a certain point, or for any specified area of any shape. The profile can show how a certain area has changed demographically over the past several years, how it is predicted to change over the next few years, and its present description. It also can show how it compares demographically to other areas of a city, county, state, nation, or other comparative base. Search capabilities may also be built into the software that will show all the areas with certain similar characteristics.

Several denominational groups have purchased this service and have it available for the churches of their constituency.[16] Individuals, local churches, or judicatory bodies can purchase the service from the various suppliers. The ACORN profile report from Dallas, Texas (see Figure 5) illustrates the kind of information available for any area, large or small.

MORE ABOUT PSYCHOGRAPHIC PROFILES Psychographic profiles, as has been indicated, go beyond even the most sophisticated demographics. Psychographics offer a more personal view of the people inside the houses identified by demographic profiles. What are their motivations? What do they seek? What values are important to them? What are their felt needs? With an understanding of a psychographic profile of a community, one can almost feel one knows the people personally, without ever having met them. Such knowledge enables the church planter to develop programs and ministries for a new church more effectively.

There are several ways of segmenting people psychographically. For purposes of this chapter, however, the SRI International system, VALS 2, is the subject of study. One attractive feature of VALS 2 is that (like VALS) it can be linked geodemographically to CACI, NDS, Claritas, and other demographic data systems. Thus, a VALS 2 profile can be obtained for any geographical area for which a demographic profile can be obtained.

Inter-connected life-style segments. The eight life-styles are shown on the following sample VALS 2 profile of Dallas,

FIGURE 5. ACORN Area Profile Report for Dallas, Texas

ACORN Type	1989	Percent	U.S. %	Index
Wealthy Metropolitan Communities				
A1 Old Money	34,792	1.4%	0.5	274
A2 Conspicuous Consumers	42,323	1.7%	1.0	157
A3 Cosmopolitan Wealth	49,596	2.0%	2.4	21
Trend-Setting Suburban Neighborhoods				
B4 Upper Middle Income Families	187,140	7.4%	2.8	263
B5 Empty Nesters	44,828	1.8%	2.5	73
B6 Baby Boomers with Families	324,430	12.8%	3.6	355
B7 Middle Americans in New Homes	151,216	6.0%	5.3	112
B8 Skilled Craft and Office Workers	100,129	3.9%	4.4	90
Apartment House and College Areas				
C9 Condominium Dwellers	29,923	1.2%	2.0	59
C10 Fast-Track Young Adults	297,239	11.7%	8.0	195
C11 College Undergraduates	9,509	0.4%	0.3	125
C12 Older Students and Professionals	77,474	3.1%	1.8	170
Big-City Urban Neighborhoods				
D13 Urbanites in High Rises	3,407	0.1%	1.2	11
D14 Big-City Working Class	1,302	0.1%	1.7	3
Hispanic and Multiracial Neighborhoods				
E15 Mainstream Hispanic Americans	94,958	3.7%	2.3	163
E16 Large Hispanic Families	47,049	1.9%	1.5	124
E17 Working-Class Single Adults	8,300	0.3%	1.5	22
E18 Families in Prewar Rentals	40,740	1.0%	1.1	148
E19 Third-World Melting Pot	83	0.0%	1.0	0
Black Neighborhoods				
F20 Mainstream Family Homeowners	185,846	7.3%	3.1	336
F21 Trend-Conscious Families	32,253	1.3%	1.9	67
F22 Low-Income Families	47,836	1.9%	0.9	210

Young Middle Class Families

G23 Settled Families	74,420	2.9%	3.4	80
G24 Start-Up Families	281,723	11.1%	5.0	222

Blue-Collar Families in Small Towns

H25 Family Sports and Leisure Lovers	26,459	1.0%	2.1	50
H26 Secure Factory and Farm Workers	5,998	0.2%	2.0	12
H27 Family-Centered Blue-Collar	8,783	0.3%	3.2	13
H28 Minimum-Wage White Families	58,591	2.3%	4.0	58

Mature Adults in Stable Neighborhoods

I29 Golden Years Retirees	26,751	1.1%	2.5	42
I30 Adults in Prewar Housing	20,568	0.8%	5.1	16
I31 Small-Town Families	43,873	1.7%	6.2	25
I32 Nostalgic Retirees and Adults	0	0.0%	1.0	0
I33 Home-Oriented Senior Citizens	13,109	0.5%	2.0	26
I34 Old Families in Prewar Homes	2,951	0.1%	4.3	3

Season and Mobile Home Communities

J35 Resort Vacationers and Locals	0	0.0%	0.8	0
J36 Mobile Home Dwellers	18,504	0.7%	1.3	56

Agriculturally-Oriented Communities

K37 Farm Families	158	0.0%	0.6	1
K38 Young, Active Country Families	141	0.0%	0.3	2

Older Depressed Rural Towns

L39 Low-Income Retirees and Youth	125,435	4.9%	3.3	160
L40 Rural Displaced Workers	88	0.0%	0.3	3
L41 Factory Worker Families	2,793	0.1%	2.7	4
L42 Poor Young Families	8,770	0.3%	0.4	88

Special Populations

M43 Military Base Families	0	0.0%	0.5	0
M44 Institutions: Residents and Staff	7,186	0.3%	0.1	283
TOTAL	2,530,720			

FIGURE 6. VALS 2 Profile of Dallas, Texas[17]

	Percent	Number	U.S. Percent	Market Index
ACTUALIZERS	10.17	258,094	8.7	117
FULFILLED	12.10	306,970	11.3	107
ACHIEVERS	16.19	410,614	13.1	124
EXPERIENCERS	12.47	316,246	12.2	102
BELIEVERS	14.67	372,117	16.2	90
STRIVERS	12.56	318,712	12.7	99
MAKERS	10.94	277,600	12.1	90
STRUGGLERS	10.90	276,463	13.7	79
TOTAL	100.00	2,536,815	100.0	

Abundant Resources	ACTUALIZERS 10.17 117

Principle Oriented	Status Oriented	Action Oriented
FULFILLED 12.10 107	ACHIEVERS 16.19 124	EXPERIENCERS 12.47 102
BELIEVERS 14.67 90	STRIVERS 12.56 99	MAKERS 10.94 90

Minimal Resources	STRUGGLERS 10.9 79

Texas (see Figure 6).[18] When one becomes familiar with the characteristics of each of these VALS 2 types, they become somewhat recognizable in the course of normal daily contacts with people.

VALS 2 helps one understand a group's social self-image and its felt needs. In the starting and growth of new churches, this technology is especially useful in helping the church planter and the church-planting team know how they can bring Jesus Christ to bear on the felt needs in the target community.

CHURCH APPLICATION OF DEMOGRAPHIC INFORMATION Application of demographic information will vary according to whether it is being used by one church; by an association, conference, or presbytery; or by a larger judicatory body or convention on the state, regional, or national level. The demographic profile helps one to visualize a community without actually seeing it, simply by statistically examining the ages and values of the houses, the household income levels, the ages and occupations of the people, the ages of their children, and similar information.

Special needs in the area may also be discovered. For instance, if a large number of the population is of a certain ethnic group, consideration might be given to starting a church for that group. If college students are numerous, ministries could be planned accordingly. If income is low for an area, social ministries could be developed. Perhaps a church is planning to begin a ministry for senior adults. It should examine the church field demographically to be sure there is a real need for that ministry. One church felt it should have a stronger youth ministry because few teenagers were attending. In examining their church field, however, church leaders discovered few teenagers lived there. Most of the people were forty-five years old and older. They saw the need for a senior-adult ministry instead. They began that ministry and experienced growth. In areas with predominantly young families with young children, churches should plan ministries to relate to those needs. One church offered "potty-training" classes because there were so many parents with young children in the area, and that ministry became an effective outreach tool. Many needs for special ministries can be discovered through a demographic report.

Socioeconomic changes in an area may signal the need for new churches. For example, a town in Iowa showed a significant change in the number of households in the highest income levels. In 1980, only 4.8 percent of the population were shown in the highest income categories. The 1988 data showed 20.7 percent in those levels with a projection that, by 1993, 31.7 percent of households would be at that level. A Missions Development Council saw the population change and guessed that new people were moving into town and new homes were being built. Going to the town to explore the need for a new church to reach these people, they stopped at a realtor's office and asked the locations where new subdivisions were being developed. Without hesitation, the realtor responded with specific directions to the new areas.

The council had discovered a possible need for a new church simply by looking at a demographic profile. Since they knew that new churches grow best in growing areas, the prospects looked promising. Even though the total population showed growth of less than 10 percent between 1980 and 1993, the potential for a new church was good because some areas of town were growing rapidly. The council also recognized that a storefront church probably would not be the best approach since the group with highest potential for church growth was the higher income group.

If the same council, however, had been planning a social ministry to the poor, they might have wanted to reconsider. Although in 1980, 12.3 percent of the households were in the lowest income level, by 1988 and 1993 only 5.7 percent and 3.8 percent respectively were in that level. Another factor that was apparent to the council from the demographic report was that the community's economy was improving. As the council expected, new businesses and shopping areas were being built. Projected socioeconomic growth and decline are important considerations for long-range ministry planning and church planting.

Concentrations of a certain type of population are as important as total numbers of population. In one town, the Hispanic population is 3,076, or 7.1 percent of the town's total population. It is projected to reach 8.3 percent in the next three years. A much larger town nearby has about the same total number of Hispanics, but they account for only about one percent of the population. The best place to start an Hispanic congregation is in the smaller town where a higher percentage is Hispanic.

When a local church, parachurch agency, or denominational agency is targeting a region for pioneer church planting, the best strategy may be to start churches that can become financially self-supporting quickly and that can then contribute money for the areas still needing churches. This would, according to this strategic approach, be a better investment of missions dollars than spending the same money to support a church planter in an area that is not likely to have adequate financial resources to help fund the overall strategy of church planting. Just as the Apostle Paul used the strategy of taking the gospel first to the trade centers, we should also consider following a strategy of church planting in several phases, focusing first on the areas that can likely fund the later phases of work in lower income areas. Demographic profiles can identify these various areas.

However, a strategic decision by leaders of the mission agency (local church, parachurch, or denominational) may choose to focus on responsive peoples. Their research may show that new churches targeted for middle- and upper-income communities are not flourishing. They may discover that the most unchurched areas are among the black and ethnic communities of a region, for instance. They may choose to use bivocational church planters so that the new congregations can move quickly toward self-support. Demographic profiles can identify these communities as well.

CHURCH APPLICATION OF PSYCHOGRAPHIC INFORMATION Church application of psychographic information is not yet as widespread as demographic application, but it offers exciting new possibilities in ministry awareness. Some psychographic application is done naturally, drawing on experience. However, understanding people is the goal of psychographic information. When people are understood, their needs can be met. Various ministries and programs can be designed to respond to the driving motivations and felt needs of a specific group of people. The VALS 2 topology provides a structured framework for understanding people's basic motivations. By considering the variable factors in communities, church planters can design ministries to relate to the lifestyles and deeply held values of the people to whom ministry is targeted.

Ministry design. Certain questions can be asked by the denominational strategist or the church planter to determine the kind of church that should be started in a particular group. Once the makeup of a particular community is identified, psychographic data can provide some answers. For example, what style of church should be planted among a particular VALS 2 segment? What vision for the new congregation will best motivate a particular VALS 2 segment of the population? *Actualizers* may be challenged with a dream to establish a citywide, high-quality worship ministry. *Fulfilleds* and *Actualizers* might work to meet social needs. *Believers* and *Makers* want a friendly church where they and others feel at home and close lasting friendships can develop.

What size congregation will they prefer? *Believers, Makers,* and *Strugglers* are probably content in small congregations. Many small rural churches are made up mostly of people from these three segments. *Believers* are also quite comfortable in larger churches where they carry out many routine responsibilities necessary to make a larger church operate smoothly. *Actualizers* and *Achievers* likely prefer these larger churches with more activities and organizations than smaller churches offer. *Actualizers* usually are the main decision makers in these larger churches.

What methodological style will the target group prefer? Tradition is important to *Strugglers, Believers,* and *Makers.* *Believers* hardly trust anything that is not traditional. *Achievers* appreciate the value of tradition, but they also are concerned about results (What is effective?) and quality (Was it done with excellence?). These traits are seen in the types of music they appreciate; the style, efficiency, and effectiveness of the worship service; the quality of leadership they expect; and the growth and progress they desire for the church.

Actualizers value quality and contemporary atmosphere more than tradition. They may feel the traditional ways of doing things are ineffective and should be improved. Aesthetic qualities are even more important to *Actualizers* and *Fulfilleds* than to *Achievers,* but both groups might give up their desire for beauty in worship if they are working to fulfill a mission they feel is important. *Actualizers* seek personal spiritual growth and inner experience with God more than other groups.

Governance and decision making. How will decisions be made and the new congregation be governed? This is an important question because church conflict often centers around decisions. *Believers* probably require the longest time to make major decisions. They like to talk about things privately and informally before committing themselves to definite decisions. *Achievers* decide much more quickly. They are usually accustomed to making major decisions, and they make good ones. They are able to sort out the issues quickly, evaluate, and make the best choice, often in minutes, if they are provided with thorough and accurate information.

Actualizers and *Fulfilleds* have a more holistic approach to decision making. They follow their own values and show others respect for their personal values also. Though they could personally decide rather quickly, for the sake of the group they prefer making decisions by consensus. If not everyone is satisfied with a decision, they wait until a choice can be found that is acceptable to everyone. It takes longer, however, and can be frustrating to others who prefer to decide more quickly.

Other questions could be asked for each psychographic life-style group. What style of worship is preferred? What kinds of sermons best meet their needs? How does the pastor develop trust and gain leadership acceptance with these people? What kind of image should the pastor present to be effective in this community? What types of advertisements, brochures, and media information speak to these people?

What church property characteristics are important to them? What financial considerations are important to recognize about this group? Church-planting models and church ministry designs could be developed that would demonstrate sensitivity to the life-styles of those the new congregation is intended to reach. Pastors and church planters should consider these variables as they minister among various types of people. Denominational offices could give new pastors a psychographic profile of their target areas, along with an interpretation of the meaning of the data. Psychographic interpretation and application can improve the time of orientation for a new assignment. Seminaries may consider offering courses in this area to help student church leaders serve people more effectively. Since a church planter must learn so many things on a new field, some insight into the psychographic dimensions of the area would be beneficial. Perhaps the greatest benefit would be that of learning that people really are different from one another and different values are important to them. Church leaders must consider these differences if they would meet the felt needs of a group of people and reach them with the message of Christ.

The New Testament world of the missionary church planter Paul was characterized by social diversity and change. He sought to plant churches that were indigenous to the culture and social context of the people. He used every means available that he might effectively communicate the gospel of Jesus Christ, basing his strategy on the felt needs of the people rather than his own.

Never have we had the variety of tools, including demographic and psychographic segmentation, by which to better understand a community and the needs of its population.

Harnessing this technology for the kingdom will result in the planting of information-based, life-style-conscious, people-sensitive new churches that can communicate the gospel to this generation.

7

Creating a Climate for Planting New Churches

Being a real
New Testament church
means believing and doing
what the New Testament
church did.
It means planting
new churches as the
New Testament church did . . .
Church multiplication
was an essential part of
New Testament life.

Donald A. McGavran, 1977

In 1776, there were less than 3,000 churches
in America. There are more than 350,000 in 1990.
"Enough is enough!" many people are saying. Some Christian leaders have been saying that all of this century. The
division of the Christian population into many local congregations, large and small, is part of the scandal of modern Christianity, they maintain. "If anything is true," these
people say, "we have too many churches."

In the last chapter I discussed several factors that have
contributed to the prevailing mental climate that the time
for planting new churches in America has passed. Let me
summarize them.

1. Superior roadways and rapid transportation—both
private and public—have made established meeting houses
accessible to people from distant communities.

2. Our struggle to overcome social, cultural, and racial
segregation within churches has idealized conglomerate
churches and mitigated against starting churches in the various segments of society.

3. The prevalent infatuation with "giant" churches—from whatever motivation—has caused many church leaders to resist the planting of new churches as a threat to empire.

4. Ecclesiastical détente among American Christians in this century has produced something of a "religious settlement" among the various denominations. It has become unthinkable for Southern Baptists, for example, to consider gathering churches where there are no people with a Southern Baptist heritage. Everyone, this mentality suggests, has some preference. To attempt to win a person to active allegiance to Christ and add him to a congregation different from his preference or different from the one nearest his home is unabashedly called "proselyting" and "sheep stealing."

Given this milieu, is it possible to create a climate for church planting within a congregation? Can a church be prepared for motherhood? How is the apostolate of the New Testament church to be actualized, personalized, and localized in this era of the turning of the twenty-first century?

I'm not sure that I can answer these questions with any degree of finality. Anything I will say must be considered tentative and temporal. It must be considered tentative because the church leadership may attempt all the things I suggest and still find the church unwilling to commit itself to new work. We cannot examine many intangibles for lack of time, and others I cannot analyze for lack of skill. What I say must be considered temporal because churches are subject to change, even though some people despair that certain churches will ever change. What might work now may be ineffectual in five years. I do hope, however, to discuss some principles that are supratemporal.

THE SPIRITUAL PREPARATION OF THE CHURCH

How do you lay a spiritual foundation for starting new churches in a modern American congregation? What steps can be taken to develop a passion for church planting? I will suggest five:

1. *Set church planting in biblical perspective.* The mission of the church succinctly stated is, I insist, to proclaim the Good News of Jesus Christ in the power of the Holy Spirit among all the social groupings of mankind, and to gather those who respond into churches. Planting churches is at the heart of the apostolate of the church of the New Testament. Planting churches is the essence of the apostolic gift. Evangelicals in America, and in all places during periods of significant growth, have majored on this task. Evangelism (winning to commitment to Christ) is not complete until churches are gathered. In recent years the social establishment of evangelicals has been recognized, and we have made rapid strides toward affluence and rock-ribbed respectability. In this situation, we have lost sight of this central biblical perspective. In preaching and teaching, the importance and centrality of church planting needs to be embedded in the congregation.

2. *Magnify the ministry of the laity.* The task of church planting can never be achieved by, nor should it be conceived as, the labor of clergy. Adequate spiritual preparation should include a clear concept of the significance of the ministry of all the people of God. Men and women in churches are called to meaningful spiritual ministry, not just to menial "secular" tasks. Biblically and historically it has been the laity, mobilized and motivated to spiritual ministry, which has produced the spontaneous expansion of the church.

3. *Maximize the central place of the Holy Spirit* in the mission of the church, and emphasize the necessity and possibility for every believer to be filled and led by the Spirit of God. The Spirit of God is the Spirit of missions. It is he who is the executor of God's mission to the world in Christ. The purpose of God in redemption, the plan of God for the ages, is to be actualized by the ministry of the Spirit working in and through the Church.

Agreement on the central place of the Spirit is easily

secured. Personal, experiential acquaintance with the Holy Spirit's work in the individual Christian's life has been more difficult to find among many evangelicals since the rise of Pentecostalism during the first decade of this century. Nevertheless, adequate spiritual preparation for church planting in a local congregation demands that we teach and preach:

  a. the necessity for all believers to be filled with and to work in the Spirit.
  b. the need for all Christians to be led by the Spirit in their daily lives and to surrender themselves to God as instruments of righteousness, and then to become productive members of the body of Christ.
  c. the responsibility of each believer to attempt to discover the particular gift given him or her by the Spirit, and to exercise this gift so that the church can be built up and continue to grow.
  d. that the Holy Spirit empowers the most backward Christian for effective ministry and witness.[1]

4. *Provide opportunity for periodic renewal.* The need to re-create must be met if a church is to maintain the spiritual dynamic essential to church planting. The body of Christ must be built up as well as added to. Edification and evangelism are the twin tasks that constantly face the Church. Retreats and small groups meeting for Bible study and prayer are two excellent ways to pursue this step; there are many others.

5. *Major on direct evangelism.* Churches grow in only three ways: by baptism of the children of members; by addition of those who transfer from other churches; and by conversions from the world. The first two will never win the world to Christ, but a church that regularly wins men and women to Christ from the world can plant another church that will do the same. Effective and habitual efforts in direct evangelism will also contribute to the spiritual foundation essential to getting a church ready for church planting.

THE MENTAL PREPARATION OF THE CHURCH

How do you develop a mentality for beginning new churches in a contemporary American congregation? What steps can be taken to create a mental climate for church planting? Several matters deserve attention:

1. *Actualize mission philosophy.* It is amazing how many "missionary" churches are not missionary. They may have a stated policy of missionary concern and have a limited commitment to the financial support of overseas missions, but they never have considered putting their missionary philosophy into action through direct support and personal involvement. The missionary nature of the congregation is only a rumor. One way a local church can be prepared for church planting is to specify the mission philosophy of the church—first in words and then in concrete challenges. The church should focus on real opportunities for its membership to practice what is preached in missionary terms.

2. *Be realistic about social, cultural, and geographical boundaries.* A church—no matter how large—cannot adequately minister to a community more than a hundred miles away and across a megacity, no matter how strong the bus ministry or how dedicated the workers. Nor can a church thoroughly evangelize a large city or county with a television ministry, no matter how professionally and winsomely presented. As obvious as that may be, there are hundreds of evangelical churches that are presently attempting these strategies, and many others aspire to do so.

Cultural and social boundaries are just as real as geographical boundaries. There are conglomerate churches—composed of groupings from various socioeconomic, racial, and cultural strata—but these are few, and the men who can hold them together and lead them to grow are rare. Most of us do our most effective ministry within certain related pieces of the mosaic of human society. We do not communicate effectively across cultural lines.

This is not a defense of racial segregation, cultural

exclusivism, or social snobbery within churches. If a church does not address the gospel to everyone in its community (not just welcome them if they come, but actively evangelize them), it is in danger of vitiating its New Testament character. Refusal to offer Christ aggressively to everyone in a church's community is a mutation of New Testament Christianity just as surely as doctrinal heresy. It is an attempt, however, to underline the facts that people do not like to cross cultural and social barriers to become Christians, that we most readily and effectively witness to our peers, and that churches grow most naturally along these larger family lines. This principle needs to be recognized as reality so that the sponsoring church can see the need for planting churches within every segment of human society. It is patently un-Christian to insist, de facto, that the only way a garbage man can become a Christian and an active church member is in the church where the president of the bank is a principal leader.

3. *Combat local-church myopia.* There is an innate short-sightedness in mankind, a tendency to look at the local, at what is ours, and to focus full energies in that direction. One's own community, no matter how needy, is not the whole world. Believers develop something akin to militant nationalism in reference to their own church. It is extremely rational to many people to say, "Why should we preach the gospel in other places when we have not won our own community as yet?" Such a philosophy would have confined Christianity to Judea and Galilee as an insignificant sect of Judaism.

4. *Be honest about small-church efficiency.* We are living in a big-church era. Church and church staff size have become status symbols. Recent statistics among Southern Baptist Convention churches bear that out. The facts are illustrative, I believe, of every other evangelical or mainline denomination. Huge churches have not historically characterized Southern Baptists. There were only seventeen SBC

churches with more than 2,000 members in 1924. By 1940, however, there were more than 100. In 1979, 563 SBC churches had more than 2,000 members; 187 of these counted more than 3,000 members. By 1990, 772 churches had more than 2,000 members; 297 of them had exceeded 3,000 in membership.

Small churches are much more efficient in terms of evangelism than large churches in the Southern Baptist Convention. In 1988, for instance, SBC churches between 2,000 and 2,999 in membership averaged 52 baptisms. That same year the churches with memberships of 200–299 averaged 7 baptisms. Ten of the small churches (200–299) would have baptized 18 more people than one large church (2,000–2,999). Georgia, where I now live, is the home of many very effective large churches. The number of large churches will significantly increase during the next twenty-five years. However, it is also a state with many small Southern Baptist churches. In 1990, very small churches (1–49 members) baptized 5.5 persons for each 100 resident members. Let's say that is about 2.7 persons per church. Larger churches (1,000–1,499 in membership) baptized 3 persons for each 100 resident members. That is about 45 persons for each church. Thirty churches with 49 members each would have won to Christ almost 80 percent more people than one church with 1,499 members (81 persons baptized as to 45 persons baptized).[2]

This requires mental toughness in a day of big-church romance. Information like this needs to be shared over and over again with the budding mother church.

5. *Develop a congregational strategy for church planting.* Long-range planning has come of age among most Protestants. While churches are setting goals, determining actions, and assigning responsibility for such growth as in membership, building development, and Sunday school attendance, each church should also develop a long-range strategy for church planting over the years.

Evangelical leaders are doing tough thinking about church growth, and a precise language has been developed

about the subject. Many powerful books have been written
from almost every denominational perspective. Begin passing this information on to the membership of your congregation. Four kinds of church growth have been identified.[3] I
believe that most churches can be involved in all four types
simultaneously.

Internal growth is growth in grace. Goals should be set
and a strategy should be developed to help the church
members grow toward Christlikeness and to help them
learn how to be led by the Holy Spirit. To focus only on
this kind of growth is a tragic mistake that leads to "holy
snobbery" and a spiritual ghetto mentality. To do this is a
very strong temptation, especially to those of us who have
been shaped by the nineteenth-century Holiness movement. A church can strangle on a total inward focus.

Expansion growth is the numerical increase of the church
within its own community. This is desirable and essential.
Most planning will focus on this kind of growth. It is, however, an overweening concern for this kind of growth as
the only way a church can grow numerically that hinders
church planting among evangelicals today.

Extension growth is that which takes place when a church
plants a daughter church among people of the same general
homogeneous group as the mother church. This, too, is
church growth and is, in fact, the quickest way to turn the
growth graph of a local church upward. Extension growth
multiplies the church's ministry in a dramatic way. It is the
church growing in another locale. It must not be seen as competition. A strategy for extension growth should be developed.

Bridging growth is that which takes place when a church
plants a daughter congregation in a radically different cultural, linguistic, or racial community. It might be in
another geographical area, or in the same community
where the mother church is scattered. It might meet in the
same building. Steps should be taken to identify and to
plant new churches in these cultural and racial pockets.

6. *Cultivate the spirit of winning.* A positive mental

attitude is essential to constant achievement. The church is called to victory, to growth, and to the multiplication of units. A church whose members believe that, under God, they can, can! One of the most essential factors to proper mental preparation for church planting is a spirit of faith, victory, and confidence permeating the congregation and its leaders. A church that expects great things from God can attempt great things for God.

PREPARING THE CHURCH ORGANIZATIONALLY

How do you devise an organizational foundation for church planting? Can steps be taken to develop a congregational structure for starting new churches? How can this structure contribute to a church extension climate in the congregation? I will suggest five guidelines.

1. *Make specific assignments for leadership* in church planting to responsible members of the congregation. Select a missions committee, a missionary board, a church-extension task force, or a missions development council within the congregation. Whatever form you choose, place the responsibility for this significant function of the church on the shoulders of lay leaders. It is tragic, but true, that in the minds of most evangelicals in America, Matthew 28:19-20 has been the exclusive domain of the overseas mission. At least this has been characteristic since 1886. This idea has given a distorted view of the mission of the church to the average church member. By making missions the sole responsibility of those especially called and trained for cross-cultural evangelism and of national and regional boards and societies, usually in distant cities, churches as a whole have been robbed of the glory of direct involvement in the most primary of all mission tasks—that of gathering new disciples of Christ into new, growing congregations.

Some churches, especially committed to the multiplication of congregations and other ministries, are now employing a fully salaried staff person to give leadership to this function of the church. These persons enlist and equip lay leaders and give strategic direction to the task. The focus continues to be on lay persons.

Assigning specific responsibilities to lay leaders will also counteract a most unscriptural notion that the responsibility for starting new churches in the American context belongs to state, regional, and national boards or societies and is divorced from the essential duties of churches or individuals.

2. *Give the church-planting task force (CPT) status in the congregation.* It should rank along with the board of Christian education, the budget and finance committee, the youth council, and other such groups as a primary organization in the administration of the total ministry of the church.

3. *Choose members for the CPT who will provide creative, forceful leadership.* Too often, all other leadership positions in the church organizations are filled first. Then, those positions structured with responsibility beyond the immediate community of the church are manned by the unwilling or inept. Persons chosen for the CPT should have a missionary and evangelical passion and a personal faith that is contagious. They should be able and willing to devote time to gathering and analyzing data about community needs. They should command the attention and respect of the congregation when they speak.

4. *Train the CPT for its job.* Begin with bare essentials. Do not share all the minute details at a one-and-only training session. Let the CPT begin to function, and then provide continual training opportunities that are dictated by functional needs. This approach vastly increases the relevancy of training information and provides high motivation for training opportunities.

5. *Turn the CPT loose to function.* There are at least five primary functions for a CPT:

a. A prophetic function. Churches have, since the Jerusalem church of Acts, tended to become ingrown, exclusive, self-centered, and institutionalized. The CPT, by reminding the church of the biblical mandate and by sharing the needs of communities, calls it back to its spiritual purpose.

b. A planning function. The CPT must develop church-extension eyes just as a student pilot must develop navigational eyes. It must be able to recognize evidence of unreached pockets of people. This function is not primarily intuitive. It requires study of census data and housing and economic patterns. Recognition is only the beginning. The CPT must develop strategies to penetrate unreached populations and gather new congregations. The strategies must be communicated to the congregation.

c. A promotion function. The findings and recommendations of the CPT should be publicized, reported, discussed, and gossiped throughout the entire membership. Do not restrict the reports to the meetings of the congregation. Both need and potential should be emphasized. The CPT should make a church-planting project as exciting and pervasive as an every-member financial canvass, an evangelistic campaign, or a building program.

d. An enlistment function. Churches have within their membership individuals and families who have particular gifts for church planting. The CPT should in every possible way attempt to discover people with those gifts and interests. They should share the church-planting needs and their plans with the congregation in such a way as to evoke such gifts that might be latent in individuals.

e. An implementation function. The CPT must have authority, resources, and initiative to see that plans are carried out, evaluated, and reshaped until they prove to be effective.[4]

By these or other similar steps, an organizational structure can be formalized within a congregation with responsibility for planting new churches. This structure can and should become a potent force in creating a climate for church extension.

PREPARING THE CHURCH PRAGMATICALLY

How do you secure concrete involvement from a potential sponsoring congregation in the task of beginning new churches? What steps can be taken to call for commitment to church planting? Commitment should be secured in at least four areas:

1. Commitment in terms of prayer. Undergird the project with prayer. Prayer must not be viewed as exotic and mystical, but essential and pragmatic. It is the place to begin, continue, and end any ministry of witness or service in the name of Jesus. Specific plans should be made, and individuals and organizations in the church should be enlisted for concerted, sustained, and explicit prayer support for the undertaking.

Practically speaking, the first concrete commitment of the church should be in a program of persistent and fervent prayer.

2. Commitment in terms of training. Equip the congregation with the skills necessary for gathering new churches. Most church training programs—except for some devised in very recent years—have been basically maintenance-oriented. We have produced a host of workers who know how to conduct a business meeting and what is the latest in educational psychology. But we have produced very few who make personal witnessing a way of life, who are always touching others with Christ. In the meantime our training programs have died. A host of lay training organizations that equip laymen for spiritual ministry has arisen outside the churches.

Do an evaluation of all the unsalaried leaders in your

church. How many exert their principal energy in ministry to those in the church? How many are actually trained and assigned toward ministry in the world? This assessment will reveal the area where there is greatest need.

Provide training for various outreach strategies. Most outreach training has been in only two areas: personal evangelism and bus ministry. We must provide training for other options: Bible study fellowships, evangelistic speaking, coffee fellowships, Bible clubs, and various other community ministries.

Let me emphasize one thing: This practical training must be tied directly to spiritual preparation. It is impossible to share life-at-its-best if you are not experiencing life-at-its-best. The two must go hand in hand. Pragmatically, new churches demand relevant training opportunities.

3. Commitment in terms of money. Underwrite the project with necessary funding. I am not speaking here of total support. I know of churches that have refused to sponsor a new work because they could not buy a site, erect a first unit, and put a full-time seminary graduate on the field. That is not what I am calling for. I know of other churches who will sponsor a new work only if it requires no support in terms of money or people. To both extremes I call for the commitment of necessary funding.

In funding, priorities need to be established. People are much more important than places. Many new churches have been aborted because no worthy meeting place could be found for rent or because no place could be found to build a building. The best money will be spent on personnel. Halls should be rented only when homes are unavailable or too small. Buildings should be erected only as a last resort.

Pragmatically, new churches demand financial commitment just as other programs demand monetary resources.

4. Commitment in terms of people. Ask the church to commit people—individuals and families—to church planting just as it commits people to Bible study organizations, to

organizations for missionary education and music, or to social activism.

Many denominations have begun new churches with sponsorship in name only, and I'm sure many more will start this way, even though it is less than desirable. Under such "sponsorship" no people and no dollars are committed. It is much better when a church invests part of its life in a new work by providing at least part of the nucleus in the new community.

"But that will weaken the sponsoring church!" is the first reaction. "All this does is divide a fairly strong church and produce two weak ones!" is another.

The worst way to begin a new work is with a church division. If sponsoring churches could be led to see that a new church multiplies their ministry, perhaps this could be overcome. I often say to a pastor, "What would you do if two families in your church were transferred to other cities by their employers?" "We would go on and seek other members." That is just the way the church should look at the investment of people in new churches. Expect and look for others whom God will send to fill their places.

The New Testament pattern in evangelism was not to make many new disciples and leave them unrelated to other Christians. That is why the local church is of crucial importance. Nor is the biblical pattern to enlarge existing churches until their membership numbers in the thousands. The biblical pattern is to move converts into new churches, let them meet in homes, and then multiply the number of such churches. In an analogy of biological cells and churches, Howard Snyder said, "Normal growth comes by the division of cells, not by the unlimited expansion of existing cells. The growth of individual cells beyond a certain point is pathological."[5]

The only way to increase the ratio of Christians to population in any nation is to multiply the number of churches. If evangelicals are to make significant progress in bringing America to Christ, the number of churches must be multiplied.

These remarks are from many years of experience as a pastor in northern Illinois, where very often the churches nearest the areas of need were least able, in terms of money and personnel, to sponsor new churches adequately. This same thing may not be true in many areas of the nation or for other evangelical groups. But there is still much reluctance to plant people in new units.

Finally, there can be commitment of personnel on other than a permanent or semipermanent basis. Groups of men, women, and young people can be enlisted for community events and ministries, for surveys, special projects, and evangelistic campaigns. Involvement of the whole church in the project over several years is very desirable.

Pragmatically, new churches demand the involvement of people in service and witness.

I have not even touched upon one very fundamental problem involved in creating a climate for planting new congregations. I have assumed that the pastor is sympathetic with growth by the multiplication of churches. This is very often not the case. In fact, he is often the point of primary resistance. How to deal with the problem is a crucial matter. Nevertheless, if a pastor is committed to multiplying churches in every segment of society, an environment for church planting can usually be brought into existence in a local church.

8

Getting Off to a Big Start

by David Putman
Regional Church Starter Strategist
Georgia Baptist Convention

There is only one way
the Great Commission
can be fulfilled,
and that is by establishing
gospel-preaching
congregations
in every community
on the face of the earth.

David Womack, 1973

One of the great advances in church planting
over the last decade has been achieved by the informed use
of direct marketing tools and communication technolo-
gies. The proper use of these tools has enabled some new
churches, it seems to some, to step full grown into their
ministry. For generations new churches have struggled to
break the plateau that comes when attendance reaches 35,
then 75, then 125.

These plateaus are related to structure and organization.
Each plateau shapes a certain vision of the future in the
minds of members of the congregation. Structures can
stunt and discourage the new church, causing it to despair
of greater effectiveness in penetrating its community.

"Starting big" enables the new congregation to bound
over those plateaus in one big leap.

David Putman has himself planted several churches that
have broken the 125 barrier within eighteen months.
There is no instant church. But he provides clear, practical
instruction about how to build a network of methodologies beyond the use of direct marketing by phone. This

kind of network is especially important if you are attempting to "start big" in an area that does not lend itself to thirty thousand calls.

A few years ago, I arrived in a major metropolitan area with the assignment to start new churches. I immediately began by approaching other church starters with the question, "How?" One church starter encouraged me to "take time to get to know God." Another gave me a lot of demographical information and resources. Finally, a church starter suggested that I take time to meet all of the pastors in the area.

All of these people gave me excellent advice. Churches cannot be started effectively without a personal relationship with Jesus Christ, a good demographic perspective of the area, and a proper relationship with existing churches. However, I still had the same question, "How do you start a church?"

In reality, as I thought about it, the question became, "How do you start a church that will guarantee its best possible future?" One answer to the second question, I have come to believe, is to get off to a big start. The purpose of this chapter is to discuss the "how to's" of a big start.

ADVANTAGES OF A BIG START

God is doing something significant in church starting today. Until recently, a new church with two hundred to three hundred in attendance on the first Sunday was unheard of. Today, new churches with two hundred or more in attendance from the beginning are springing up in every city and in every denomination. Modern urban society lends itself to starting larger churches. Mission leaders should look long and hard at this phenomenon as they develop church-starting strategies for the 1990s and beyond. Several factors prompt us to take this possibility to heart. Getting off to a big start can help us in our task.

GREATER SURVIVAL RATE Little hard data exists concerning how many new churches fail to survive their first few years of existence. However, there are clear indications that in my own denomination, the Southern Baptist Convention (SBC), many churches fail to survive their first few years. From 1972 to 1987, the SBC organized 5,095 churches. Of these churches, 750 (14.7 percent) were dropped from SBC rolls during this same time frame.[1] This does not take into account new congregations that were not yet independently constituted and added to the SBC affiliated churches. From this data, it is clear that there are a significant number of new churches that do not survive. A number of reasons could explain this fact.

In a similar study of 1,181 Southern Baptist churches organized between 1972 and 1982, data clearly indicates that the larger the number of charter members, the less likely the new church will fail. Table 1 indicates that 93 of 1,181 churches included in the report began with 150 or more members. Not one of these 93 churches failed within five years. On the other hand, of the 196 that began with fewer than 25 members, 25 percent were unreported in five years. Churches that begin big have a greater survival rate.

GREATER GROWTH POTENTIAL In the same study of 1,181 churches organized between 1972 and 1982, a clear relationship exists between initial size and growth cycles. Table 1 demonstrates that among those churches beginning with fewer than 25 members, only 26 percent were in a growth cycle. Of the churches that began with 150 or more members, 49.5 percent were in a growth cycle.

Several reasons explain this pattern. Church growth researchers have discovered growth plateaus in a church's history. Each attendance plateau has unique characteristics and requires a unique plan of action to overcome it. Harry H. Fowler identifies these plateaus as 25–35; 65–75; 125–135; 175–200; 325–350; and 900–925.[2] Fuller Theological

TABLE ONE

STATUS OF CHURCHES ORGANIZED 1972 TO 1982
AFTER FIVE YEARS OF EXISTENCE

Status after Five Years of Existence Based
on Change in Membership

Initial Size of Church in Resident Members	Dropped from SBC	Declining (Less than 10 %)	Plateaued (-10 % to + 10%)	Growing (10% to 99%)	Super Growing (100% or More)	Total
1-24						
Number	49	14	13	51	69	196
Percent	25%	7.1%	6.6%	26%	35.2%	100%
25-49						
Number	59	22	27	102	120	330
Percent	17.9%	6.7%	8.2%	30.9%	36.4%	100%
50-99						
Number	32	35	38	158	96	359
Percent	8.9%	9.8%	10.6%	44%	26.7%	100%
100-149						
Number	6	7	12	61	44	130
Percent	4.6%	5.4%	9.2%	46.9%	33.9	100%
150+						
Number	0	7	14	46	26	93
Percent	0%	7.5%	15.1%	49.5%	28.8%	100%
Total						
Number	14.6	85	104	418	355	1108*
Percent	13.2%	7.7%	9.4%	37.7%	32%	100%

Source: Research Division, Home Mission Board

*Current records indicate 3,705 churches were started from 1972 to 1982; however, only 1,181 of these filed Uniform Church Letter reports during their first year of existence, and since 73 churches filed incomplete UCL records, only 1,108 churches can be traced for their first five years of existence.

Seminary also recognizes a variety of natural barriers and is now offering seminars on how to overcome them. Given today's evolving methodologies for starting new churches, it is conceivable that congregations may be started that surpass the first three or four barriers at the first public meetings, producing a greater potential for growth.

GREATER FINANCIAL BASE New churches require adequate financial bases. Locating the sources of adequate financial foundations can often be a problem. However, when starting "big," churches have stronger financial bases from the beginning.

Yet, just because one gathers a large number of people for the first public meeting of a new church does not necessarily secure a strong financial base. If the big start is a good balance of churched and unchurched people, then the financial base is likely to be strong. On the other hand, if the original group is largely unchurched people, then the financial base is likely to be weaker, but yet significant. It takes time to develop givers and tithers.

A good example of what can happen is the Crossroads Baptist Church in Coweta County, Georgia. After only a few weeks of existence, its first budget was planned based on what the church was taking in weekly. It totaled more than $50,000 annually. Within a few months the budget was revised upward to more than $70,000. This new church began with 178 mostly unchurched people in its first service.

The Greentree Church was started in a neighboring county six months later with a similar number in attendance. It included more churched than unchurched people in its beginning congregation. Its first budget amounted to more than $85,000 annually.

GREATER NETWORK FOR EVANGELISM I have asked hundreds of unchurched people the question, "What is the one thing you would look for in a church?" That simple research indicates that more than anything else, people want to build meaningful relationships. As Christians, we know that people ultimately are looking for relationships with God. In today's world, if the church is going to reach the unchurched, it must build bridges of relationships. In a new start with a balance of churched and unchurched people, the potential for evangelism is obvious. The larger the start-up of the new church, the greater the potential for networking through relationships for evangelism.

GREATER PEOPLE RESOURCES On several occasions, I have heard the statement "The resources are in the harvest." In getting off to a big start with a new church, amazingly, God seems to bring many talented people into the new congregation. Often there are people "sitting in the pews" of the mother church with wonderful untapped potential. Through starting a new church, these people are identified. In my own experience, I have been informed of potential members of the core group that I would not want to use for one reason or another. Later those people would become vital members of the new church.

Many of the jobs needed in a new church are not necessary in an established church. Many, if not most, of these jobs can be filled with people who attend the first worship service. You may discover people who wouldn't qualify for leadership positions, but who could do excellent jobs in greeting people, in setting up chairs and furniture, in running sound systems, and in a host of other activities. One of the best ways to assimilate new people is to give them tasks to perform.

GREATER MOMENTUM Everyone wants to be a part of a success story. Whether true or not, people usually equate success with numbers. With a big start for a new church, people take note, and momentum is created. It is easier to get a community's attention with a big bang than with a little pop, regardless of whether the people in the community are churched or unchurched.

Today's unchurched people are more open to attending a new church that has an attendance large enough for them to maintain their anonymity. Therefore, starting big can give the necessary momentum the new church needs for reaching the unchurched population.

SELECTING AN AREA

It is essential to be "at the right place at the right time" in getting a new church off to a big start. Even with everything else in place, if timing and location are off, the church is destined for difficulty. In selecting an area, consider five criteria. When these five criteria are met, the potential of a big start is great.

LOOK FOR A GROWING POPULATION The suburbs around the great urban centers of America are prime locations for growing populations. People continue to move to the suburbs, creating unparalleled opportunities for church starting. Francis M. Dubose stated, "The modern era has witnessed the greatest suburban development in history."[3]

This phenomenon is just beginning. *Missions USA* magazine reported that "by the year 2000, 95 percent of the American people will live on 10 percent of the land."[4]

One key to getting off to a big start is identifying these growing suburbs and starting new churches on the fringes of their development. Unfortunately, we often wait until an area is saturated with development before planting a church. When this happens, we lose the advantage of timing, and the work becomes more difficult. To be good stewards and obedient to the Great Commission, we must begin our church-starting efforts in the suburbs as they are being developed.

To determine an area's growth potential, people and institutions in the community are the best resources. Key people who can help you make this determination are planning commission members, developers, builders, school boards, and local politicians. All of these groups should be able to help you develop an overall perspective of current trends and events in an area. However, all of the planning in the world does not guarantee that an area is going to grow. Information must be verified after it is gathered by being compared with what is actually happening. A key tool for verifying this kind of information is readily available. Check the number of actual residential building permits issued within the study area in a given period of time.

LOOK FOR A CHANGING POPULATION Change comes in many forms. Change usually presents us with a unique opportunity for starting new churches. People in transition are often more open to a new church. One obvious form of change is *racial* change within a community. From 1970 until 1980, the black population increased from 6,880 to more than 50,000 in the area I served in the southwestern part of suburban Atlanta. At the same time, the total population of this area experienced only a slight increase. This presents a prime example of a changing community with a great potential for a new start. Many of the new black residents were looking for new congregations.

A second type of population change is often overlooked. When an area goes from *rural to urban,* few people notice. Dubose noted that "a hundred years ago, the typical American family was the rural family . . . today it is the suburban family."[5] People with rural orientations and people with urban orientations differ greatly. Areas where this change is taking place can be targeted for a new church with a big start.

A third example of change that dovetails with the rural-urban change is *economic.* Today's affluent are creating unique communities just beyond the suburbs known as exurbia.[6] The exurbia is often made up of wealth and power obtained from the great urban centers, but the affluent choose to live beyond the urban centers in a country-club setting.

These represent three types of change that we look for

in starting new churches. Many different types of change produce key opportunities for a big start.

LOOK FOR UNMET NEEDS Both growing populations and changing populations create unmet needs. This is significant because, as Harvie M. Conn suggests,

The church needs to recognize that in most cases each separate group will require churches of its own kind and style in order to develop and enjoy culturally and socially authentic expressions of Christian worship, community life-style, theology, ethics, and evangelism. People must be able to say, "God speaks my language." In churches where that occurs, growth may often be fast and sure.[7]

Based on this assessment, we should ask: "Is there a church in a targeted area that is allowing God to speak the community's language?" For example, in *Megatrends 2000,* John Naisbitt and Patricia Aburdene state that "nearly 70 percent of baby boomers believe in God or 'a positive, active spiritual force.' . . . A 1988 Gallup poll showed that 59 percent complained their churches or synagogues are too concerned with 'organizational as opposed to theological or spiritual issues.'"[8] Is it possible, in light of these facts, that we have not sufficiently addressed the needs of the unchurched baby boomer? Baby boomers represent only one example of large segments of population with unmet needs.

LOOK FOR INTERESTED PEOPLE In a study of 750 congregations started between 1979 and 1984, lay leaders proved to be essential. The report stated that "among missions (i.e., new congregations) that constituted, 43 percent told us that they had ten or more significant lay people. On the other hand, among missions that disbanded, only 8 percent told us that they had ten or more significant lay persons."[9] In starting a new church, several key families should have a vision for starting that church. In a new community, it is not uncommon to find people that are moving into the area that have yet to settle into an established church. These are the people who can and often will play an important role in the development of a new church.

On one occasion, I found a family during a survey who were in the process of moving into their new home. After a brief conversation, I discovered that they were moving into the area from out of state and were looking for a church home. After telling them about the church we were starting, they attended the sponsoring church and became the first family to become a part of the new church. They stated later, "Now we know why God moved us to this area." In today's mobile society, God has many missionaries in transition. To utilize these people, we must go into the community, find them, and plug them into a new church.

SENSE A BURDEN God knows where his church belongs. Church starters must depend on the Holy Spirit. All of the superficial conditions may exist for a big start, but the bottom line remains. Is it God's will at this time for a church to be started in this location? I believe it is God's will for churches to be started, and not nearly enough of them are being started. However, God may want the work to be started in a different location. When I am ready to weep over an area, I know I am where the Lord would have me to be. God is sovereign, and we must depend on his leadership.

When these five criteria are met, the potential for a big start for the new church is great. This list is not exhaustive. I have found these to be key elements in the new churches I have planted. The stronger these elements are, the more likelihood there is of a big start. Keep in mind there are areas in which churches should be started, but these churches will never start big or grow to be big. Yet these churches are crucial to the kingdom of God. On the other hand, there are areas in which we must start churches with the intention of beginning big and growing big, simply because the needs of the community demand it.

DEFINING A TARGET

A key to getting off to a big start is asking "the right people the right questions." Remember, the church is for the unchurched in a new start situation. Therefore, it is important to direct our questions to those who are not involved actively in a local New Testament congregation.

If the unchurched are the right people, what are the right questions? Three basic questions help us define our target: (1) Where are the unchurched? (2) Who are the unchurched? and (3) Why are they unchurched?

WHERE ARE THE UNCHURCHED? Research suggests that 83 percent of church attenders travel twenty-five minutes or less to attend church.[10] Therefore, it is important to determine where the unchurched are located. In essence, we are determining who constitutes our church field and where it is located. To do this, we should consider two things: (1) How many people live within a twenty-five-minute drive of the new church? and (2) How many of these people are unchurched?

A new congregation often makes the mistake of locating outside of its targeted community. This makes it very difficult to establish an effective work. If possible, the new congregation should secure a facility within the targeted area. This is important in order for the community to perceive that the new congregation exists for them.

In most cases, at least 50 percent of the targeted area is unchurched. This is a conservative estimate, and the unchurched population usually surpasses this. It is not unusual for an area to be 70 to 80 percent unchurched.

This can be determined by studying the present membership and attendance of existing churches within the targeted area. By determining the unchurched population,
the new congregation can get a handle on its potential.
Knowing the unchurched population helps the new congregation's leaders establish criteria for an effective ministry.

WHO ARE THE UNCHURCHED? In our diverse world, we
can no longer assume that all people are the same within a
given area. We must determine ways of identifying exactly
who are the unchurched. Two important considerations
help determine this: (1) demographic considerations and
(2) cultural considerations.

Through a demographic study, three key factors are identified: (1) population projections, (2) age distribution, and
(3) income distribution. Whereas population projections do
not tell us who the unchurched are, they do tell us where
they are. In determining who the unchurched are, age distribution and income distribution are key factors. Both of
these affect our approach to reaching people. This demographic information can be gathered from a variety of
sources, including the U.S. Census Bureau, school boards,
county and city planning departments, marketing companies, and other sources discussed in chapter 6.

The second key to understanding who the unchurched
are is the cultural consideration. Webster defines culture
as "behavior typical of a group or class."[11] In defining the
target culturally, we are trying to get a grasp on the life-
style of the population segment we are targeting. Many
resources are available for gathering this type of data.
One such resource is National Decision Systems out of
Encinitas, California. Through their Vision Marketing
Guide, they break the population up into forty-eight different segments. Each of these segments is presented with
a summary, demographic, socioeconomic, and housing
profile, along with location and a comparison with the

U.S. average. This information can be used in understanding and developing a strategy to reach the targeted community. (See chapter 6 for a full discussion on market segmentation and Values and Life-styles [VALS] information and their use in church planting.)

WHY ARE THEY UNCHURCHED? If we are planning to reach the unchurched, we need to understand why they are unchurched. Once this understanding has been established, a strategic plan can be put into action. Only one way exists for determining why people are unchurched. We must ask them.

At this point, it is important to ask the right questions of the right people. Researchers today are successful with opinion polls that get to the heart of this issue. Rick Warren of Saddleback Valley Community Church in Orange County, California, has popularized the following questions that many are using effectively in this way.

1. *Are you an active member of a nearby church?*
2. *What do you think is the greatest need among the people in this area?*
3. *Why do you think most people here don't attend church?*
4. *If you were looking for a church, what kinds of things would you look for?*
5. *What advice would you give me as the pastor of a new church in this community?* [12]

Once the reasons people are unchurched have been discovered, an effective people-centered strategy can be developed. Keep in mind that a strategy should always begin with the unchurched in mind.

DEVELOPING A STRATEGY

In the development of a strategy for beginning a new congregation, the target people should be the determining factor.

The key is to have "the right plan with the right goal." The right goal is to get those on the outside, inside. The future will show, in my opinion, that one of the most effective evangelistic methods is a worship service clearly designed with the unchurched in mind. When we provide a nonthreatening place for "seekers" to discover the gospel in a contemporary and relevant fashion, we will see more "seekers" become "finders."

FOCUS ON THE UNCHURCHED The worship service should be designed for the unchurched in a new start situation. Today, more new churches are being started that target the unchurched in their worship services. To accomplish this means doing church differently. Seekers and believers differ in distinct ways. These basic differences should be kept in mind when we focus on the unchurched. Believers identify with the congregation and wish to know and be known. They are more apt to sing; they may speak out; they are more likely to support the work of the church. They tend to take the Bible seriously and try to apply it to life. Those who are seeking God probably will not wish to identify themselves and may not desire to meet others. They are often reluctant to sing, speak up, or give to support the church. They will judge the Bible from the viewpoint of relevance. (See Table 2.)

Obviously, worship with these differences in mind takes on a different look.

TABLE 2

Seeker	Believer
1. Anonymity	Belongingness
2. Silence (no singing)	Singing
3. No speaking	Speaking
4. No giving	Giving
5. From relevance to revelation	From revelation to relevance
6. To initiate	To be initiated towards

*Source: "Strategies for Starting New Churches," seminar notebook for Fuller Institute, 1989.

NEUTRALIZE THE UNCHURCHED NEGATIVES From the use of this opinion poll, while starting Saddleback Valley Community Church, Orange County, California, Rick Warren reported that the four major reasons people gave for not attending church were: (1) sermons are boring and don't relate, (2) members are unfriendly, (3) too much emphasis on money, and (4) poor child care.[13] A significant part of our strategy should be to neutralize these and other objections we discover.

Everything we do helps either neutralize or strengthen the objections of the unchurched. The Greentree Church in Fayette County, Georgia, for example, takes neutralizing the objectives of the unchurched seriously. They began services in a catfish restaurant that was closed on Sundays. To accommodate preschoolers, they rented a nearby building and completely remodeled it before they had their first worship service. Whenever an unchurched person attends the Greentree Church with a preschooler, he or she is met by a smiling face, and basic information about the child is taken to assure quality child care with a personal touch.

MAJOR ON RELATIONSHIPS The world is changing. When I grew up, all of my relationships centered around my extended family. To visit my grandparents required a quick ride across town. My first cousin was my best friend throughout my school days. In today's mobile society, things are quite different. My children are not acquainted with most of their relatives and often spend months between visits to their grandparents.

My story is not unique. It is a typical picture of the lifestyle of the American family. Neighborhoods have been replaced with subdivisions and neighbors with strangers. The average person pushes the garage door opener as he or she turns into the driveway and disappears until the next day.

This isolation has created a tremendous opportunity for the church. In my experience with opinion polls, I find the most common responses indicating needs almost always center around relationship. An effective strategy builds on these needs. The great example of this kind of strategy is the Incarnation. God transcended all barriers and became man in order to make possible a personal relationship with each man or woman.

Relationship building can be introduced into a church start in several ways. As founding pastor, I tried to do this by example. On Sunday mornings, I was always in the parking lot greeting our guests and attenders as they got out of their cars. I also promoted informal, celebration-oriented worship. The more informal the service, the easier it becomes to be relational.

TARGET PEOPLE EXPERIENCING CHANGE Win Arn has said, "A proven principle of church growth is that unchurched people are more responsive to becoming Christians and responsible church members during periods of transition . . . times of transition in the lives of unchurched individuals are great opportunities for ministering to people in need."[14] C. Peter Wagner said, "The nature of the change is not as significant as the change itself."[15]

When beginning a new church, we need to keep our eyes open to those experiencing change. The most common type of change in a fast-growing suburban community is the change of address. For this reason, to get on the fringe of growth, not where the development is already saturated, is one key to a big start. An effective church-starting strategy must be sensitive to all types of changes.

MINISTER TO THE FELT NEEDS OF THE UNCHURCHED Jesus always met people right where they were. By the expression, "minister to the felt needs of the unchurched," I am talking about the same thing. A "baby boom" mom may see her need as a crash course in parenting. Actually her real need may be an attitude change produced by a relationship with

Jesus. In this case, the new congregation should attempt to help her at the point of her felt need and then move her toward her ultimate need. It is important to begin at the point of relevance and move toward revelation in the life of the unchurched person. This is a key component in the strategy of a new church.

To minister to the felt needs of unchurched people requires creativity and diversity in programming, with the entire family in mind. This requirement presents new churches with a unique challenge. Given the diversity of today's society, new churches that offer a smorgasbord of programs to meet people's felt needs will be the churches that grow and endure into the twenty-first century.

BUILDING A TEAM

By *team*, I refer to what others have called a core group. *Team* is preferable because it expresses the concept of task and the necessity of cooperation. The model for church planting that I advocate calls for targeting a date and launching the new church on that date. The team should be built prior to the new church start. This team is crucial to rapid growth and stability. To discover "the right leaders with the right influence" is, therefore, a salient concern for starting big.

RECRUITING The recruitment of the church-starting team is crucial. Charles R. Swindoll has described the types of people needed on the church-planting team:

Instead of just going for big names or starting with a few hotshots, look for some comers, achievers in process, truly trustworthy folks . . . love 'em to their full potential as you cultivate a long-haul friendship. Give your heart in unrestrained affection! Then watch God work. A team drawn together by love and held together by grace has staying power.[16]

Three primary sources exist from which the church-planting team can be recruited: (1) the community, (2) the sponsoring church, and (3) a network of sponsoring churches. The most effective team is drawn from the community. During the survey, interested families usually can be identified that already have a good level of spiritual maturity and are not yet plugged into an existing church. This team must be composed of people who have already been won to Christ and added to his Church. This team becomes the "movers and shakers" of the new congregation. If the situation requires a starting team from an unchurched background, time should be spent discipling the team.

The remaining two possible sources for the church-starting team come from the sponsoring church or a network of sponsoring churches. From these sources, team members may be enlisted for the long haul or committed for a designated period of time. Many committed people are called out of their churches by God to be a part of a new church. However, please note that there are well-intentioned people who leave their established churches to go to new congregations with the purpose of doing church their way or no way. Because this is true, it is important to establish pastoral leadership as early as possible.

In recruiting a team, size considerations are also important. Remember that the new church is for the unchurched. Therefore, a church-starting team that is too large can be a negative. Five to eight committed families is ideal. Such a number provides enough people to staff the preschool, run the sound system, greet the people, set up the worship center, and perform the many other duties involved in a church start.

TIMING Time is important in building a team. The team should spend about eight weeks together before the start of the congregation. This period should be followed by one week of rehearsal; then the actual launch of the new church should take place. It takes about six weeks for a team to start bonding. By the eighth week, the excitement should be peaking in most cases. The time to strike is when the iron is hot. Waiting may mean loss of momentum.

DREAMING The primary role of the pastor at the beginning of the church can be described as building and communicating a dream. The eight weeks of team building should be filled with vision sharing, a time when the church planter presents his dream to the church-starting team. It is a time to clarify the dream. By the time the new congregation is launched, the team should have a clear understanding of what direction God would have them go.

The dreaming stage is also a time of "unpacking and repacking our baggage." All people go into a new congregation with preconceived ideas. Some of these ideas are great; others need to go. This must be a time of complete openness, a time when the team becomes willing to look at new ways of doing things. During these weeks, the team should ask why things have been done as they have in the past. During this time, team members should openly examine their lives and motives for being a part of a new church. The bottom line when this team-building and dream-building stage is complete is, Do we agree about the direction God wants us to go? Are we convinced that our primary motive for being a part of a new church is to honor and glorify God?

IMPLEMENTING This team-building stage is also a time in which implementation of strategy begins. During the team-building stage, much of the logistical detail of the worship celebration should be completed. Responsibilities can be delegated and details ironed out at this point. A significant part of this process is the discovery of the areas of giftedness within the church-starting team.

PRAYING A major emphasis should always be placed on prayer. A church that begins on the foundation of prayer will continue to be a praying church. Prayer should be an important part of the team-building stage. In fact, nothing builds a team or a church like prayer.

During my first church-planting experience, I worked very hard to get all of the strategies in place for an effective church start. We had a strategy for everything. However, one strategy was left out—a prayer strategy. I quickly corrected that by sending out fifty letters to people I could count on to pray all over the country. Within days, things began to happen. Doors that were closed, opened, and people began calling us in expectation of a new church. Prayer makes a difference.

NETWORKING THE COMMUNITY The goal to achieve by networking the community is to persuade a significant number of the unchurched within the targeted community to attend the first worship service. The axiom that guides their effort is, "The right information produces the right response." Networking is getting the right information out in order to get the right response from the unchurched. In short, it is marketing the new congregation. The potential for networking a community is unlimited, and only a few of the approaches may be discussed.

TELEMARKETING A popular form of networking the community today is telemarketing. Norm Whan has created a telemarketing program called "The Phone's for You!" This program is a step-by-step phone campaign for starting a church of one hundred or more in ten weeks without a core group. This telemarketing program has been used effectively in North America. The fact that this program is designed to target the unchurched makes it especially attractive. The first question of the phone script is, "Are you currently involved in a local church?"

My experience with this program suggests that it is effective, but it should not be the only strategy employed. One issue in telemarketing is how to assimilate the first-time attenders. It is not uncommon for a large number of unchurched to be attracted to the first worship service. It is also not uncommon that most of them will be lost over the next few weeks. One church was started through this program in suburban Atlanta with more than 240 first-time attenders. Within a few months, the attendance had dropped to fewer than 50. The blame was not with "The Phone's for You!" program. The story illustrates the necessity of having clear strategy for assimilating the attenders.

DIRECT MAIL Direct mail is another effective means for networking a community. Direct mail can come in the form of a letter, coupon, brochure, newsletter, or a variety of other forms. Creativity and sensitivity to the community are important in developing direct mail pieces. Direct mail should be a part of a continuing strategy. Six general guidelines for a direct mail program will help keep it on target.

Target the unchurched with your marketing. Understanding the target group in direct mailing is important if we are to communicate effectively. In a church start, seek to target the unchurched. But all unchurched people are not the same. Therefore, it is essential to define the target before attempting to network the community with direct mail.

Develop your mailings around the unchurched mind-set. It is easy for believers to assume that the unchurched world understands church language and common ways of doing things. This is rarely the case. To develop a piece for mail, use an unchurched person to evaluate it. Recently I prepared a mailing that I liked. I asked my unchurched advertising agent what she thought of it. She responded that if she received it, she wouldn't bother to read it. She then designed a piece she would read. Through this process, we were able to target the unchurched more effectively. Jesus always met people where they were; so should we.

Make a commitment to excellence. In all probability, your direct mail piece will be accompanied by many others. If your piece is going to be read, it is important to produce the best-quality piece your budget can afford. It is better not to use direct mail than to do it poorly. For many people, this is your only opportunity to get into their homes. Direct mail becomes even more important in higher income areas. Often an additional second or third color on a mailout can change the appearance of the piece completely.

Give people an opportunity to respond. In direct mail, you can reserve or add space for a return card. This gives the target group an excellent opportunity to request additional information without having to attend a service. For many people, a second or third contact is required before they attend. The card should be easily detached and return postage paid. If you depend on people to cut out the card, place it in an envelope, and stamp it, you may never see the card again.

Measure your results. Include in your Sunday worship registration card a place for your attenders to tell you how they became aware of the church. If you use various means of marketing, include each of these separately. Also take the time to personally interview people concerning the way they discovered the new congregation. To determine the most effective marketing technique in your community is extremely important.

Select the best possible time for your direct mailing. At key times during the year, people are more open to attending a church. Easter is probably the best time in the year to use direct mail. In starting churches, early fall is often targeted. For parents with children in school, this presents a good time for getting into a new routine. New Year's, Christmas, Thanksgiving, and Independence Day are other dates to consider.

Consider the best day of the week to target a community. Walter Mueller states, "Tests performed by several direct mail organizations reveal that mail that arrives on Tuesday is usually most effective."[17]

Plan your direct mail far enough in advance to be aware of the schedules of other churches in your community that use direct mail. Since few churches do direct mail, this can be accomplished easily. If possible, do your mailing at a time when your church is the only one with a piece in the mail.

NEWSPAPER Another excellent means of networking the community is the newspaper. In most cases, this can be accomplished in two ways: spot ads and articles. Most communities have a local newspaper that the majority of its population subscribes to for information. By placing spot ads in the newspapers, a number of contacts can be made without a large cost. When starting a new church, try to place positive ads a week before the first service. As with other marketing, this should be placed in nonreligious sections of the newspaper where the unchurched will more likely see it. A positive introduction to the church and an invitation for the community to attend are all that is needed for an effective ad.

Most newspapers are willing to write articles about the beginning of a church in a community. These articles don't cost a dime and are priceless in giving the new church credibility with the community. Plan to have these articles in the newspaper the week before the first worship celebration.

RADIO Non-Christian radio can be an excellent way of networking the unchurched community. Often people living in a community listen to the same radio station. This can be verified by surveying the community. Once this has been done, a well-stated announcement at the right time can be effective. If possible, place radio ads during the time most people are en route to work.

RELATIONSHIPS As stated earlier, relationships are a key part of any strategy. In networking the community, this holds true also. Research shows conclusively that most people who attend churches became involved through personal relationships. Each team member should have a network of five or six unchurched families to relate to in the new community. These networks of relationships can be established in a number of places. Through coaching ball teams, attending parent-teacher association meetings, working in the community, and any number of other ways, team members can initiate relationships with unchurched people. I recently met many of my new neighbors by taking my children "trick-or-treating" on Halloween. People were open to our introduction, and many invited us back.

Church planters and church-planting teams should grasp the importance of all of these methods to provide an effective network into the community. The more effective we are with each of these components, the more effective we will be in getting the unchurched to attend the first worship service of a new congregation.

LAUNCHING THE EVENT

Usually it takes around four to five months of getting ready and ten to fifteen thousand dollars of funding to get to the point of launching the new church. The cost can be divided into two parts: marketing and equipment. This varies, depending on each circumstance.

The time required can also be divided into two parts: pre-networking phase and networking phase. The pre-networking phase is spent primarily defining your target and recruiting your church-starting team. The networking phase is spent building your church-starting team and networking your community. At this point, it is important to have "the right substance and style" to reach the unchurched.

BE READY A lot of time and energy have been spent before the first public worship service. It is important to be ready for the unchurched in that first worship service. Much care should be given to providing a comfortable facility and efficient equipment. The impression you make at that first worship service is a lasting impression.

Rehearsal. A rehearsal service should be planned for the Sunday before the first worship service. This is a time for ironing out the wrinkles. It is an exciting time for the church-starting team. The rehearsal service is helpful in providing the necessary confidence for the first worship service. This worship rehearsal should also be a time for sharing God's Word and prayer.

Part of being ready is making sure that all of the proper equipment is in place and functioning properly. This requires setting everything up during the rehearsal as if it were the actual first worship service. This includes setting up the preschool facility and becoming familiar with the logistics of assimilating preschoolers. Preschool care is a sensitive area. It is essential to provide the type of child care that puts parents at ease.

Greeting. An important factor is the way people are greeted when they arrive. They should be assimilated into the worship center. Greeting should begin in the parking lot and continue into the worship service. Parking lot attendants, welcome-center attendants, greeters, and ushers are all important. In short, by the time the first-time guest gets to his or her seat, the guest should have been assisted by at least four people.

Name tags. Name tags are a helpful part of the greeting process. At the welcome center, the guests are greeted and everyone in attendance is given a name tag. The effect of being able to communicate with one another on a first-name basis is amazing. This becomes an important part of assimilating and building a fellowship. Name tags should be used every week by everyone in attendance.

Worship registration. A practical tool for a new start is the worship registration card. This card should be placed in every seat and filled out every week by everyone in attendance.

This card is designed to do a number of things. It registers each attender and at the same time replaces the visitor's card and avoids singling out the guest. On the card, people can indicate how they learned of the new church. The card may also be used to register responses during the invitation. This is a very versatile tool and a key part of being ready.

Bible study. If the church is begun with a Bible study, it is important to work out the details in order to provide quality. The Sunday school is important for assimilating purposes. I prefer, however, to start on the Sunday school program the second week. This permits the first service to be focused totally on one event. To get unchurched people to attend a large-group setting the first time is often difficult. To persuade them to attend a small-group setting also is next to impossible. The worship service is becoming more and more the entry point into the church for today's unchurched people. The same is true for new churches.

BE FLEXIBLE Rarely does everything work out exactly as planned. Therefore, expect the unexpected and be ready to improvise. When the Crossroads Baptist Church outside Atlanta started, 178 people attended the first worship service. Of the 178, approximately 130 were unchurched. I felt sure that many of them would respond during the traditional time of invitation. However, not one responded. In the middle of that invitation, I realized I was asking most of them to do something they had never seen before in front of a group of people they had never seen before. I made a quick course correction. I invited them to register their decisions on their worship registration cards. These cards were placed in the offering plates at the end of the worship service. Thirty-one responses were registered that day. A lack of flexibility would have caused us to miss thirty-one opportunities for follow-up and ministry.

BE REALISTIC Lower your expectations. Psychologically, it is much better to surpass a goal than to fail to reach a goal. In one new church, I expected more than 250 people at the first worship service. This figure was based on the percentage of people contacted. Actually, 183 people attended the first worship service. I was disappointed. The church-starting team was disappointed. As I look back, it was foolish to be disappointed with 183 in attendance at an opening service of a new church. Because my expectations were so high, I was disappointed. It would have been better for me to underestimate rather than to overestimate.

BE EXCITED Enthusiasm, it is said, is caught—not taught. It is important to be excited and expectant about the new church. How could anyone come this far and not be excited? Sometimes it is possible to get so caught up in making sure everything goes off as planned that the excitement is lost. Ultimately God is the one who is in charge, so leaders should just sit back and enjoy what God is going to do.

ASSIMILATING THE ATTENDER

Drawing a crowd is not the problem. The problem is, How do you keep a crowd once you have gotten them to the first service? The assimilating process is just as important as getting the unchurched to the first worship service. If a new congregation's leaders do not have the resources to assimilate attenders, they should postpone the launch day. An axiom that guides us is, "The right relationship produces the right commitment." This axiom is on target when considering the most effective ways to assimilate attenders.

RELATIONSHIPS The key to keeping formerly unchurched people and leading them to a personal relationship with Christ is closely related to the ability of leaders to build relationships. The need for new worship attenders to form relationships with the pastor, church-starting team, and other new worshipers is great. When this occurs, growth is often fast and certain.

The pastor. Without a doubt, the key person in assimilating attenders is the pastor. A common mistake among those who plant churches is to start the congregation without a permanent pastor in place. If this takes place, one or two things usually happen. The attenders may decide not to attend a second or third time because they don't want to make a commitment to something that is uncertain. Or, they may get attached to the person serving as temporary pastor and, after he leaves, they drop out.

This pastor should be able to communicate effectively, understand the needs of the unchurched, and know how to relate to unchurched people in a contemporary and relevant fashion. When these elements occur, assimilation and new growth usually follow. A major part of reaching the unchurched is by building bridges of relationships. The pastor is the first person to have opportunity to do this in a new congregation. These relationships must develop.

The church-starting team. The church-starting team is also an important part of the assimilating process. In addition to the pastor, the church-starting team must initiate relationships with attenders. This assimilation process is two-sided. The church-starting team must bond with the attenders, and the attenders must bond with the church-starting team. Many effective ways exist for developing these relationships. The need for the church to develop sound relationships with the attenders in the worship and ministry setting is crucial. For this reason, the logistics of getting people from their cars to the worship center and back is important. Even this time should be given to building relationships.

The church-starting team should also relate to attenders in settings away from the worship services. Personal visits, hosting attenders in the homes of team members, phone calls, or just genuine friendliness accomplish this goal.

Openness and flexibility aid the process of getting to know attenders.

Attenders. A third key to assimilation is to get attenders to relate to one another. This can be accomplished by offering activities that allow people the opportunity to get to know each other. One of the best means to do this is by getting attenders together for a meal. In Acts 2, part of the assimilating process in the new Jerusalem church was the sharing of a meal together. In the life of Christ, eating together was an important part of his ministry. Many methods can be found to get attenders together. The important point is that they be brought together. Only then can assimilation take place.

FOLLOW-UP

After the first service has taken place, effective follow-up strategy should be in place. On Sunday afternoon following the first service, each guest should be called by the pastor. That afternoon, if possible, a quick visit by one of the church-starting team would be appropriate. This should be a doorstep visit in which the attender is thanked for his or her attendance. By Monday, the guest should receive a phone call from his or her Bible study leader, if the new congregation is being started with a Sunday morning Bible study. By Wednesday, a informal thank-you letter from the pastor should be in each mail box. By Friday, a newsletter from the new church should arrive. This procedure allows for five nonthreatening contacts the week following the first service. Follow-up visits should be planned at this point based on their responses.

SMALL GROUPS

When attempting to start big, the large-group setting is the entry point for attenders to the new church. However, the small-group setting is the assimilating arm of the new church. As soon as possible, each attender should be assigned to a small group. This may be a traditional Sunday school program, a nontraditional Sunday morning Bible-study group, or a cell group that meets on its own sometime during the week. In cases when small groups are impossible, a midweek Bible-study group, led by the pastor, can add much to follow-up.

Getting people together in order to start forming relationships with one another is important. If this doesn't take place, the large group soon becomes a small group.

Many pastors, denominational leaders, and church planters today want an instant church. Churches don't come into existence that way. Within four to six months, a large crowd can be gathered for a worship service with this model. However, it takes months of hard work to assimilate people into the spiritual family that becomes a church. When many of the new attenders have been totally unchurched, it may take months to bring them to a point of decision for Christ. The hard work actually begins once you have had the big day. At least a year is needed to reach out and bring in those who attend the first big service. With adequate preparation, hard work, and vision, new churches can be started today that will transcend the clutches of smallness. It is possible to start big.

9

Spontaneous Church Planting in the Inner City

*One of the strange,
weird, perplexing,
and paradoxical
miracles of history
is the origin of the
black church on
the North American
continent.*

W. J. Hodge, 1972

The proliferation of Pentecostal congregations
is the greatest global church-planting story in the twentieth
century. There were no Pentecostal holiness churches on January 1, 1901. (I do not speak, of course, of the Pentecostal
Holiness Church.) When one looks at the rise of Pentecostal
churches around the world in less than ninety years, he is
astounded. In terms of sheer numbers and the relatively successful penetration of just about every "ethclass"[1] in the
United States, the multiplication of Pentecostal churches is a
most impressive church-planting success story.

This story has received a great deal of notice from
church growth and mission researchers, and that recognition is justified. Other Christians have much to learn from
what God has done through Pentecostal people in the last
nine decades. However, there is a second story that has
been almost totally overlooked—the rise and growth of
black churches, especially black Baptist churches. Students
of church growth and practitioners of church extension
have hardly stopped to take more than a passing glance at
what has been accomplished by these people.

The most dramatic rise and growth of black churches has occurred in the great industrial and commercial centers of America during this century. To this subject we turn our attention in this chapter. What I am going to share is not the result of careful research but rather of careful observation in one of the great industrial states of America and in the nation's third largest city. These observations will describe the situation in most northern and western cities and probably will not be too far away from that of cities of the South and Southwest.

PURPOSE OF THIS STUDY

I hope to accomplish four things with this investigation. First, I hope to stimulate further interest in a relatively new field of American church growth research, one from which I am convinced we have a great deal to learn.

There are several reasons why so little has been done in this area. Most of those people passionately interested in how and why American churches grow or do not grow have been white themselves and leaders of predominantly white churches, denominations, or missionary or educational agencies. During the same period that the church growth movement has become a reality, most prominent black church leaders have been committed to problems of racial and social justice in this country. Church growth has taken place, I think, and church planting has continued, but it has not received major emphasis or paramount attention. In fact, some principles of church growth have been extremely threatening to men who have been committed to integration, equality, and justice.

Another problem, of course, is the dearth of reliable statistics for black churches, especially for black Baptist churches. The National Baptist denominational groups were not included in the Glenmary study of American churches and church membership up to 1990 because the most reliable figures for numbers of churches and

members were only estimates.[2] Still, the research needs to
be done. I doubt that there were fully reliable statistics
for Pentecostals in Latin America in the sixties. Nevertheless, it is remarkable what was discovered about the
growth of churches when a huge investment of man-
hours was devoted to that research. This same commitment of man-hours and money will have to be made in
order to discover how church growth has occurred in the
American black community.

Further, someone needs to discover for us what kind of
growth has actually taken place. There can be no doubt
that the rise of black Baptists in American industrial centers is a great church-planting story. However, whether
there has been significant growth of the Body of Jesus
Christ in the whole process has not been established. From
1915 to 1930, a great migratory flood took place. It consisted of "the movement of members of the Negro population from rural to urban centers and from the urban South
to the urban North."[3] The process began again with the
outbreak of World War II and did not abate until the
Nixon recession of the early seventies.

Much of the growth of black churches has been biological and transfer growth. We have no way of knowing or
judging how well these new black congregations have done
in penetrating the pagan pools within the black community. We may have a salient illustration of how big
churches—as well as many small churches—come from
small rural churches. This in no way detracts from the
achievements of those stalwarts of the gospel of Christ,
who have produced thousands of churches that now exist
in the inner cities of America. They have done this in spite
of hardships, lack of monetary assistance, and scant academic or theological training. The story begs for a full and
thorough examination in every city.

The second thing I hope to accomplish with this investigation is to call attention to those countless men who have
been God's instruments in accomplishing tremendous feats

in church planting. They are unknown to nearly all church historians, to denominational and mission executives, and to church growth and church extension leaders. While church historians have been writing about the demise of Protestantism in the inner cities, these men have been gathering the new populations of those cities into Protestant churches. While denominational and mission executives have been spending thousands of dollars trying to keep the doors of church buildings open (in communities from which the churches that once met in the buildings have long since departed) and have been going through all kinds of contortions to hold on to inner-city real estate, these men have been planting churches without the benefit of real estate, endowments, or mission dollars. While church extension and church-growth specialists have focused on the declining membership of great, old, rich ecclesiastical institutions and on the people who have moved out, and while they have tried to solve the problems of prejudice, paternalism, and property, these men and women have focused on the newcomers. These newcomers were, they conceived, the future of these transitional communities. The new arrivals were uprooted and looking for a fellowship where they could be themselves and where they could worship God the Father and encounter Christ the Son among their peers.

These church planters have been inconspicuous and ignored. They may have been highly articulate among their peers, but considered inarticulate by those who have overlooked them. Leaders from the Protestant establishment have talked about the Christlike sacrifice of those who have commuted from the suburbs to keep the churches open. These church planters have lived in the ghettos and the transitional communities, have identified with the people, and have, in fact, been of the peoples there. They have worked by day or night to make their own living while these new churches were being started. "People blindness" expresses itself in many different ways, and Protestant leaders have overlooked these church planters.

Third, I hope this discussion will prepare the way for church leaders to consider another option for dealing with communities in transition. Very often, church planters focus upon the transitional churches as institutions rather than as people. They are concerned with how to guarantee survival of the institution, rather than how most effectively to evangelize and to congregationalize the new peoples who are coming into the community, and how most effectively to conserve those for Christ and his Church who have moved from the changing communities. I will go into these in more detail from the perspective of the community in transition in the following chapter. Here, however, I want to suggest church planting in transitional communities as a viable, purposeful way to be faithful to Christ.

Fourth, I hope the material presented here will stimulate an aggressive strategy of church multiplication on the part of black leaders and congregations. What has been achieved is significant, but these leaders agree that in most cases it could have been done more easily and efficiently.

METHOD OF THE STUDY

My method will be very simple. First, I will set the story in historical perspective and look briefly at the growth of black Baptist churches over the last century, especially as this growth has developed in Chicago. I will then expose the church-planting methods that were used, or at least the methods being used today, by introducing five pastors who have planted black Baptist churches in Chicago during the past fifteen years. These churches all happen to be a part of the Southern Baptist Convention, and I have had close association and contact with them over several years. You will get a good picture of what I mean when I speak of "spontaneous church planting in the inner city" as you meet these men. Several reflections will need to be made about what we discover. Finally, I want to challenge leaders of predominantly black churches. I want to call them to deliberate, planned church planting in the decades ahead as a major strategy for bringing America to the feet of Jesus.

HISTORICAL DEVELOPMENTS OF BLACK BAPTISTS First, we will look at black Baptist churches from a statistical and historical perspective.

When the Southern Baptist Convention was organized in 1845, there were, it has been alleged, more blacks in the membership of those churches than whites.[4] Twenty years later, however, the Civil War was over, and the process of organizing black Baptist churches with black leadership swelled to a flood stage. By 1890 there were 12,856 black Baptist churches, with 1,350,000 members, and at the same time the U.S. Bureau of Census found that there were 17,209 Southern Baptist churches with only 1,280,000 members. Ninety percent of all the black Christians were in twelve southern states in 1890. This means, of course, that black Baptists and Southern Baptists essentially occupied the same territory. By 1906, both groups had made significant gains. That year the Bureau of Census found that Southern Baptists had added 4,866 congregations since 1890, so they were up to 21,075 churches and slightly more than 2,000,000 members. The National Baptist Convention had been formed in 1894 with 18,534 affiliated churches. When you add black Free Will Baptists and black Primitive Baptists, the total of black Baptist churches was 19,582, an increase of more than 6,000 congregations between 1890 and 1906. Total membership reached 2,311,000. Again 87 percent of the black church members were in the twelve southern states.[5] (See graphs 1 and 2.)

When the U.S. government took its next census of religious bodies in 1916, there were 21,213 black Baptist churches with a total membership approaching 2,900,000. The great population shift from the rural South to the urban North continued at full flood, except for the years during the Great Depression, until shortly after 1970.

GRAPH 1. **Number of Churches: All black Baptist Churches and Southern Baptist Convention Churches**

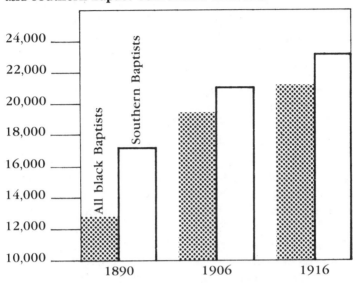

GRAPH 2. **Total Membership: All black Baptist Churches and Southern Baptist Convention Churches**

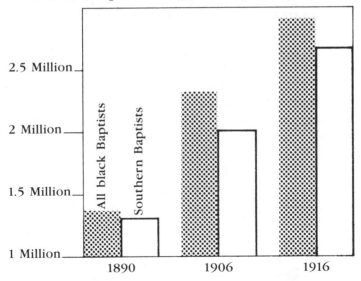

In 1899, only five black churches were reported in Chicago, although the black population was near 30,000. In 1920, the Chicago Commission on Race Relations made a very careful study of the Chicago black community. It received the assignment as a response to the great race riot of 1919, and the commissioners reported that there were 19 "regular" Baptist churches in the city (congregations occupying more-or-less-permanent church-type buildings) and 67 storefront churches, a total of only 86 Baptist congregations among a population of 109,000.[6] In 1940, although migration had been slowed down for ten years, there were 278,000 blacks in Chicago's black community. When Drake and Cayton (1940) were finishing the book *Black Metropolis,* they found that "Bronzeville" (their term for the black belt in Chicago) had about 250 black churches with more than 135,000 members.[7] I believe this to be a very conservative figure.

This pattern was general in all the major cities of the industrial North during this period. In 1916, there were only 127 black Baptist churches in Chicago, Detroit, Cincinnati, Philadelphia, and Baltimore. By 1936, the Bureau of Census counted 319 churches in those five cities.[8] However, the reliability of the census figures should be questioned. Mays and Nicholson (1933), who wrote an excellent book, *The Negro's Church,* in the early thirties, used the Federal Census of Religious Bodies for 1926. They had their own research team. They reported:

Since the number of Negro churches located during this study by a street canvass is so much greater than the number given in the Federal Census of Religious Bodies in 1926, it is safe to conclude that the census reports are probably too conservative and that many churches recorded in this study were not reported to the government in 1926.[9]

If Chicago is typical of other cities, and if we are willing to take storefront churches seriously, current estimates of the number of churches continue to be low.

By 1950, the black population had grown to 492,000. By 1970, the black community in Cook County had multiplied 2.3 times to 1,183,000. The migration had been so significant that there were more blacks in Cook County in 1970 than in Alabama and Mississippi combined. No one has the exact figures about the number of black Baptist churches in Chicago today. Counting "regular," storefront, and house churches, probably there are close to 1,750 black Baptist churches, with 350,000 members. Multiply this kind of pattern by all the American cities where there are large black communities—especially black communities that have developed since 1945—and you'll have a picture of the accomplishment in church planting that has taken place.

CHURCH-PLANTING METHODS In 1972, when the Illinois Baptist State Association (IBSA) began to take a hard statistical look at Illinois, we were face to face with a community of 1.4 million to whom we as a denomination had never addressed the gospel. We had made loud claims about preaching the gospel to the whole state. We had a magnificent rhetoric, but we had totally ignored the black community in Illinois. As a denomination we did, I believe, consciously accept responsibility to assist in starting and developing Baptist churches among these peoples as well as others in the state. We have adopted a long-range strategy for the black community that was taken seriously. For several years the IBSA had a number of fully salaried church planters over the state. Three of the church planters, at the end of the 1970s, were blacks who were attempting to plant churches in underchurched black communities. No effort was made to encourage churches aligned with National Baptist Conventions to affiliate with us. A few did. Most of the black churches affiliated with the Southern Baptist Convention in the Metro East St. Louis area hold dual alignment. Very few are dually aligned in the Chicago area. There are now sixty black churches across the state.

The Home Mission Board, SBC, now has a unit called the Division of Black Church Extension. It pursues a national strategy for planting churches in predominantly black communities. Leaders of predominantly black SBC churches and denominational programs expect to have four thousand churches by A.D. 2000.

Where will these churches come from? Very few of them will be started by fully salaried church planters. Most of the growth will come from newly organized, unaligned churches that are being formed in new black communities or among the new residents of black communities in transition. Church and denominational leaders often think of transitional communities only as black to white, or white to black, but there is a continuous wave of transition that is black to black as well.

These congregations will start in homes and will graduate to storefront churches. In a few years, they will acquire more church-type buildings and affiliate with one of our local associations of churches. They will seek affiliation because of a desperate need for community, for organizational and educational know-how, and some because of a hope of realizing some monetary assistance, probably in terms of building loans. These churches will arise much like the five I am about to describe, along with the six remarkable men who began them.

I will start with *Claude Tears.* He is pastor of the First Corinthians Baptist Church, south of 113th Street, on State Street. Claude is a tremendous singer. He is the chief singer in his church, and his wife is a fantastic organist. He came to Chicago from Tennessee in his teenage years, part of the post-World War II migratory pattern. His wife was born in Chicago. Claude was very much involved in the music program of a large black church in Chicago when God called him to preach. In order to get to church, he drove through a changing community where new young black families were moving in. He became convinced that God was calling him to that community. He, his wife, and

two other families began meeting there in July 1966.
When they first started having Sunday services, they
rented a school building; then they purchased a former
supermarket building. They affiliated with the Southern
Baptist Convention in 1972. In 1973, they purchased a
very substantial building with considerable educational
space and a pastor's home. Their auditorium will seat
about five hundred. They did not get any assistance from
Southern Baptists for the purchase of the property. They
have had a radio ministry, a bus ministry, and a fantastic
ministry of witness and service on the streets of their community. They now have more than twelve hundred members and more than one thousand in attendance on special
days. The First Corinthians Baptist Church is one of the
largest Southern Baptist churches in Illinois.

The second man I want you to meet is *Don Sharp*. He is
pastor of Faith Tabernacle Missionary Baptist Church, on
South Cornell in Chicago. He began to hold weekly Bible
studies in the homes of friends in 1964. The fellowship
was so good that somebody said, "Why don't we start a
church?" He talked with his pastor about it and received a
somewhat reluctant permission. In August, the group
organized into a church with twelve members. Don said,
"Nobody helped us. We didn't begin with mission status.
Boom! We were just a church—sink or swim." For five
years they met in what had been a warehouse. Then they
began to rent space from Cornell Avenue Baptist Church—
a church that had previously been named the First Southern Baptist Church of Chicago. Faith Tabernacle began its
worship service at noon. Later, the two Sunday schools
were combined. Still later, Cornell Avenue Baptist Church
relocated in the Hyde Park community, and Faith Tabernacle purchased the church building. The growth of the
church has been fairly slow, but very stable. They now have
over six hundred resident members.

The third person is *Abraham Picou*, who grew up in
New Orleans and went to work at Walgreen's as a boy. He

was transferred by the company to Chicago in 1960, as Walgreen's deliberately began to develop stores in the black community. He didn't come looking for work. He was so valuable that his company sent him to Chicago to help in the marketing process in Chicago's black community. Soon he was sent to Cincinnati. He opened the first black Walgreen's store outside the city of Chicago. In 1967, the company transferred him back to Chicago to the corporate offices. A Baptist preacher working as the porter in his office witnessed to him regularly. Picou was eventually led to Christ through his custodian's witness. Picou started attending the church this man served as pastor. In 1968, Abraham Picou was called into the ministry—called to preach. That was very threatening to his pastor, so Picou moved to another church, the Antioch Missionary Baptist Church, and was there about a year when the pastor left. The Antioch Church then called him as pastor. At that time, the church was sixteen years old, but it had only 25 members. It now has 275 members. Picou gave up his management job and took a $350 monthly cut in salary to take a five-day-a-week job so that he could continue to serve as pastor of the church. In 1985, Picou was called by a church in Louisville, Kentucky. The Antioch church continues to grow with new leadership, but is no longer active in Southern Baptist Convention life.

The fourth man is *Joseph Rainey,* pastor of Christian Fellowship Missionary Baptist Church. He moved to Chicago from Tennessee in 1956. He has worked for the Post Office in Tennessee and Chicago for a total of twenty-eight years. He served as deacon and Sunday school superintendent in a Chicago church, and he helped plant the Haven of Rest Baptist Church in Chicago. He was called to preach in 1970. When he told his pastor, the pastor was greatly disturbed. He finally did consent to let him preach the following November. Soon his pastor suggested that he start holding worship services in the basement of his home. He began to do that but quickly needed more space. This new congregation had a great struggle getting a place to meet. When city inspectors refused to permit the use of a storefront building for worship services, the church defied the ruling. Rainey was threatened with jail. The church was locked out by the Chicago police. In 1976, they finally secured a permanent building. Now they have more than three hundred members and still need larger facilities, and the pastor continues to be bivocational.

The fifth person is *Eugene Gibson,* pastor of the Mission of Faith Baptist Church. Gibson worked for a number of years for Speigel, Inc., in management. He was bumped when Speigel merged with a larger company and he went to work for Chicago City College to develop a job survival curriculum for that school. Although he was pastor of a church, he didn't feel that he was accomplishing much. He was struck down by a heart attack that required a triple bypass operation. During convalescence he felt a call from God to develop a black church that would be, as he says, "based on faith and a strong Bible teaching program." The Bible teaching program in black Baptist churches has typically been weak, and the black pastors are very concerned about this. After Gibson's convalescence, he resigned as pastor and started a new church in a funeral home. Fantastic things have happened for that congregation during the two years since it began. This middle-class black church has acquired a beautiful building without assistance from the denomination. They have developed one of the strongest Sunday school programs in the nation among predominantly black SBC churches. They had 789 enrolled in 1990, with an average attendance of 413. The church has over four hundred resident members. Gibson has received national recognition as a Sunday school leader in the convention. This is a very aggressive and progressive church.

Clarence Hopson is pastor of the Broadview Missionary Baptist Church, Broadview, Illinois. Broadview is one of the larger Chicago suburbs developed in the first part of this century. The church was organized in 1972 as a mission of the

Northwest Missionary Baptist Church. The sponsoring church was predominantly white, composed mainly of people from eastern Kentucky and Tennessee who came to Chicago in the Eisenhower recession of the 1950s.

Northwest Missionary was a prolific mother of SBC churches all over the Chicago area in the 1960s and 1970s. Broadview was started in the Chicago Metro Baptist Association's office building, then located in Broadview.

In 1974, when the Broadview congregation had less than fifty members, and only one male member, Clarence Hopson was called as pastor. Though not the first pastor, he has been God's man to nurture and develop what had only barely begun.

Hopson had moved from Mississippi to Chicago with a young family in 1953. He had been converted in a small church outside of Jackson and had been active in the New Hope Missionary Baptist Church in Jackson before coming to Chicago. In Chicago, he joined the Pilgrim's Rest Missionary Baptist Church, was called to preach, was ordained, and served an active apprenticeship.

He moved to Melrose Park, in suburban Chicago, in 1970 and joined the Southern Baptist church in that city. When the Broadview church became vacant, he was called as pastor. It has been his only church.

Broadview Baptist is now the largest SBC church in Illinois in resident members (2,600) and worship attendance (1,400). Several years ago they purchased the Messiah Baptist Church building. It has been remodeled, enlarged, and put to multiple use, and it is still too small.

On an average Sunday at Broadview, 675 people will attend the 8:15 A.M. service; about 600, many adult men and women, will be involved in a graded Sunday school program; and then more than 700 will crowd into the 11:00 A.M. service. The range of ministries conducted by the church is vast, determined by the felt needs in the community. However, the emphasis is on evangelism. "Everything in a church should be evangelistic," Hopson says.

His church led all SBC churches in Illinois in baptisms for eleven years consecutively.

OBSERVATIONS

Let me make some observations about the personal stories of these men and the churches they have developed.

1. For most of the black Baptist pastors that I know, and these in particular, the call to preach is a very objective—as opposed to a subjective—experience. Joseph Rainey, for example, was in Los Angeles on vacation. He had been struggling with an inner call to preach. He and his wife attended a Church of God in Christ worship service, and the pastor of that church walked down to him—a stranger—and said, "God has called you to preach and will prepare the way for you to do it. What are you waiting for?" When he went back home, he told his pastor, announced his call publicly, and was soon preaching in his own home.

2. For these men, to be called to preach is tantamount to being called to gather a congregation. Black pastors are not usually comfortable with having another preacher in the church except in an apprentice role. Multiple staff roles in black Baptist churches are just developing. To be able to gather a congregation is the seal of one's call. Thus, planting churches has been spontaneous rather than planned.

3. Founding pastors plant and serve their churches for several years with little or no remuneration. For the first five years the pastor usually puts his own money into the church and its program at a much higher rate than he receives in remuneration. Joseph Rainey was the pastor of his church for eight years before he received one penny in salary.

4. All of these congregations were started in new black communities with young families. These communities, from the point of view of whites, were in transition and decline. Much of the present discussion about transitional

communities is an expression of cultural chauvinism. It issues from the viewpoint of the people in flight rather than from the newcomers.

5. The story of these churches is usually an incredible struggle to get property, to get adequate facilities. This struggle and the kind of permanent buildings they get shape the character and personality of the church.

6. Planting a church is always a great step of faith, a bold act of obedience. It is an opportunity to see God at work. It is like crossing the Red Sea—something the congregation continually looks back to and usually celebrates each year.

7. The church is usually established on some spiritual axiom or watchword. At First Corinthians, the people's bedrock principle is "There's nothing too hard for God." They keep pounding away at that idea, proving that it's true.

8. Without exception, these new churches came about as a result of a God-given vision. The vision is most often in the form of a mental and emotional conviction that God wants to build a church in a certain place on certain principles. Sometimes, however, the preacher passes through a mystical encounter with Christ and emerges with a flint-hard conviction that God will raise up a church if the pastor will only be faithful in hardship. Gene Gibson received such a vision while he was in the hospital recovering from heart surgery. When he delayed, hoping to bring the church that he served as pastor up to the new principles on which he felt called to found the church, he says that the Lord spoke to him again. It happened to him at the stroke of midnight, on New Year's Eve, while he was praying as the old year passed. He said, "The Lord spoke to me almost audibly saying 'Gibson, when are you going to do what I told you to do?'" So, he got up from his knees, went home, called his wife in Philadelphia, and told her he was going to resign as pastor of the old church and build a new church founded on faith and sound Bible teaching. He did that immediately.

9. These new churches, and the majority of black Baptist churches, develop along larger family lines. Don Sharp says that very often his church penetrates a family through children. The children come, they get involved, and then the mother decides she should be where her child is. The mother will become a member—and maybe the father will begin to attend—and then the mother's sister will come, and then the sister's husband. Perhaps he will become a deacon, and then they will get the nieces and nephews. The growth goes on and on, along larger family lines.

The next four observations are not as directly related to these five men as the previous ones were, but they represent significant truth for inner-city church planting.

10. The most responsive people to the gospel are generally those who are recently uprooted and who are attempting to get started in a new area. This period of responsiveness does not last forever. It has its limits, and we need to have the most effective evangelistic strategy possible for a changing community during that period of time. New black churches are most often brought to birth in new black communities.

11. Contrary to the opinion of most whites, the black community is not a social monolith. Like the white community, it is a mosaic of many pieces. There are southerners and northerners, rich and poor, middle class and lower class, educated and uneducated, working and professional classes. Any strategy for church planting must take the cultural and social pattern of the community into consideration. Denominational leaders, white and black, need to develop an entirely different attitude toward new black church development in the inner city, an attitude instructed by this truth. It plays a big part in the way these new churches get under way.

12. Denominational executives, church planters, and church-growth specialists need to be taught by these black church planters. What they have been doing in the inner city is far superior to what white Protestants have been doing. We have a lot more to learn from those who are

building churches in the inner city than from those who are dismantling churches there. Someone needs to develop a major research project to study the growth of the Church in the black communities of great American cities. Much of what I say is only conjecture. I hope students of church growth, white and black, will explore this whole church-growth galaxy.

13. Black Southern Baptist churches in the Chicago area, almost without exception, are experiencing significant membership growth. The number of churches is also increasing. Many of them seem to be making a wholesome adaptation of SBC organizational methods while retaining the spontaneous, celebrative character of black worship. This, too, deserves study.

TO LEADERS OF BLACK CHURCHES

Since I first began exploring this subject and sharing my observations with others, I have had a number of opportunities to speak specifically with leaders of predominantly black churches, both individually and in groups. What implications does this wonderful story of achievement have for black churches today? At least three suggestions may be helpful:

First, take a realistic look at all of the community where your church is located. Culturally, black churches have not been parish-oriented but pastor-oriented. Nevertheless, God surely holds us especially accountable for those people immediately around us.

Black church members and leaders have been very sensitive to social needs in communities and have become increasingly involved with political structures and community organizations in efforts to effect change. Pastors and other leaders, no matter where they live, have tended to become involved in the community where the church building is located. This is commendable and has, in my opinion, contributed to the growth of black churches during the last quarter century. Historians will undoubtedly record that the most important contribution of Christianity to American life in the twentieth century has been the leadership given by black churches to the civil rights movement and the social revolution that was its aftermath.

However, black churches generally need to take a hard look at their community in reference to its ethnic and socioeconomic character. In many predominantly black communities the racial and cultural mix is considerable. This cultural pluralism is always a fact in those communities in process of transition.

As an illustration, try to imagine a community where the population is 65 percent black. Thirty-five percent of the population is divided primarily into three other people-groups. Fifteen percent of the population is older whites, a declining number. A growing Hispanic community composes another 14 percent of the total. A small Southeast Asian community, mostly ethnic Chinese, makes up 4 percent of the population. Many other small groups equal about 2 percent of the populace. This kind of racial mix can be found in many black communities in our larger cities.

Furthermore, the black community itself is a conglomeration of very distinct subgroups. These would range from a number of "Afro-philes," those who have so idealized African roots as to totally reject Christianity as a denial of blackness, to a small group of "Afro-Saxons," those so assimilated with white, middle-class culture as to be uncomfortable within the typical black church. Among these various subgroups would be a community of French-speaking Haitians. The largest group by far, however, would be those black Americans who can easily be evangelized by existing black churches.

Taking this kind of look at one's community will enable leaders of black churches to see the need for and possibility of cross-cultural ministries and cross-cultural church planting within the community where the black church exists. Most existing black communities in

America have an abundance of churches. I counted, on one occasion, as many as ten storefront churches on both sides of the street in one block of Roosevelt Road in Chicago. However, these churches address themselves to the various subcultures of the black community. The day has come, I believe, for vibrant black churches to see the ethnic diversity that is around them and to begin intentionally to engage in cross-cultural church planting in their own immediate communities.

Second, be alert to new black communities that are being formed in our major cities and their suburbs and deliberately and enthusiastically plant new churches in those places.

Communities in transition will have new churches. The growing black populace of many suburbs will have predominantly black churches with black leaders. The spontaneous methods that have been used to generate black churches during this century have been effective but painful. They have been painful both in terms of strained relationships and in terms of the difficulty of getting started without aid from a mother church. Much stronger churches more strategically located could have been formed had there been planning and intentional efforts to sponsor and support new congregations.

There is no reason for the same pattern to continue with all of its hardships. Those methods that have proven effective but emotionally costly can be improved. Improvement can take place if leaders of black churches will be alert to areas where new black churches are needed and lead their churches to multiply themselves in these new communities through daughter churches.

Third, commit yourselves to plant the vigorous faith and vitality of black churches among all the people-groups that make up America. This is a challenge to cross-cultural evangelism and church planting in the American context.

In most discussions about Christianity and the American city, and always in dialogues about missionary strategy for the city, the focus is on designing a plan to get the resources of the suburbs to the central cities. There is a need and place for that concern. However, I am more concerned about transmitting spiritual vitality than I am about sharing material resources and learned leadership skills. Churches with spiritual vitality are needed among all the people-groups of the American population.

Spiritual vitality is present within thousands of black churches. Research has shown that blacks are more likely to be evangelical than whites. Overall, blacks make up about 10 percent of the U.S. population and about 15 percent of all evangelicals. Nor does evangelical Christianity reside mostly in the suburbs. Actually, suburbs, with only 16 percent of the evangelicals and 27 percent of the populace, are less evangelical than the nonmetropolitan cities, small towns, rural areas, and inner cities of this nation. The central cities of America, alleged by many to be barren deserts as far as evangelical Christianity is concerned, have about one-third of the nation's total population. They also have one-third of America's evangelicals.[10] A principle reason for this is the tremendous achievement in evangelism and church planting carried on by black churches and black church leaders throughout this century.

Black churches have yet to awaken to their responsibility to communicate the gospel to white, English-speaking communities or to other language-culture groups. Given the vitality that is within black evangelical Christianity, this responsibility shouts for recognition and response. Several black churches are now leading the way in this endeavor. If someone objects that such missionary action is impossible because the black Christian community lacks the resources to evangelize and congregationalize among peoples materially richer than themselves, I respond that in the first-century the gospel was habitually passed from the "have-nots" to the "haves." I suggest that black churches adopt the model of the first-century churches in modern America. In truth, the rich, vibrant, personal faith of black churches needs to be shared with all the various peoples that make up North America.

10

Church Planting: An Apostolic Opportunity in Urban Transitional Communities

Metropolitan transitional areas
should become mission fields
in the same way other
under-churched areas of the country
are considered mission fields.

George W. Bullard, Jr., 1976

Dilemmas and frustrations are a way of life for most churches in communities in transition.[1] No other single concern has consumed as much time for church and denominational planners over the last generation.

Transitional communities are likely to continue to make inordinate time demands. Heretofore the general assumption has been that transitional communities were in the inner cities and consisted primarily of ethnic and racial change. Indeed, this chapter essentially discusses the transitional community from that point of view. But the assumption is no longer completely valid. Communities undergoing radical changes can be found in all parts of the nation, rural and urban, and the nature of the change experienced varies over a wide range of social characteristics.

Central city areas will continue to be a major port of entry for refugees and immigrants, but they may not continue to be so for migrants from nonmetropolitan areas of the country. Some suburbs now constitute major transitional areas in North America, and now many rural areas are experiencing radical change. But the inner city remains the most obvious transitional area. Principles enunciated here should apply to any type of transitional community.

Tied up with this problem in the central city is a wide range of ethical issues, from "sheep stealing" to racial injustice. Furthermore, the pride, stability, and strength of whole denominations are threatened by the problem. The great prestigious churches in the cities, the bastions of the Protestant hegemony of the past, have been depleted and defeated, and hundreds have died. Many more will die in the future. This demise of great city churches has been one of the factors contributing to the severe decline of world mission giving among many Protestant groups. The massive decline of mainline Protestant groups in North America in the last thirty years, of which decline in urban transitional communities is a major contributor, has been studied and is being addressed by every denomination.[2]

As yet no ultimate solution to the problem has been found. As was indicated in the last chapter, in terms of the growth of the Body of Christ, the problem is not really as serious as many have suggested. A Gallup survey has shown that the inner cities of America have a greater proportion of evangelicals to population than do the suburbs of our large cities.[3] Where many churches have died, many more have been planted.

One way of meeting the need, until the last decade, was seldom explored by those who do research and spend time deliberately attempting to build strategies for transitional communities. Along with other strategies, now some groups have intentional plans to plant churches among some of the new peoples in transitional communities.[4] However, it must be said honestly, this alternative is still not the method preferred by church and denominational leaders for solving this problem.

THE SCENARIO AND ITS OPTIONS

Before addressing this subject directly, let me outline the constellation of factors that produces the multisided problem that church leaders usually face in transitional communities.

The church leader finds himself serving a congregation that is, in the main, not a part of the community where its building is located. Many of these members have moved away from the building, but some have never lived in the area. The pastor and other staff members are likely to be in this latter group. The congregation was originally composed of one sociocultural group, and this character is still evident in the congregation, especially in the key leadership positions.

The building in which the church meets is often old, expensive to maintain, energy-inefficient, ill-suited to present-day congregational needs, and almost impossible to renovate or remodel.

Most of the membership of the church—especially the leadership, including the pastor—is in a socioeconomic group that is significantly different from the people living near the building.

Attendance, membership, and financial support have been in decline for several years. This decline probably began well before the present pastor and staff came on the scene. They inherited a set of problems already in existence.

The general expectation, however, from both the congregation and the denomination, is that the pastor and staff should produce a successful and effective church. "Successful and effective" usually means (1) that the church is solvent, (2) that it is able to contribute fairly significantly to the denomination's missionary and benevolent programs, and (3) that the congregation is growing in numbers.

Given this definition of "successful and effective," the pastor and staff must choose between (1) giving primary consideration to the commuters who, at considerable sacrifice and with commendable dedication, continue to man and support the church's organizations and ministries and (2) giving primary attention to evangelism and to ministries aimed at people in the immediate community where the church meets for worship. A salient dilemma arises here. Should the pastor (and to a lesser degree, the staff) spend most of his time with those who provide leadership and financial support or with the people in the immediate community of the church building? Whatever option is exercised, the church will fail to be "successful and effective."

The question of programming provides another dilemma for pastor and staff. Should the programs of the church be designed for the stalwart commuters or for people near the church building? The roles of pastor and staff are made more difficult by the fact that there often is a conflict between their views about the church and its mission and those of many members of the congregation. To their amazement, also, they often find that prejudice, distrust, and bigotry are just as ingrained in the people who have moved into the community as in those who have fled because of change or who remain out of necessity.

The situation is further complicated by problems of relationship and understanding. The pastor and staff probably feel alienated from or forgotten by denominational leaders and peers in churches whose communities are not undergoing significant change. Relationships are often strained; a communicated empathy is rare; peer support is almost nonexistent.

This description could be enlarged upon in many directions. In general terms it describes the situation in several thousand churches in America today and delineates the future of many other congregations.[5]

Addressing this kind of situation, churches have operated under one of several options open to them when they face these problems:

1. A congregation can choose to die a lingering, and often painful, death. Many churches have made this decision.

Refusing to change, hostile to the new residents, disappointed at those who no longer drive in from afar, and always talking about the good old days when Dr. Great Preacher was pastor, they lock themselves up behind fortress walls and pass away.

2. A church can choose to die a sudden death. It can sell or give its property away, urge its members to join other churches, and officially vote to disband. This provides immediate deliverance from the horns of the dilemma, but it really solves few problems and usually is done only after gaping wounds have been inflicted and considerable agony of soul has been experienced. I believe, however, it is to be preferred to the first option.

3. A church may choose to merge with another congregation in the same community for any of several reasons. If the merger is to combine resources to perpetuate the fortress mentality, this option is just an extension of option number one.

4. A church may choose to die with dignity. Some churches have decided to give the last years of their life to meeting the physical and social needs of the peoples of the changing community. They commit their resources, facilities, and staff to this kind of ministry. The bulk of the membership is usually not directly involved. In the main, it is ministry by proxy. No real effort is made and no expectation is harbored that any of the people receiving these ministries will ever become a significant part of the membership of the church.

All four of these options could be reduced to one: a decision to die—for whatever reason and in whatever manner.

5. A fifth option is to relocate the meeting place of the church. There are two ways to go about this. The first is to merge with an already-existing church in another community. A second is to buy property in another community and build a new building, begin to meet there, and attempt to develop a ministry in the new community.

This decision may be made at any one of several stages. The church may relocate early, when the influx of new people and the exodus of members from the community first begins. In this case, the building is usually sold and the resources used to erect a new building. At times a church will begin a satellite congregation in the community where it plans to relocate.

Second, the church may seek to develop another congregation or permit someone else to develop another congregation indigenous to the people moving into the community, using its own building as a meeting place. When the original church moves, it either sells or gives the building to the new congregation. Most strongly prefer to sell.

Third, if the community has become highly multiethnic or multiracial, the church may opt before it departs to develop several congregations that meet within its building. In fact, part of the original congregation may stay to become one of the several congregations that meet in the building.[6]

Fourth, a church may wait, maintaining a fortress mentality until death is near, and then attempt to sell and move. In this case it must sell; it no longer has the vitality to begin from scratch again in a new community. Also, the residences of the members in such a case are not usually grouped in any one place. Such a move often ends in failure to continue the life and ministry of the church. Attempting to save its life, it has lost it.

As Lyle Schaller (1979), Ezra Earl Jones (1976), and Gaylord Noyce (1975) have all intimated, there are good reasons for relocation. Extraordinary care should be taken to avoid laying a load of guilt on those churches and church leaders who opt for this course of action.[7]

6. A church may decide to continue to meet in the transitional community, to minister to and evangelize the people in the community, to integrate the membership with new members from the new residents of the commu-

nity, and eventually to become indigenous to the community-as-it-has-become. This probably is considered the most ideal and "Christian" option. It is being advocated by many church and denominational leaders, attempted by many churches, and carried on successfully by a small but growing number. Even if this is done successfully, it has some pitfalls; if unsuccessful, it has many pitfalls.

7. A church may attempt type-transformation. For example, a neighborhood church may deny it is a neighborhood church and insist that it is a "metropolitan" church with a ministry to the whole city. By "whole city" it usually means those of the particular socioeconomic and racial group to which the bulk of its commuters belong. This is another form of fortress mentality. If the church is successful in drawing new people from the larger city, it continues to ignore and be isolated from the community in the immediate area of its building. An "old First Church" may attempt to regain its lost glory through adopting a "metropolitan" or "special purpose" church style. This is another way that this option is often exercised.

8. A congregation may choose to make a more deliberate, quicker, and cleaner transition to a church relevant to the community-as-it-has-become. C. Peter Wager has outlined this approach, modeled after a plan to "indigenize" a national denominational body on an overseas mission field.[8] With this approach a date would be set two years in advance, at which time a transition of leadership would be made from the people who commute to those who have been recruited from the new arrivals in the community. A co-pastor indigenous to the new people would be called, and intensive evangelistic efforts for the next two years would be made among the new residents. On a certain predetermined date, the original pastor would resign, along with commuter church officers, and a total transition of leadership would be made.

Few churches have used this approach. It has many

inherent problems. In churches with congregational government—and almost all American churches tend toward
congregationalism—it would be next to impossible to
achieve. It makes no provision for the protection and care
of the original leadership, it seems to assume some higher
authority which could order such action, and it would
surely lead to many church divisions.

9. A church may choose to reproduce itself in the various cultures or subcultures of the community where it
meets. I speak here of more than the various possibilities
mentioned above for the church that opts to move. This
option can be used in tandem with any of the options
numbered four through seven. My thesis is that it should
be used along with the other options.

For a church to opt to maintain only its meeting place
in a community without aggressively addressing the gospel
of Christ to the community and attempting to serve the
people of the community in Jesus' name is most unfortun-
ate and threatens the apostolic character of the congregation as a church of Jesus Christ. It is an option of needless,
purposeless death. To merge in order to take longer to die
just prolongs the agony. In most cases, to disband is not
the best option either.

Whichever of the other options is chosen, the congregation that meets in a changing community can multiply its
own witness and ministry among the new residents by
planting new congregations. Such a plan should be part of
a comprehensive strategy for that changing or, better,
"new" community. No strategy can be comprehensive that
does not include this option.

It is easy enough to see how this option can combine with
the option to move as described above. What is more difficult to see is how this option can and should be combined
with the decision to die through ministry (option four), the
decision to make a speedy and forced transition (option
seven), or, especially, the decision to minister, evangelize,

and eventually become indigenous to the new people in the community. Surely, with this last option, leaders tend to rationalize, the decision to reproduce one's church in its own community through daughter churches would be counter-productive.

Not at all. Let me repeat again, it is impossible to have a comprehensive strategy without planting new congregations. The strategies we have been using—even the "best" and "most Christian" ones—have subtle inadequacies. Very often they do not take seriously enough the social realities created by the arrival of new people and the flight of former residents.

WHAT WE HAVE BEEN DOING: A CRITIQUE

Let me suggest several areas, both practical and conceptual, where our most advocated strategies can be faulted. Anemic motivation and distorted viewpoints have subtle ways of diluting even the highest ideals. All of these areas overlap, and one leads, quite naturally, to another.

1. Most of the reasoned exhortation about the church in the transitional community confuses the building where the church meets with the body of believers. The literature on the subject has repeated impassioned pleas for the church to "stay and serve," while, in fact, the church has, in the main, already moved. That is just the problem. The church only meets for worship and to conduct social ministries in the community. The call to "stay and serve" is most often a call to commute and serve.

Ezra Earl Jones, who is usually very careful to speak precisely about all subjects, has a few sentences that illustrate the point. "But to remove a church from a community for the sole reason of maintaining it as an institution is unacceptable. . . . A church should never be relocated from a community in transition when it is the only remaining church."[9] This is clear confusion of the church with the church house. To keep a church building open in a community only to maintain an institution is unacceptable also.

2. Related to the tendency to confuse the building with the church is an inconsistency concerning enlistment and support. Members of the old church in the transitional community are urged to continue to return to the community from which they have moved for worship and ministry. In fact, members are often accused of racism and escapism, of disloyalty and inadequate dedication if they consider uniting with a church in the community where they live. Their continued support in organizational roles, in various social ministries, and in monetary contributions, they are often told, is absolutely necessary if the congregation is to continue to survive and to minister.

At the same time, leaders do all they can to enlist new members from those newly arrived in the community. Most of the literature—most of our concern, I will suggest later—is for these older, prestigious churches, the flagships of our denominations, that are about to be lost. Little or no thought and no space in literature are given to those little congregations that meet in storefronts and remodeled warehouses, churches in which a large number of the new residents either hold membership or have given some level of support.

If our concern is for the whole Body of Christ (and not just for the "flagship" churches), in fairness, shouldn't these new arrivals be urged to go back to their old communities in order to support their former storefront churches with bivocational pastors? I have never read that position supported in any of the literature.

Most individuals responding to this question will insist that the varied and more holistic ministries offered by the larger, most stable churches and the more balanced leadership of a well-trained, professional staff are adequate reasons for urging newcomers to identify with the well-established congregations in their new community. The same arguments are used by leaders of growing suburban churches to attract those who have fled racially changing communities.

Isn't the basic problem that we can't bear to lose the great old institutions with their rich traditions and stately buildings?

3. Much of the literature about churches in transition reflects an inordinate concern for real estate. B. Carlisle Driggers is one of the most sensitive people I have ever met. He has demonstrated his compassion for and interest in persons as persons through years of leadership in churches attempting to minister in transitional communities. His book, *The Church in the Changing Community: Crisis or Opportunity,* is a passionate plea for Southern Baptists to "stay and minister" in changing communities. But he, too, falls into the real-estate trap.

If we lose the great cities of our land, only chaos will be the result. . . . At some time in the future Southern Baptists may try to move back into the cities and relocate churches. When this occurs . . . it might be discovered that (1) property will be scarce and practically unavailable; (2) the properties which might be available will be anything but choice for church buildings or will have exorbitant price tags; and (3) the people living in the neighborhoods will not desire for Southern Baptist churches to be there at all because Southern Baptists departed them in the past when they were needed most. [10]

The major impact of this paragraph is "stay and hold on to the property!" The truth is that imposing, ornate, expensive buildings may appear so foreboding to the new arrivals that they effectively keep them from Christ and identification with his Church.

One of the early studies of churches in transitional communities was made by Robert L. Wilson and James H. Davis in the mid-sixties. At the end of the book they considered the dilemma of denominational administrators who, among American Protestants at least, have little control over the action of local congregations. Conserving hard-won real estate was a major concern. The first question to be asked, according to Wilson and Davis, in an effort to discover guidelines for effective administrative procedures was, "What can be done to conserve the property assets of the churches located in communities which have completed their racial changes?"[11] This concern is just below the surface in much of the literature discussing this issue. Its presence leaves one feeling that property is sometimes more important than people in our strategies for transitional churches.

4. Most of the published rhetoric and philosophy on transitional communities and churches is focused on the people who are leaving the community, not on those who are moving into the community. Communities are described according to the classical sociological categories. They move from the new development stage to the post-transitional stage.[12] The life cycle of institutions is applied to churches and collated with the stages of community development. The whole picture is one of decline and deterioration and decay, moving inevitably toward death.

This is all true from the point of view of the long-term residents. But from the perspective of the new residents, the community is one of hope, not despair. They are moving to better homes, leaving less-desirable conditions. Jere Allen and George W. Bullard, Jr. have noted this condition in a well-done book, *Shaping the Future for the Church in the Changing Community.*

The post transitional stage . . . can be the newly developing stage of the incoming community in disguise. The cycle of the community stages begins again, and new patterns of relating . . . are established. . . . This is the real opportunity for the church in the changing community, i.e., the ability to perceive the new community which is emerging and to shape the future of the church based upon it.[13]

Failure to see the social situation from the viewpoint of the newcomer has tended to divert strategies toward maintenance and survival goals. Evangelistic and servant ministries addressed to newcomers are seen as a way to perpetuate the institutions. The spiritual and moral reasons for getting involved in these ministries are adulterated.

5. Consequently, much that has been done in local churches has been motivated more by a concern for sustaining the existing institutions than for meeting the needs of people in the transitional community. Institutional requirements—debt retirement, proper maintenance of extensive buildings, staff to lead sophisticated, middle-class programs, the support necessary to guarantee open doors—easily intermingle with Christlike concern for the unsaved and action toward those who are hurting. Motivations become mixed and unclear. The situation is often perceived early by newcomers. They feel they are being used, and at times they are.

The solution is not to abandon evangelistic and servant ministries. The solution is to commit ourselves to the most effective means for achieving goals related to these ministries. Those who are already Christians need to be enlisted and conserved. Those who are not Christians need to find Christ. Individuals and groups in transitional areas have open, aching wounds, spiritual and physical, that need to be bound. For many of these people the best way to help will not be to incorporate them into the existing WASP congregations. Many will be culturally uncomfortable in existing churches. If they were to join, they would be involved in the support of institutions (facilities, traditions, and goals) with which they do not identify. They would be expected to express their commitment to Christ in worship patterns largely alien to their culture. Other options need to be found.

6. Strategies used by old churches in transitional communities often express a cultural imperialism that is both

offensive and oppressive to newcomers. We have tended to approach the whole matter of reaching new peoples from our perspective, for our needs, and with our methods. We have expected these new people, when they have become involved in our church, to adopt our worship patterns. Even though congregations make some concessions toward diversity in music, very few churches have moved to true pluralism in forms of worship.

Our strategy often reflects an assumption that the way in which the existing, established church worships is culturally acceptable to newcomers. We may assume that they will prefer it. Lurking in the back of our corporate ecclesiastical cranium is a firm conviction that when these newcomers are properly assimilated into our churches, they will appreciate the grand worship patterns we presently enjoy. Bach is, after all, better than the Blackwood Brothers. The gospel songs of the eighteenth century are superior to the gospel soul music of the twentieth century.

7. The strategies that we advocate, though we have the best of intentions, are often paternalistic at best and can be racist in their most extreme expressions. This is the most subtle of all the pitfalls I have mentioned.

The problem is not with what is done, but with the attitude that pervades it. Too often, the ministries in which we engage are only deeds we do for the "poor folks." Our evangelistic efforts are like much of the county jail evangelism in which I have often shared. No mutual repentance, no confession of sin is expressed on the part of the witnesses. Our message too often sounds like, "Be good like us," rather than, "Turn to Christ." Beneath ministries that we perform, there can be a subtle paternalism or prejudice based on race, class, national origin, or life-style.

What we do may be altruistic. We ourselves may be engaged in a terrible battle with overt racism. We may detest paternalism with a passion. We may give ourselves in selfless abandon to serving people. Yet our basic attitude and approach are demeaning to those who receive our ministry. The end result is that the newcomers are not built up but belittled. There is no affirmation of their culture, no appreciation of their roots. Thus, much that we do, even though it actually brings substantial help to those who receive it, turns them away from Jesus Christ rather than attracting them to him.

TOWARD A MORE COMPREHENSIVE AND EFFECTIVE STRATEGY

Alerted to some of the pitfalls that plague the various solutions that have been fashioned for churches in transitional communities, we can move on to explore church planting as a manageable and major option in these rapidly changing urban areas.

Everyone concerned with this problem agrees that a more effective and extensive strategy is needed. Such a strategy should also be theologically and culturally aware. It should avoid as far as possible the subtle weaknesses of existing strategy models. Action plans we have developed for urban transitional areas have too often been ineffective and have never been comprehensive.

A bold determination to begin new congregations among some of the new residents, I assert, is part of the answer. A church-planting plan will enable a church to design a more holistic strategy. This more comprehensive strategy should be aimed at the penetration of every significant social segment within the church's community, a community that has probably become increasingly pluralistic.

First, let me identify a basic assumption upon which this discussion is based. I assume that the churches we are discussing have abandoned any serious commitment to racial exclusivism in their membership.

This has been made clear in earlier chapters of this book. Nevertheless, it must be restated here. The concepts I advocate must not be construed as defenses for racially or socially segregated churches. Every church should win to Christ and incorporate into its membership as many as it can from the various racial, social, and language-culture groups within the community where it meets for worship. I agree with Donald A. McGavran, who wrote:

Nothing I have said justifies injustice and intolerance, or the strong enforcing segregation against the weak. My own considered opinion is that, in the United States, the refusal of any congregation to admit Negroes as members is sin.[14]

A church that is not willing to evangelize, baptize, and welcome into its membership those of other races and classes is as heretical as those that deny that Jesus Christ died for our sins and was raised for our justification.

The question with which we struggle is not how to inculcate the principles of Christian brotherhood in a congregation. That is a serious problem within many congregations and should be addressed. But that is not the problem we address here. If a church is racially segregated in a racially changing community, it must either flee or die. I assume in this discussion that the churches have already passed the Rubicon and are committed to evangelizing and ministering effectively to all peoples.

The question we address is not, How should Christians act toward peoples of different races and cultures? but How can a church in a transitional community effectively communicate Christ to all the various cultures and subcultures of that community?

I assume that the problem is not with the policy of the church. The problem is with the sociocultural attitudes and feelings of the new residents of the community. A church may be eager to receive anyone into its fellowship who gives evidence of knowing Christ and wants to follow him in daily life, and still find it impossible to disciple the new arrivals effectively.

In response to this problem I make three suggestions

that will move toward a more comprehensive and effective strategy in transitional communities.

1. *Develop a people-vision.* In America we tend to idealize the individual and perceive society as essentially composed of isolated or, at best, loosely related individuals. The programs most often suggested for churches in transitional communities reflect this basic viewpoint. They are designed for and directed toward individuals, without serious reference to the social structures found in the transitional community. There are numerous reasons why this is true.

Most often Americans are taught that differences are bad; that we should refuse to be stereotyped; that each of us is a unique individual, and not merely a member of a group.[15]

We have been nurtured on two myths. The first is that America is a melting pot where different ethnic and social groups lose their distinctiveness. The second is that the cultural distinctives are to be lost in "Anglo conformity."[16] In site of gargantuan efforts to make it so, America is not a melting pot but, as Andrew M. Greeley has suggested, a stewpot.[17] Components remain distinct.

Ethnic pluralism in America is an accepted reality in most academic disciplines and in the political, educational, and business communities of the nation. In denominational and local church planning, ethnic realities have been but slowly recognized. The new ethnic consciousness that arose out of the civil rights movement of the sixties makes many of us uneasy. We have difficulty recognizing the various people groups created by racial, cultural, and social distinctives. When we do perceive these groups, we often do not appreciate and adequately value those things that define their peoplehood.[18]

In a changing urban community, the first step toward developing a comprehensive strategy is to take these distinctions seriously. We must develop a sensitivity to peoples rather than just to individuals. We must begin to ask ourselves how we can reach a whole people rather than individuals.

2. *Recognize the diversity within people groups.* While it is crucial to develop an eye for discerning groups of people within a community, it is equally important that we recognize the heterogeneity within these larger homogeneous groups.[19] Church leaders tend to think that any people group different from their own is a cultural monolith. That is, of course, a type of people-blindness. Strategies developed that do not give serious consideration to in-group diversity will be ineffective.

Each people group moving into a transitional community can be described and graphed in terms of its predictable responsiveness to the church already meeting in that community. By defining the level of ethnic consciousness among the newcomers, an acceptable estimate of responsiveness to a different group can be obtained.

Daniel R. Sanchez, in his seminal effort to develop a five-year growth plan for the Baptist Convention of New York, first formulated the following hypothesis: "The assimilation status of a group determines the degree of cultural awareness that will be present in the church established by the group."[20] Adapting from Andrew M. Greeley, he carried his study much beyond Greeley in his doctoral studies at Oxford University. There he categorized four types of ethnic adaptation to a host culture as:

(1) *Total Ethnics: those explicitly and self-consciously concerned about ethnic traditions;*
(2) *Median Ethnics: those to whom ethnicity is a relatively important part of self-conscious identification;*
(3) *Marginal Ethnics: those who occasionally think of themselves as ethnics; and*
(4) *Assimilated Ethnics: those who explicitly and self-consciously exclude themselves from ethnic collectivity.*[21]

These general categories are descriptive of the various subcultures among any significant people group moving to a community in transition. With them in mind, I wish to formulate a corollary to Sanchez's hypothesis: *The degree of assimilation among a new people group will determine its openness to integration with existing churches in urban transitional communities.*

What does this mean? First, churches in transitional communities can realistically expect only a certain portion of a new people group to identify with the existing WASP church. They can expect to evangelize effectively that portion of the people group that is "assimilated." With some adjustments in style and leadership, they may expect to reach a portion of those classified as "marginal." The second thing it means is that a game plan is needed for the remainder of the people group that will include efforts in addition to those designed to attach people to the existing churches.

The predictable responsiveness can be depicted by use of a Gaussian graph. Karl Friedrich Gauss, a German mathematician, discovered that most human characteristics, when plotted against populations, produce a curve that looks like a gently sloping, round-topped mountain.[22]

The four degrees of assimilation discussed above will be distributed in different proportions for different people groups. The size of each subgroup will be determined by certain related factors, such as racial identification, national origin, religion, economic status, vocation, formal schooling, regional identification, or length of time in America.[23] Figure 1 shows how the four categories might be distributed among a typical American black people group. Figure 2 represents the distribution among a Hispanic group. Figure 3 pictures a people group of Southeast Asian refugees.

3. *Adopt a balanced strategy* designed to communicate Christ to all the peoples of the transitional community.

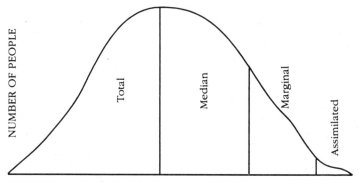

FIGURE 1. **Assimilation Factors among Blacks**

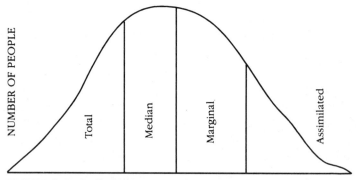

FIGURE 2. **Assimilation Factors among Hispanics**

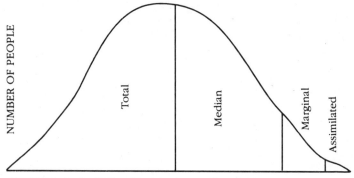

FIGURE 3. **Assimilation Factors among Laotians**

What are the missiological implications for what has been said?[24]

    a. The transitional church should make every effort to win the "assimilated" subgroup to Christ, to enlist them into its membership, and then to incorporate them into its leadership. Both evangelistic and ministry strategies should be formulated to focus on these persons with the intent of full integration within the church.

    b. To reach for Christ those described as "marginal," the transitional church will need to alter its ministry style. A staff member from the people group and an effort to include some worship forms from the culture of the newcomers may suffice if the number in this subgroup is relatively small. If a significant number of the people group are at this level of assimilation or if there are multiple people groups within the community, the transitional church may need to become a multiculture church or organize a new multiculture congregation. An alternative may be to constitute several monoculture churches that will share its building.

    c. Those newcomers who are classified as "median ethnics" require a bilingual or bicultural church to respond most easily to the claims of Christ. In this kind of church "median ethnics" can express their Christianity most naturally and exercise their leadership most comfortably. This subgroup will probably eventually require a new congregation. If the newcomers are part of a language-culture group, the way to begin may be with a separate department. If they are from an English-speaking racial group, "median ethnics" will probably require their own congregation from the beginning. Starting new congregations may prove to be the most effective method of bringing this group as a whole to Christ.

d. Those who are unassimilated, the "total ethnic" type, require a church indigenous in language, culture, and, as far as possible, leadership. A new congregation is an absolute necessity for the most effective evangelism with this group. They demand a church that looks, sounds, and functions as part of their culture. Church planting is the only faithful response to the missionary command of Jesus among these people.

The complex social structure of transitional communities demands a complex missionary strategy. A strategy is needed that will consider the social diversity within the community in all of its aspects. To penetrate each people group with Christ's Good News and to gather those who believe into responsible churches should be the primary goal of the strategy. To maintain the existing institution should not be the first consideration. The diversity within people groups will permit both effective evangelism and a continued vigorous life for existing churches. A complex strategy makes it possible for a church to respond realistically to the community-as-it-is-becoming.

George W. Bullard, Jr., in a dissertation that should be required reading for those who wrestle with the problems of churches in transitional communities, studied one hundred selected Southern Baptist churches in metropolitan transitional communities in 1975. These one hundred churches had been studied in 1965 by G. Willis Bennett.[25] Bullard set out to update the social research on the churches after ten years, to discover trends and make suggestions for future ministry.[26] One of his conclusions was that "churches with a perceived ministry style of evangelism tend not to decline statistically."[27]

Bullard found that the way a church perceived itself and its various ministries was of more importance than what the church did. Churches that did not decline statistically were, along with many that did decline, involved in intensive community ministries. The nondeclining churches perceived various community ministries as a means to obey Christ's evangelistic mandate. These churches served in order to win to faith in Christ. They understood themselves to be meeting needs in the name of Christ so that they could legitimately call people to faith in Christ. Commitment to a comprehensive evangelistic strategy will tend toward both missionary obedience and institutional longevity.

The rechurching of American inner cities is under way, but slowly. Most of it has been spontaneous, unplanned, and often unowned by the most prominent councilor and evangelical denominations. Few comprehensive program designs for the churches in the transitional communities have included intentional church planting as one of their action plans. Church planting remains an untried and overlooked option for the urban transitional community. The day for its consideration is long past due.

Urban transitional communities need to be considered mission fields in the same way that other underchurched areas of America are considered mission fields.[28] But the responsibility for congregationalizing the new people groups in urban transitional areas should rest first of all on the existing churches, not on the regional or national judiciaries and agencies of denominations.

Both interdenominational and intradenominational cooperation are still necessary, however, in addressing the transitional communities of our nation. Existing churches should adopt a comprehensive and pluralistic strategy as early as possible in the process of change. Church planting enables churches in transitional communities to have a balanced and effective approach to the total community.

ENDNOTES

Chapter 1

1. For a more detailed discussion, see Charles Chaney, "Garden or Wilderness: The Mission to America in Historical and Personal Perspective," *The Birth of Missions in America* (South Pasadena, Calif.: William Carey Library, 1976), 281-304.
2. See Franklin H. Littell, *From State Church to Pluralism* (Garden City, N.Y.: Anchor Books; Doubleday and Company, Inc., 1962), 29-36.
3. See *Baptist History and Heritage,* vol. X , no. 1 (January, 1975), an excellent introduction to Landmarkism and its relationship to the Southern Baptist Convention.
4. B. H. Carroll, *Baptists and Their Doctrines* (New York: Fleming H. Revell Company, 1913), 37-62.
5. W. O. Carver, "Introduction," in Duke K. McCall, *What Is the Church?* (Nashville: Broadman Press, 1958), 3.
6. W. O. Carver, *The Glory of God in the Christian Calling* (Nashville: Broadman Press, 1949), 43.
7. Roland Allen, *Missionary Principles* (Grand Rapids: Wm. B. Eerdmans Publishing Company, 1964), 67-100.
8. Carver, *Glory of God,* 201.
9. Melvin Hodges, *A Guide to Church Planting* (Chicago: Moody Press, 1973), 16. Darrell Robinson, *Total Church Life* (Nashville: Broadman Press), suggests this same purpose.
10. See Francis Schaeffer, *The Church at the End of the 20th Century* (Downers Grove, Ill.: InterVarsity Press, 1970), 9-25, for example.
11. K. Livgren, "Dust in the Wind," *Point of Know Return* by Kansas (CBS, Inc.: LP ZK34929, 1977).
12. See Leslie Newbigin, *Trinitarian Faith and Today's Mission* (Richmond, Va.: John Knox Press, 1964).
13. W. O. Carver, *Missions in the Plan of the Ages* (New York: Fleming H. Revell Company, 1909), 12.
14. George Eldon Ladd, *The Gospel of the Kingdom* (Grand Rapids: Wm. B. Eerdmans Publishing Company, 1918), 117.
15. Melvin Hodges, *Build My Church* (Chicago: Moody Press, 1957), 97.
16. J. Terry Young, "The Holy Spirit and the Birth of Churches," in *The Birth of Churches,* ed. Talmadge R. Amberson (Nashville: Broadman Press, 1979), 163.

17. Harold Lindsell, *An Evangelical Theology of Missions* (Grand Rapids: Zondervan Publishing House, 1970), 190.

18. John R. Mott, *The Decisive Hour of Christian Missions* (New York: Laymen's Missionary Movement, 1910), 193.

Chapter 2

1. See Roland Allen, *Missionary Methods: St. Paul's or Ours?* (Grand Rapids: William B. Eerdmans Publishing Company, 1962), 17, where this is one of Paul's "strategic points."

2. A.T. Robertson, *Epochs in the Life of Paul* (New York: Charles Scribner's, 1930), 145.

3. See Ron Johnson, Joseph W. Hinkle, and Charles M. Lowry, *Oikos: A Practical Approach to Family Evangelism* (Nashville: Broadman Press, 1982) and W. Oscar Thompson, Jr., *Concentric Circles of Concern* (Nashville: Broadman Press, 1981).

4. I am not trying to raise the issue of the ordination of women. In my own opinion, there is little, if any, scriptural basis for ordination of men or women as it is practiced in the church today within any denominational group.

5. Dean S. Gilliland, *Pauline Theology and Mission Practice* (Grand Rapids: Baker Book House, 1983), 54.

6. Allen, *Missionary Methods,* 87-101.

7. Melvin L. Hodges, *The Indigenous Church* (Springfield, Mo.: Gospel Publishing House, 1953), 17-18.

8. William O. Carver, *The Glory of God in the Christian Calling* (Nashville: Broadman Press, 1949), 53.

9. Ibid., 123-124.

10. Ibid., 56.

11. Allen, *Missionary Methods,* 131.

12. Gilliland, *Pauline Theology,* 211.

13. C. Kirk Hadaway, et al, *Home Cell Groups and House Churches* (Nashville: Broadman Press, 1987), 38.

14. Paul Yonggi Cho, *Successful Home Cell Groups* (Seoul: Church Growth International, 1981), 16.

15. Gilliland, *Pauline Theology,* 209.

16. James F. Engel and Wilbert Norton, *What's Gone Wrong with the Harvest?* (Grand Rapids: Zondervan Publishing House, 1975), 143-144.

Chapter 3

1. See Ezra Earl Jones, *Strategies for New Churches* (New York: Harper and Row Publishers, 1976), 101, for a suggestion much like this definition.

2. See Donald A. McGavran, "Church Growth in America through Planting New Congregations," the closing address of the Consultation on Evangelism and Church Growth, October 1976, Kansas City, Mo., and Charles L. Chaney, "Why Multiply Churches?" paper presented to the National Extension Leadership Conference, HMB, SBC, Chicago, Ill., February 25, 1991.

3. I assume that these two terms that have arisen from the Church Growth movement do not need definition.

4. See Clay L. Price, "A Brief Study of the North Central States 1980 to 1988." Unpublished report, Research Division, Home Mission Board, SBC, Atlanta, Ga., September 1989.

5. These figures and those in the narrative have been compiled from several sources: Clay L. Price, *op. cit.;* Phillip B. Jones and Richard C. Stanley, "HMB Environmental Indicators," Research Division, HMB, Atlanta, October 1990; the 1973 and 1990 annuals of the fellowships and conventions; and two papers I prepared in 1974, "Take a Good Look," and "Challenge 1990: A Strategy for Doubling Southern Baptist Work in Seven North Central States by 1990." The 1990 figures come from a report from state missions directors, December 1990, compiled by Tom Biles. Tommy Coy's "Data Model for North Central States," with its attached statistical tables, has been invaluable.

6. Price, "A Brief Study," 7.

7. See Jones and Stanley, "HMB Environmental Indicators," 49-50.

Chapter 5

1. Jack Redford, *Planting New Churches* (Nashville: Broadman Press, 1979), 22-23.

2. See William A. Lumpkin, *Baptist Foundations in the South* (Nashville: Broadman Press, 1961), for the full story of this remarkable church. H. Leon McBeth, *The Baptist Heritage* (Nashville: Broadman Press, 1987) 227-235, also tells this story well.

3. Though he does not stress megachurches, Peter Wagner has said that one vital sign of a healthy church is that it is "big enough." By "big enough," he meant large enough for the functioning of its own philosophy of ministry and for extension growth. See *Your Church Can Grow* (Glendale, Calif.: Regal Books, 1976), 84, 93.

4. Two excellent books called attention to this development: Lyle E. Schaller, *44 Questions for Church Planters* (Nashville: Abingdon Press, 1991), 13-36, 163-188; and C. Peter Wagner, *Church Planting for a Greater Harvest* (Ventura, Calif.: Regal Books, 1990), 11-25.

5. Clay Price and Phillip Jones, "A Study of the Relationship of Church Size and Church Age to Number of Baptisms and Baptism Rates" (mimeographed document, prepared for Department of Church Extension, Home Mission Board, Southern Baptist Convention, Atlanta, Ga., 1978).

6. See Sherri Brown, "The Search for Saddleback Sam," *MissionsUSA* 59 (July-August 1988) 4, 6-19, for a good succinct account of the first nine years.

7. Wagner, *Church Planting,* 16-17.

8. See *MissionsUSA Video Magazine,* vol. 7, no. 1, and Sarah Zimmerman, "Leader of the Band," *MissionsUSA* 62 (May-June 1991) 5, 17-26.

Chapter 6

1. Louis Luzbetak, *The Church and Cultures* (Maryknoll, N.Y.: Orbis Books, 1988), 69.

2. Ibid., 44.

3. Art Weinstein, *Market Segmentation* (Chicago: Probus Publishing Co., 1987), 4.

4. James F. Engel and Wilbert Norton, *What's Gone Wrong with the Harvest?* (Grand Rapids: Zondervan Publishing House, 1975), 37.

5. Edward Dayton and David Fraser, *Planning Strategies for World Evangelization* (Grand Rapids: William B. Eerdmans Publishing Company, 1980), 125.

6. David Hesselgrave, *Planting Churches Cross-Culturally* (Grand Rapids: Baker Book House, 1980), 207.

7. *Christian Marketing Perspective,* Barna Research Group, Glendale, Calif., 1989.

8. Ray Bakke, Urban Training Cooperative of the Home Mission Board, Chicago, Ill., August 1988.

9. Michael J. Weiss, *The Clustering of America* (New York: Harper and Row, 1988), 6.

10. Claritas Corporation, Alexandria, Va., PRIZM slide presentation, 1989.

11. Weiss, *Clustering of America,* 1.

12. Weiss, Ibid., 140.

13. A. H. Maslow, *Motivation and Personality* (New York: Harper and Row, 1954).

14. David Reisman, Nathan Glazer, and Reuel Denney, *The Lonely Crowd* (New Haven, Conn.: Yale University Press, 1950).

15. All this material is adapted from Maria Martin, "Characteristics of the VALS 2 Segments," *SRI Report 78,* May 1989, 8-31.

16. For example, the Home Mission Board of the Southern Baptist Convention (HMB/SBC) and several state Baptist conventions have access to CACI's market segmentation data. The Research Division of the HMB/SBC will provide the demographic data for any targeted community in the nation if the request comes through the missions director of one of the forty-one state or regional conventions that are part of the SBC family.

17. The market index in this figure and the Index in Figure 5 are derived by dividing the percentage in the target area by the percentage in the base area, in this case the USA, and then multiplying by 100. Thus, if the percentages were the same, the market index would be 100, or average. An index of 200 would indicate that one is twice as likely to find that type in this area as in the population at large.

18. Arnold Mitchell, *The Nine American Life-Styles* (New York: Warner Books, 1983), 165.

Chapter 7

1. This is an adaptation from Hodges, *A Guide to Church Planting* (Chicago: Moody Press, 1973), 27.

2. See *The Quarterly Review* (July-September, 1989), 21.

3. I have used the terminology used by the School of World Missions, Fuller Theological Seminary, because I think it is essential that we use terminology with a precise definition.

4. I have adapted materials from *The Church Missions Committee Manual* (Atlanta: Home Mission Board, SBC, 1976) and *The Associational Missions Committee Manual* (Atlanta: Home Mission Board, SBC, 1975) for use in this section. This process is now contained in the Missions Development Council materials available from the Home Mission Board, SBC, 1350 Spring St., NW, Atlanta, GA 30367.
5. Howard A. Snyder, "The Church as God's Agent in Evangelism," in *Let the Earth Hear His Voice,* ed. J. D. Douglas (Minneapolis: World Wide Publications, 1975), 332-333.

Chapter 8

1. Clay L. Price and Philip B. Jones, "Update of Church Lifecycle Study: New Churches Added to the Southern Baptist Convention, 1982-1987" (Atlanta: Home Mission Board, SBC, 1988), 6.
2. Harry H. Fowler, *Breaking Barriers of New Church Growth* (Rocky Mount, N.C.: Creative Growth Dynamics, 1988), 21.
3. Francis M. Dubose, *How Churches Grow in an Urban World* (Nashville: Broadman Press, 1978), 25.
4. Everett Hullum, Kathy Choy, and Sherri Brown, "The Cities," *MissionsUSA,* July-August 1987, 40.
5. Dubose, *How Churches Grow,* 26.
6. Ibid., 26.
7. Harvie M. Conn, *A Clarified Vision for Urban Mission* (Grand Rapids: Zondervan Publishing House, 1987), 217.
8. John Naisbitt and Patricia Aburdene, *Megatrends 2000* (New York: William Morrow and Company, Inc., 1990), 275.
9. Rudee Devon Boan, "Factors Influencing the Outcome of Church-Type Missions" (Research Report for the Home Mission Board, Atlanta, 1986), 6.
10. *The Win Arn Growth Report,* Number 20, published by the Institute of American Church Growth, Pasadena, California.
11. *Webster's Seventh New Collegiate Dictionary,* rev. ed., s.v. "cultural."
12. Sherri Brown, "The Search for Saddleback Sam," *MissionsUSA 59,* July-August 1988, 14.
13. Ibid.
14. *The Win Arn Growth Report,* Number 10, n.d., 2-3, quoted in C. Peter Wagner, *Strategies for Church Growth* (Ventura, Calif.: Regal Books, 1987), 82.
15. C. Peter Wagner, *Strategies for Church Growth* (Ventura, Calif.: Regal Books, 1987), 81.
16. Charles R. Swindoll, *The Quest for Character* (Portland, Oreg.: Multnomah Press, 1988), 164.
17. Walter Mueller, *Direct Mail Ministry* (Nashville: Abingdon Press, 1989), 67.

Chapter 9

1. See C. Peter Wagner, *Our Kind of People* (Atlanta: John Knox Press, 1979), 61-74, for a full definition and discussion of this term.

2. See Paul R. Picard and Bernard Quinn, *Churches and Church Membership in the United States: 1971* (Washington, D.C.: Glenmary Research Center, 1974.)

3. Benjamin E. Mays and Joseph W. Nicholson, *The Negro's Church* (New York: Russell and Russell, 1933), 33.

4. Edward L. Wheeler, "Understanding and Relating to the Black Community," in B. Carlisle Driggers, compiler, *Churches in Racially Changing Communities,* mimeographed proceedings of the National Leadership Conference, Department of Cooperative Ministries with National Baptists, Home Mission Board, Southern Baptist Convention, Atlanta, Ga., 1978, 180.

5. See U.S. Bureau of Census, *Census of Religious Bodies,* 1906, 10ff., as the source of this information.

6. Chicago Commission on Race Relations, *The Negro in Chicago* (Chicago: University of Chicago Press, 1922), 142ff.

7. St. Clair Drake and Horace R. Cayton, *Black Metropolis* (New York: Harcourt, Brace and Company, 1962), 416ff.

8. U.S. Bureau of Census, *Religious Bodies: 1936 Selected Statistics, Table 1;* 16ff. See also Mays and Nicholson, *The Negro's Church,* 96.

9. Mays and Nicholson, *The Negro's Church,* 97.

10. *Christianity Today,* 21 December 1979, 18.

Chapter 10

1. Ezra Earl Jones, "Identifying the Church in the Racially Changing Community," in *Churches in Racially Changing Communities,* Proceedings of the National Leadership Conference, Department of Cooperative Ministries with National Baptists, Home Mission Board, Southern Baptist Convention, 1978, 33, defines churches in transitional communities as "congregations located in geographical areas . . . where change is occurring that is basic to the character of the community; where change is widespread, and where the fundamental nature of the community . . . will be radically different for at least a generation."

2. See Dean R. Hodge and David R. Roozen, eds., *Understanding Church Growth and Decline: 1950-1978* (New York: Pilgrim Press, 1979).

3. PRRC *Emerging Trends* 2, 1, 2.

4. For example, Ezra Earl Jones, "Rationale Question, and Assumptions," in *New Church Development in the Eighties,* ed. Ezra Earl Jones (New York: National Division, Board of Global Ministries, the United Methodist Church, 1976), 8-9, seems to promise a great deal, but in his later book, *Strategies for New Churches* (New York: Harper & Row, Publishers, 1976), 168-170, he gives very little attention to the possibility. Lyle E. Schaller raised this possibility in his early book, *Planning for Protestantism in Urban America* (Nashville: Abingdon Press, 1965), 154-156, but concluded that the need in declining communities was for more professional staff—not more churches. C. Peter Wagner in *Your Church Can Be Healthy* (Nashville: Abingdon Press, 1979) does not mention this as a major option for a church with "ethnikitus," but a church-planting model is described in

his *Our Kind of People* (Atlanta: John Knox Press, 1979), 158-163. Several works in the last decade have proposed this option. The best is Jere Allen and George W. Bullard, Jr., *Shaping the Future for the Church in the Changing Community* (Atlanta: Home Mission Board, SBC, 1981), 21-26. See also Jere Allen, "Stages in Transition," *Urban Review* (October 1985), 4-12, and C. Kirk Hadaway, "Types of Growing Churches in Transition," Ibid., 13-22. Raymond J. Bakke and Samuel K. Roberts, *The Expanded Mission of "Old First" Churches* (Valley Forge: Judson Press, 1986) gives slight attention to this option. The same is true for Keith Anderson, *Dying for Change* (Minneapolis: Bethany House Publishers, 1990), Lloyd M. Perry and Gilbert A. Peterson, *Churches in Crises* (Chicago: Moody Press, 1981), and Ray Bakke, *The Urban Christian* (Downers Grove, Ill.: InterVarsity Press, 1987). Francis M. DuBose, *How Churches Grow in an Urban World* (Nashville: Broadman Press, 1978), 153-178, continues to be ahead of his time in this regard.

5. For more adequate descriptions of the problems that arise in transitional communities see Schaller, *Planning for Protestantism*, 157-161; Robert Lee, ed., *Cities and Churches: Reading on the Urban Church* (Philadelphia: The Westminster Press, 1962), 85-124; *Review and Expositor* LXIII (Summer 1966), a whole issue given to "The Church in the Changing Community"; G. Willis Bennett, *Confronting a Crisis* (Atlanta: Home Mission Board, SBC, 1967), 1-13; George A. Torney, ed., *Toward Creative Urban Strategy* (Waco, Tex.: Word Books, Publisher, 1970), 5-23; Lyle E. Schaller, *Hey, That's Our Church* (Nashville: Abingdon Press, 1975), 39ff.; Gaylor B. Noyce, *Survival and Mission for the City Church* (Philadelphia: The Westminster Press, 1975), 68ff.; Walter E. Ziegenhals, *Urban Churches in Transition* (New York: The Pilgrim Press, 1978), 13ff.; Ezra Earl Jones and Robert L. Wilson, *What's Ahead for Old First Church* (New York: Harper and Row, Publishers, 1974), 9-50; Robert L. Wilson and James H. Davis, *The Church in the Racially Changing Community* (Nashville: Abingdon Press, 1966), 19ff.; Murray H. Leiffer, *The Effective City Church* (Nashville: Abingdon-Cokesbury Press, 1946) 82ff.; Ezra Earl Jones, "The Church That Wants to Remain in the Changing Community," *Churches in Racially Changing Communities*, 1978, 57-89; B. Carlisle Driggers, *The Church in the Changing Community: Crisis or Opportunity* (Atlanta: Home Mission Board, SBC, 1977), 14-21; George W. Bullard, Jr., "An Analysis of Change in Selected Southern Baptist Churches in Metropolitan Transitional Communities" (Th.M. diss., Southern Baptist Theological Seminary, 1976), 14ff.; B. Carlisle Driggers, *Models of Metropolitan Ministry* (Nashville: Broadman Press, 1979); Francis M. DuBose, *How Churches Grow,* 145ff.; C. Peter Wagner, *Your Church Can Be Healthy,* 29ff.; Douglas Alan Walrath, *Leading Churches through Change* (Nashville: Abingdon Press, 1979); and Jere Allen and George W. Bullard, Jr., *Shaping the Future for the Church in the Changing Community*, 6-31.

6. Daniel R. Sanchez, "A Five Year Plan of Growth for the Ministry of the Baptist Convention of New York in the Area of Evangelism" (Ph.D. diss., Fuller Theological Seminary, 1979), has a very excellent discussion of this option.

7. Jones, *Strategies*, 158-161; Lyle E. Schaller, *Effective Church Planning* (Nashville: Abingdon Press, 1979), 143-145; and Noyce, *Survival and Mission*, 76-79. Note the last two especially for the guilt factor.

8. Wagner, *Your Church Can Be Healthy*, 37-39.

9. Jones, *Strategies*, 159.

10. Driggers, *Crisis or Opportunity*, 12-13.

11. Wilson and Davis, *Church in Racially Changing Community*, 143.

12. See Jones, "Identifying the Church in the Racially Changing Community," 38-45, and Jones and James D. Anderson, *The Management of Ministry* (New York: Harper and Row, Publishers, 1978), 38-41; Larry McSwain, "Stages of Community Transition," Proceedings of National Leadership Conference on Churches in Racially Changing Communities (mimeographed; Atlanta: Home Mission Board, SBC, 1979), 104-116; and Allen and Bullard, *Hope*, 13-16.

13. Allen and Bullard, *Shaping the Future for the Church*, 14. See also Jones, "Identifying the Church," 45-46.

14. Donald A. McGavran, *Understanding Church Growth* (Grand Rapids: William B. Eerdmans Publishing Company, 1970), 209.

15. Michael Novak, "Preface," *The Rise of the Unmeltable Ethnics*, paperback ed. (New York: Macmillan Publishing Co., Inc., 1975), XVI.

16. Wagner, *Our Kind of People*, 34-57.

17. Andrew M. Greeley, "Catholics Prosper while the Church Crumbles," *Psychology Today*, June 1976, 44.

18. The definition of *people* adopted by the Lausanne Committee is the background of the following discussion. A people is "a significantly large sociological grouping of individuals who perceive themselves to have a common affinity for one another." Edward R. Dayton, *That Everyone May Hear* (Monrovia, Calif.: MARC, 1979), 22.

19. The most detailed study of this social reality from a church growth point of view is Wagner, *Our Kind of People*, 58-77.

20. Sanchez, "Five Year Plan," 244.

21. Ibid., 243, 244. See Andrew M. Greeley, "Is Ethnicity Unamerican?" *New Catholic World*, 106-109. For the more extensive study, see Daniel R. Sanchez, "An Interdisciplinary Approach to Theological Contextualization with Specific Reference to Hispanic Americans," (Ph.D. diss., Oxford Centre of Mission Studies, Oxford), 91-151.

22. See Wilfred Brown, *Organization* (London: Heinemann Education Books, Ltd., 1971), 50-51.

23. Wagner, *Our Kind of People*, 61-74, describes these different factors as contributors to one's "ethclass."

24. I am indebted to Daniel Sanchez for the following discussion. Sanchez, "Five Year Plan," 244-246.

25. See Bennett, *Confronting a Crisis*.

26. Bullard, "An Analysis of Change," 1-2.

27. Ibid., 104. See also George W. Bullard, Jr., "What Is Happening with Churches in Metropolitan Transitional Areas?" *Search*, Summer 1979, 32-39.

28. Bullard, "An Analysis of Change," 106.